STRATEGIC WRITING MINI-LESSONS

for All Students, Grades 4–8

*This book is dedicated to
teachers of writing
and student writers . . .
from whom we learn so much.*

—Janet and Cindy

STRATEGIC WRITING MINI-LESSONS

for All Students, Grades 4–8

Edited by

Janet C. Richards
Cynthia A. Lassonde

Foreword by Jane Hansen

CORWIN
A SAGE Company

CORWIN
A SAGE Company

FOR INFORMATION:

Corwin

A SAGE Company

2455 Teller Road

Thousand Oaks, California 91320

(800) 233-9936

www.corwin.com

SAGE Publications Ltd.

1 Oliver's Yard

55 City Road

London EC1Y 1SP

United Kingdom

SAGE Publications India Pvt. Ltd.

B 1/I 1 Mohan Cooperative Industrial Area

Mathura Road, New Delhi 110 044

India

SAGE Publications Asia-Pacific Pte. Ltd.

3 Church Street

#10-04 Samsung Hub

Singapore 049483

Publisher: Lisa Luedeke

Acquisitions Editor: Carol Chambers Collins

Associate Editor: Megan Bedell

Editorial Assistant: Sarah Bartlett

Production Editor: Amy Schroller

Copy Editor: Linda Gray

Typesetter: C&M Digitals (P) Ltd.

Proofreader: Jeff Bryant

Indexer: Judy Hunt

Cover Designer: Karine Hovsepian

Permissions Editor: Jennifer Barton

Printed in the United States of America

A catalog record of this book is available from the Library of Congress.

ISBN 9781452235011

This book is printed on acid-free paper.

SUSTAINABLE FORESTRY INITIATIVE
Certified Chain of Custody
Promoting Sustainable Forestry
www.sfiprogram.org
SFI-01268
SFI label applies to text stock

12 13 14 15 16 10 9 8 7 6 5 4 3 2 1

Contents

Foreword   vii
Jane Hansen

**Introduction: Meeting Your Students'
Needs With Specific Writing Strategies**   1
Janet C. Richards and Cynthia A. Lassonde

SECTION I. STRATEGIC INVENTING: CONTEMPLATING IDEAS   9

1. **Color-Coding Sources**   11
   Cynthia A. Lassonde

2. **Developing Students' Awareness of
   Their Strengths as Writers With an I-Can! Chart**   18
   Joanne Durham

3. **Using a Blueprint Graphic Organizer to Build a Story**   28
   Jennifer A. Fontenot

4. **Using Genre Charts to Guide Planning and Writing**   42
   Gabriel C. Horn and Susan D. Martin

5. **Reciprocal Text Structure Mapping for Expository Writing**   55
   Joyce C. Fine

6. **Thanks for the Memories! Using a Sensory-Details
   Chart to Prepare to Write**   67
   Sandra Gandy and Mariah Kraus

7. **Organizing an Expository Essay: Using Big Idea
   Checklists to Support Writers**   78
   Allison Stone and Joyce C. Fine

SECTION II. STRATEGIC DRAFTING: PUTTING IDEAS ON PAPER   91

8. **Quilting Together an Expository Paper in Four Steps**   93
   Cynthia A. Lassonde

9. **Team Writing to Foster Students' Motivation to
   Write: Moving From Group Work to Independence**   102
   Janet C. Richards

10. **Use Your Words: Learning to Paraphrase**   **108**
   Janet C. Richards

11. **Creating Rounded Characters
   Through Cartoon Connections**   **116**
   Krishna Seunarinesingh

12. **Applying the Structure Strategy to Write Persuasive Texts**   **126**
   Bonnie J. F. Meyer, Jennifer Ireland, and Melissa Ray

13. **Buddies Build It Stronger: A Sentence-Combining Strategy**   **137**
   Todd Sundeen

**SECTION III. STRATEGIC REVISING:
ATTENDING TO ORGANIZATION AND COHESIVENESS**   **147**

14. **Deconstruct Then Reconstruct a First Draft**   **149**
   Cynthia A. Lassonde

15. **Portal Writing: Helping Writers Rethink Their Writing**   **155**
   S. Rebecca Leigh

16. **Conferring With an Avatar**   **163**
   Chase Young and Lynda Swanner

17. **Writing Aloud: A Sound-Savvy Approach to Writing**   **168**
   Sandra K. Athans

18. **A Picture Is Worth a Thousand Words:
   Revising With Photographs**   **176**
   Noreen S. Moore

SECTION IV. STRATEGIC EDITING: THE FINISHING TOUCH   **187**

19. **Revising and Editing Through Primary Sources**   **188**
   Nancy L. Williams and Kathleen Muir

20. **Code Switching: An Editing Strategy**   **196**
   Rebecca Wheeler

21. **The Imagine, Describe, Resolve, and Confirm (IDRC)
   Strategy to Develop Students' Story Writing Abilities**   **207**
   *Lindsay Sheronick Yearta, Katie Stover,
   Lynne Newton, and Karen Wood*

22. **Probable Passages: Using Story Structure to Write and
   Revise a Predictive Passage**   **218**
   Katie Stover, Jean Payne Vintinner, Crystal P. Glover, and Karen Wood

References   **229**

Index   **236**

About the Authors   **246**

About the Contributors   **247**

Foreword

Jane Hansen

Teachers of Grades 4 through 8 often worry about how to teach writing to students at varying levels of achievement, especially the students who seem to struggle as writers. How can we rev up their energy as writers? How can we set a solid groundwork so that all students, regardless of skill level, eagerly raise their hands to share their writing at the end of a class? With those types of essential questions in mind, the authors of and contributors to this book provide tips about how to tailor and differentiate instruction.

As we teach writers, we gradually become aware of their skills, set goals for their improvement, and monitor their growth. Our students are the ultimate record keepers; as they write, they provide documentation that shows what they can now accomplish compared to what they previously did. They also reveal areas in which they may struggle.

The Student Reflection section of each chapter sets the stage on which writers can become aware of potential and possibilities. Always, the students talk about what they are trying—the new territory into which they are venturing. Perhaps one writer is learning how to incorporate a chart into a draft, another is trying to write with a flashback, and another is learning how to write from a different point of view. Their time to reflect enables them to come to a clearer understanding of what they are trying to do—and they hear what others are trying, which gives them ideas for their own work, as well.

Struggling writers tend to see themselves as failures or, at best, as students who possess few strengths in writing. It may be especially important for these students to become aware of what they can do. As writing teachers, one of our most important tasks is to help all our students come to identify themselves as writers.

Importantly, the "I Can!" strategy chapter (Chapter 2) sets up writers to know what they can do. As a group, they create class charts to show what they learn from mentor texts, and writers create individual charts onto which they record their own strengths. They also see what others can do as they share these charts formally or informally with their classmates. This vision enables them to turn to each other for ideas and assistance. In so doing, their community of writers becomes increasingly strong.

Talk is also crucial to writers because it helps them determine which option to pursue at a particular time and it helps us recognize what skills they need to focus on next. As the authors of this book say, there is no sequence or prescribed list of what to teach when. It depends on the writers, so we must learn to listen to their needs and tailor our instruction accordingly.

A constant, however, is revision—of all kinds and for all reasons. One reason for revision trumps others, however: the writer's determination to become better. In some cases, students do not understand revision as literally meaning to "re-see"; instead, they tend to think of revision as editing to correct errors of punctuation, capitalization, and the like. Two refreshing ideas to aid revision may be helpful. One is for writers to study photographs as a way to see information they may not have seen in what they read (Chapter 18), and another is the idea of finding portal words, or windows through which they may be able to re-see their writing (Chapter 15).

Always essential for all writers is their use of authentic mentor texts for fiction, short stories, sports articles, the daily news, and essays. Where do students find the real essays they read so they have a mental model for what essay writers do? Do we ensure that our students study essays online, in print newspapers, and in magazines? According to the wise authors of this book, we always turn to mentor texts to provide the credibility our authentic instruction mandates.

A few of the chapters herein offer specific ideas for writers to try as they learn to incorporate references. To learn to paraphrase and quilt can be helpful because both provide students with multiple opportunities to talk extensively about what they are learning. They put their new knowledge into their own words as they tell their story about their information. When they can explain it clearly, they can write it—without looking at their references.

Character development is another complicated process for young writers. In Chapter 11, the students create cartoons to enable them to show the changes their characters experience. They begin with well-known pop culture characters—a sure way to engage young writers—and they gradually inflate a balloon to help them remember the idea of a character with several attributes. Importantly, as with all the ideas in this book, this process of creating complicated characters can be used in more than one content area.

Also, as is pointed out in every single chapter, English language learners (ELLs) may have specific difficulties with writing. They may need extra support with vocabulary and/or syntax. Significantly, they may benefit from additional opportunities to talk with teachers and classmates who appreciate approximations. It is important for ELLs to talk with not only classmates of their own language but also with English speakers who are good listeners. With these types of support, ELLs gradually become able to explain themselves to all their classmates.

When they write, ELLs may benefit from writing in their native language. As they gradually become more proficient in spoken English, their written texts will, as well, contain a larger percentage of English words. Overall, ELLs write for various trustworthy audiences who appreciate what they can do. The more our ELLs talk and write in supportive environments, the more quickly they will progress.

Strategic Writing Mini-Lessons for All Students, Grades 4–8 will enrich the teaching of teachers and the writing of writers, all of whom thrive in classrooms in which students know their thoughts are sought and honored. The chapters will inspire teachers and students to step forward to enter the conversations that surround them. It will enable them to transform their classrooms into busy workshops in which the writers use multiple processes and learn from each other—and their teachers.

Publisher's Acknowledgments

Corwin gratefully acknowledges the contributions of the following reviewers:

Marsha Basanda, 5th Grade Teacher
Bell's Crossing Elementary, Simpsonville, SC

Nancy Foote, Teacher
San Tan Elementary School, Gilbert, AZ

Aimee J. Jahns, Reading Specialist/Interventionist
Cedar Hills and Shepard Hills Elementary Schools, Oak Creek, WI

Kandace Klenz, National Board Certified Teacher
Longview Elementary, Moses Lake, WA

Paulette Moses, 5th Grade Teacher
Ballentine Elementary School, Irmo, SC

Linda Sarver, Retired Teacher
Excelsior Springs, MO

Neal Shambaugh, Associate Professor and Program Coordinator
Graduate Programs for Instructional Design and Technology, West Virginia
University, Morgantown, WV

Bonnie Snyder, Reading Specialist
Schoharie Jr./Sr. High School, Schoharie, NY

Cathern Wildey, Adjunct Professor
Nova Southeastern University, Miami, FL

Gary L. Willhite, Professor and Teacher Educator
University of Wisconsin La Crosse, La Crosse, WI

Introduction

Meeting Your Students' Needs With Specific Writing Strategies

Janet C. Richards and Cynthia A. Lassonde

S takeholders in U.S. education note the need for a thorough, wide-reaching commitment to improve student writing achievement, which has generally stayed low for more than 10 years (Troia, Shankland, & Heintz, 2010). One reason for this dismal fact is that when compared to reading and mathematics, writing instruction has been a "neglected element of American school reform" (National Commission on Writing, 2003, p. 9). In fact, the No Child Left Behind Act placed little emphasis on writing (Graham & Harris, 2005), and at this time, only a small body of work focuses on educators' professional development in writing (Troia et al., 2010). It is not surprising then, that the College Board, an organization of 4,300 colleges, warns that "students and society will be short-changed if writing is not placed squarely in the center of the school reform agenda" (Graham & Harris, 2005, p. 19).

In contrast to these gloomy facts, we know teachers are committed to improving their students' writing abilities. To meet teachers' instructional needs we offer this book to help teachers improve the writing of their students in Grades 4 through 8. Writing coaches, language arts specialists, support personnel, and students in teacher education programs will also find this book valuable.

One research-proven way to improve students' writing achievement is to model and teach strategies that foster students' self-regulated, independent writing. The strategies supplied in this book are research based, and teachers have field-tested the strategies in their classrooms. The strategies also connect to the English Language Arts Common Core Standards. On the inside the front cover of this book, you will find a chart that correlates the Common Core Standards for English Language Arts Grades 4 through 8 to the strategies presented in this book. The Standards define what all students are expected to know about writing and be able to do with writing, but they do not dictate *how* teachers should teach writing. The chapters herein offer easy-to-follow, authentic lessons that will help students in Grades 4 through 8 develop proficiency in the grade-level goals set by the Common Core and other standards.

We suggest you take time to read this introductory chapter, which provides an overview of the book, before turning to the strategy chapters. Here, we explain the benefits of individualizing writing instruction for students and describe how teachers, writing coaches, language arts specialists, and other support personnel can differentiate writing instruction by modeling and teaching strategies based on students' individual needs. We also provide some theory that supports writing strategy instruction and share how to tailor writing pedagogy for

- writers who struggle,
- English language learners,
- gifted writers, and
- students who may just need a quick review about a specific feature of writing.

Differentiating Student Writing Instruction

This practical book provides mini-lessons that you can use with any writing program. Strategy instruction does not take the place of district- or schoolwide-adopted writing plans; rather, small-group strategy mini-lessons fit nicely with any district-mandated or school-adopted writing program. The lessons described in each chapter will help teachers and other educational specialists who teach writing offer individual and small-group writing strategy instruction to all students—not just to those students who struggle with writing—in Grades 4 through 8.

WHY THIS BOOK IS NEEDED NOW

For years U.S. policymakers have highlighted writing instruction in Grades K–3. Unfortunately, after Grade 3, many schools stop teaching writing (Alliance for Excellent Education Issue Brief, 2006; Lemke et al., 2004; Olson, 2006). Yet vast numbers of students in Grades 4 through 8 need help with their writing—"a topic that has previously not received enough attention from researchers and educators" (Graham & Perin, 2007b, p. 7; also see Troia et al., 2010). In reality, many students in Grades 4 through 8 do not meet basic writing standards. And according to Gregorian (2010), their teachers and others who support students' writing often do not know how to help them. Grades 4 through 8 are a critical bridge to high school, where writing instruction is rarely individualized. These years offer a final opportunity to prevent students' continued writing failure (Strickland, Ganske, & Monroe, 2002).

A survey of teachers of Grades 4 through 8 who are also our graduate students indicate they are concerned about their students' writing problems. We think their concerns may be similar to your concerns. For example, they wrote,

My fourth-grade students lack focus. They pick up a writing assignment like it's week-old laundry—like it's a chore. I want them to get excited about writing. I've tried to think of ideas that might excite them. I want them to love to write. But all I get is, "Let's get this over with." Also, they hate to make revisions. I need strategies to motivate my fourth graders to write and then make revisions. All my students want to do is give their writing a quick once-over, and then they decide their writing is perfect and they expect an A.

My fifth graders cannot understand how to do research—to pull information from a variety of sources and then write these ideas in their own words. They don't understand that one book can say one thing and another book can say another and they have to include this information. They don't know how to organize information in a coherent way. They don't know how to get information from computer sources.

My sixth graders will go to the high school building next year. The teachers there expect them to know how to write to explain what they know and what they have learned. They write short, choppy sentences with each sentence beginning with The, A, An, or I. Not only that, they jump from one idea to another within the same paragraph. I worry about that.

My seventh-grade students need help with all phases of the writing process. They begin writing without planning because they do not think planning is worth the effort. They hate to revise because they think it is too much trouble, and they rarely edit their writing.

My eighth-grade students do not know how to elaborate and I cannot figure out how to help them use descriptive phrases, adjectives, and adverbs. In addition, they do not identify and edit errors in their writing.

Noted literacy scholar and author Gail Tompkins (2010) is also troubled about the writing abilities of students in these grades. Like Strickland et al. (2002), she believes Grades 4 through 8 are a critical period for developing students' writing expertise and that these grades may offer last-chance opportunities to remedy students' continued and personalized failure in writing. She states, "If students are unfamiliar and uncomfortable with the basics of . . . writing by the time they reach grade four, all their learning will suffer" (p. x).

Statistics also indicate there is cause for concern.

- A recent survey shows writing instruction in the United States has not received sufficient attention from researchers or educators (Cassidy & Cassidy, 2009, 2010; Cassidy & Lovelace, 2011; also see Graham & Perrin, 2007a; Strickland et al., 2002).
- Seventy percent of students in Grades 4 and above are low-achieving writers—those whose writing abilities do not satisfy grade-level writing requirements (Persky, Daane, & Jin, 2003).

- College instructors estimate that 50 percent of high school graduates are ill prepared for college writing (Achieve, Inc, 2005).
- The writing abilities of graduates in the United States are lower than their counterparts in most industrialized nations (Organisation for Economic Co-operation and Development [OECD], 2000).
- Thirty-five percent of high school graduates in the workforce think their writing is poor (Achieve, Inc, 2005).
- Nearly one-third of high school graduates are not ready for college-level English composition courses (ACT, 2005).
- Teachers of Grades 4 through 8 worry how to teach writing to students of different ability levels and how to support struggling writers (Ganske, Monroe, & Strickland, 2003).

These statistics are alarming; however, there is also hope. Recently, educators have begun to appreciate the benefits of teaching writing in small groups based on students' differing needs (Lenski & Johns, 2004). A recent report from the Carnegie Corporation of New York found that while no single approach to writing meets the instructional requirements of all students, writing strategy instruction "has shown a dramatic effect on the quality of students' writing" (Graham & Perin, 2007b, p. 15). The use of writing strategies provides necessary help for students by reducing their cognitive load as they proceed through the writing process (Olinghouse, Zheng, & Reed, 2010). Writing-strategy instruction is well supported by research and is effective for *all* students, particularly those in the intermediate grades who are low-achieving writers (De La Paz & Graham, 2002; Graham & Perin, 2007b; Troia & Graham, 2002).

HOW WE ARRANGED THIS BOOK

We have organized the chapters in this volume in four sections. Section I provides invention strategies: strategies writers use to help develop their ideas for writing. Section II presents drafting strategies: independent ways writers can get their ideas down on paper. Section III offers strategies for revision: the heart of writing. Section IV provides editing strategies: methods writers employ to fine-tune their work.

All chapters, which have been written by classroom teachers, language arts specialists, and teacher educators, follow a parallel structure for ease of use. Each contains the following sections:

- An explanation of the *purpose* of the strategy (e.g., "This strategy helps students learn how to paraphrase information an author has previously stated")
- A section on why the strategy is important
- A list of materials needed to teach the strategy
- An authentic classroom scenario that includes step-by-step guidance for teaching and modeling the strategy

- Suggestions for helping students practice the strategy, scaffolding students as they write independently, and assisting students as they reflect on how use of the strategy enhances their writing efforts
- Suggestions for adapting the strategy for diverse learners
- Suggestions for extending the strategy across content areas
- Suggestions for further reading about topics discussed in the chapter in a brief annotated bibliography

Research indicates that educators tend to adopt new practices if they are presented in classroom contexts (Borko, 2004; Fuchs & Fuchs, 2001). In addition to the real-life scenarios presented in each chapter, the strategy lessons provide explicit details for instruction that will help readers understand how to

a. model appropriate strategies that meet students' immediate writing needs,

b. assist students as they learn and practice the strategies in an interactive setting with peers,

c. engage students in discussions and dialogue about the strategies to determine their understandings and confusions, and,

d. support students as they learn to make use of the strategies as needed in authentic writing situations.

The parallel format of the chapters will help you easily locate information.

Many chapter authors use devices and techniques other than paper and pencils to help students understand writing concepts. For example, some authors include visuals in their lessons, such as an inflated balloon, drawings, charts, or photographs. Other strategies help students visualize (i.e., create mental images) about a topic or story characters. Still other chapter authors incorporate technology or assemble students in small collaborative groups or with partners. These techniques and practices enable teachers and students to move beyond traditional print-based writing instruction to engage with a wide range of possibilities geared to developing students' writing capacity.

It is important to remember that "there is no set list of 'one size fits all' strategies for writing" (Hampton & Resnick, 2009, p. 60). Following Harris and Graham's (1992) recommendation, we do not present strategy mini-lessons in a prescribed sequence that must be explicitly followed. Instead, we arranged this book so that you can easily find chapters that address your students' particular needs. The strategies are grouped according to students' developmental needs and typical writing problems. We trust you to use your professional judgment to determine what strategies to teach in meaningful mini-lessons according to students' strengths and requirements. Strategies address a wide range of needs, including these:

- How to recognize the purpose and structure of different genres
- How to paraphrase and why it's important
- How to use mentor texts to guide writing
- How to "quilt" a research paper together
- How to observe character traits and apply these observations to writing

In addition, the book contains student self-assessment checklists, charts, and rubrics that help students "reflect upon and evaluate the quality of their own writing" (Graham & Perin, 2007b, p. 27).

THE NEED TO OBSERVE STUDENTS

It is important to note that our purpose for this book is not to provide descriptions of writing strategies you should model and teach irrespective of students' needs. Rather, we aim to help you understand the value of recognizing what individual and groups of students need to learn next about writing. We encourage you to

- observe your students closely as they write and then document their writing behaviors,
- scaffold students' immediate writing requirements by providing brief collaborative lessons that promote and encourage student input, and
- help students deliberately apply these strategies to solve problems they encounter when writing independently (see Collins, 1998).

STRATEGIES THAT MEET THE WRITING INSTRUCTIONAL NEEDS OF ALL STUDENTS

As we planned this book, we recognized the following:

- "All students need to become proficient and flexible writers" (Graham & Perin, 2007, p. 7).
- Students in Grade 4 vary considerably from students in Grades 5, 6, 7, and 8.
- This book will be used by a variety of teachers and other support personnel with a wide range of students irrespective of grade level.
- Teaching contexts at any grade level vary widely and may include gifted writers, students with written language learning disabilities, students who struggle occasionally or often with certain aspects of writing or particular writing genres, and those who compose in a second language (Graham & Perin, 2007). A worrisome issue for new and experienced teachers is how to work with different levels and abilities of students, a problem that is intensified by large classes (Ganske et al., 2003).

Toward this end—and inspired by Carol Baldwin (2008), who authored the book *Teaching the Story: Fiction Writing in Grades 4–8*—we have planned this text carefully to suit the writing instructional needs of diverse learners, including English language learners, students who struggle with writing, and gifted writers. You, as a knowledgeable professional, will determine what specific writing strategies students need to learn next.

WE ADMIRE YOUR WORK

We wrote this book for busy writing educators like you who support, affirm, and mentor all their fourth- through eighth-grade students to enable them to become confident, strategic, independent, successful writers.

We would like to hear from you, so please contact us, and let us know how the strategies in this book meet your students' writing instructional needs. And thank you for all your work to ensure that your students become confident, self-directed writers.

Janet (JRichards@usf.edu) and
Cindy (cindy.lassonde@oneonta.edu)

Section I

Strategic Inventing

Contemplating Ideas

There are many steps we can take to help students fulfill their potential to create and compose high-quality, creative, and informative pieces of writing—whether they are composing in a writing workshop setting, for personal enjoyment, to respond to a prompt, to reflect, or to fulfill an assignment related to a content subject. In each case, students must begin with ideas and information that they need to process. They need to take these gemstones of knowledge and experience; hone them into substantial, meaningful thoughts; and piece them together into organized schemas that contain the rich vocabulary, organization, and insightful context we all want as writers.

This component of the writing process is what we refer to as *invention*. Typically, inventing is the way writers begin each writing experience or task. It then occurs throughout the process as writers tumble back and forth among thinking, composing, revising, organizing, and researching while they contemplate and toy with their craft. Writers invent each time they consider a new idea and determine how to include it among their other thoughts. They make the abstract more concrete as they begin to set ideas, knowledge, experiences, and eventually, words to paper.

Each of the strategies presented in this section is designed to help students

- generate and expand ideas,
- develop insight,
- organize their thinking,
- envision what their writing will entail, and
- produce as they prepare to write.

Some chapters provide reproducible charts and graphic organizers to prompt students to capture and record valuable thoughts and vocabulary as they prepare to draft. Some prompt students to think metacognitively about writing to guide their planning. Other chapters support students' thinking by reviewing and analyzing mentor texts as genre models. Each chapter offers a mini-lesson to foster students' self-regulated use of inventing strategies as writing tools.

You may wish to begin to explore this section by reading the opening paragraph in each chapter. Note: Think of the individuals in your class who might benefit from each of the mini-lessons. Then, select a mini-lesson and try it out. We think you will be amazed at how readily students latch onto the use of well-grounded inventing strategies that support their writing—and how their writing improves as a consequence.

Color-Coding Sources 1

Cynthia A. Lassonde

According to the English Language Arts Common Core Standards, students in Grades 4 through 8 are expected to start to learn how to locate and synthesize information from multiple sources to compose reports and research papers. The Color-Coding Sources strategy helps students organize ideas gathered from multiple primary and secondary sources by linking information with source citations. As students write notes, construct outlines or graphic organizers, and draft reports, they bring along the color-coding that matches the citation. This eliminates all guesswork about the material's origin.

WHY THIS STRATEGY IS IMPORTANT

As a sixth-grade English language arts teacher, I routinely collaborated with our team social studies teacher on an inquiry project in which students researched and wrote reports about ancient civilizations. One of the most difficult writing tasks for students was to keep their notes organized as they collected information from multiple sources. By the time they wrote their first draft, many could no longer remember the exact sources of each piece of information. That's when I started showing students how to color-code sources and notes. To our delight, we found that adding this visual component helped them stay organized.

THE MINI-LESSON

As I work with students on research reports, I note which writers have a system for organizing their information and which do not. To make this assessment, I simply look for citations attached to notes and ask students what they do to identify which information came from which source.

Once I've determined who would benefit from learning the Color-Coding Sources strategy, I meet with them in a small group, asking them to bring their notes and sources.

Materials Needed

- Highlighters in several different colors
- Index cards
- Class computers, prepared for use
- Example inquiry question written on a piece of paper
- Examples of notes that have been color-coded using three methods:
  - highlighters
  - colored index cards
  - differently colored fonts

In preparation for the lesson, I use a different color in some way to code each source that I will bring to our group—highlighting it, writing it on a particular colored index card, or selecting a colored font on the computer. As noted, students also bring their own resources and notes when we meet in a small group.

To begin, students take turns sharing what they've done so far, and together we look at students' processes and progress. We also discuss how essential it is to cite others' ideas and not present them as our own. One of the most beneficial parts of this strategy happens when students move their notes into their report. All they need to do is transfer their highlighting from their notes to their report as they write the first draft. This way, they can identify what notes and sources they have used and the pages from which the information came. I tell students about this advantage up front so they know why they are color-coding their notes. For this stage, however, they should focus on getting the notes they will need to inform their writing in a way that is organized and makes sense to them.

Model the Strategy

As I lead the group, I do the following:

1. I model how students might ask their question of inquiry, look for information in multiple sources, and keep a running log of citations or references for each source.

2. I ask students to take notes from one of my sources, using *the same color* that corresponds with the citation. I model this process as I explain it.

3. I demonstrate how I paraphrase. I remind students how to do this using the Use Your Own Words: Paraphrase strategy (see Chapter 10).

Here's an example of what this looks like.

Teacher: My report is about how the Ancient Egyptians used to mummify people when they died. In the part of my report that I'm working on now, I'm trying to answer my question about the process of mummification:

> How were bodies prepared for mummification? I've found these three informative resources: *Mummies & Pyramids* [Taplin, 2010], *Mummies Made in Egypt* [Aliki, 2011], and an online BBC website entry about mummification [see www.bbc.co.uk/history/ancient/Egyptians]. They each explain the process and show pictures that help me understand the procedure.

I show them the first book and continue.

> **Teacher:** I have my inquiry question written on top of the note card or paper so I know what question I'm trying to answer. That keeps my notes organized.

I point out the question on top of a piece of paper.

> **Teacher:** Then, I paraphrase or put into my own words this information about the mummification process.

I show them the following notes in three formats: typed on a computer, written on a colored index card, and written on paper and highlighted.

> **Teacher:** If I like to use the computer to take notes, I start with my first source. I type in my bibliographic information on the book first thing. That way, I have it done, and I won't have to look for all the information when it's time to get my bibliography together. I also note the page numbers where I find the information I'm paraphrasing so if I want to go back to check on something, I have that information right there. Also, if I want to quote something word for word directly from the book, I write it in quotes in my notes and put the page number. I'll need that page information to put into my report for direct quotes. I'm making things very easy for myself later by taking the time to put this information in my notes now. I know I won't remember all these details a week from now when I'm writing my final report!

As I explain all this, I point to this information in the sample notes I have displayed.

> **Teacher:** Now comes the color-coding part. When I type in the bibliographic information for this first source, I choose one color that will stand for this source only. I've chosen blue for the *Mummies and Pyramids* book because the cover is blue. You don't have to use colors to match the book cover, but I find it's just another little strategy to help me remember

> where my notes came from in case I need to go back to the book later. When I type in all my notes from this source, I will use blue. Then, I go to the second source, *Mummies Made in Egypt.* I change the color of my typing. This time, I'll use the color red to remind me of the cover. I type the bibliography for *Egyptians* in red, then type all the notes from this source in red also. Then, I go on to my third source, the BBC website entry on mummification. Again, I change to a third color; I've used green. I type my bibliography and notes from that source in that color.

After we've reviewed the three different methods, I continue modeling.

> **Teacher:** Now that I have all my notes about the process of mummification in one place, I can read through them and quilt them together into a well-written report about how Egyptians mummified people when they died.

After students complete their notes, we meet again to practice quilting together their notes into a color-coded draft. At that point, I also refer students to the Quilting Together an Expository Paper in Four Steps strategy for how to synthesize notes from three sources into their report (see Chapter 8).

When the time comes for students to write their draft, I demonstrate how to transfer the color-coded notes into a first draft. I simply use a highlighter that matches the color of the source to highlight the section that came from a particular source. If I'm working on a computer, I change the color of the font to match the notes' colors. When I'm done with my draft, I show them how to insert the reference citations by matching the color-coded information to my bibliography. When I prepare my final report, I write—or edit my typed report—so no color coding shows. Magically, no one knows my color-coding secret!

Students Practice the Strategy

As the example shows, I help students' practice the strategy by first walking them through one source. For students who need more help, I guide them with a second source and then gradually pull back my support so they can work toward independence.

Independent Writing

Students continue using the strategy with several other sources, identifying a different color for each source. I support them by observing and guiding them through the process as needed.

Student Reflection

Once students can use the strategy independently and confidently, I ask them to share how they might use this strategy in other ways. For example, how might color-coding help them organize other writing genres?

MODIFYING THE MINI-LESSON

Adaptations for Writers Who Struggle

I make it clear what style I want students to follow for their citations and report references or bibliography. For example, if I require APA (American Psychological Association, 2010), I provide examples of how to cite various types of sources, such as books, articles, and online sources. I teach students how to follow the models by replacing information from the model examples with information from their sources.

I also provide a graphic organizer for students to use to sort their sources (Figure 1.1). I adjust the number of sources I expect students to consult and refer to in their reports.

Adaptations for English Language Learners

I have found that English language learners (ELLs) require assistance mostly with putting notes from a source into their own words and synthesizing data from multiple sources into coherent ideas. For ideas on how to assist ELLs with these skills, see Use Your Own Words: Paraphrase strategy (Chapter 10) and Quilting Together an Expository Paper in Four Steps (Chapter 8).

Adaptations for Advanced Writers

I maintain high expectations for advanced writers to stretch their vocabulary as they write their reports and to explicitly follow the designated citation and bibliography style required. If writers are developmentally ready to think critically about the topic about which they are reporting, I have them add an addendum to the report that states their perspective or opinion and use the information from their notes to support their statement. Students use the Color-Coding Sources strategy to prepare this addendum.

EXTENDING THE STRATEGY ACROSS THE CONTENT AREAS

The Color-Coding Sources strategy easily applies to writing exposition in any content area. The strategy may also be used when students are working collaboratively on a project. Each student's work and ideas can be identified on a final product through color coding and cited in a final bibliography or color-coding key.

Figure 1.1 Note Chart for Sorting Sources

Inquiry Question:

Source # _____

Bibliography

Author _____ Copyright date _____

Title _____

Publisher City, State _____

Publisher _____ or website _____

Notes and Quotes

Page _____

Page _____

RESOURCES FOR FURTHER READING

➤ Richards, J. C., & Lassonde, C. A. (2011). *Writing strategies for all primary students: Scaffolding independent writing with differentiated mini-lessons.* San Francisco, CA: Jossey-Bass.

Teaching writing strategies is essential if we want students to envision how concrete mental operations occur during composing. Strategies such as Color-Coding Sources make mental actions transparent to students by demonstrating visually how to apply them. Teaching new strategies is critical to expand the knowledge base of writers in Grades 4 through 8.

➤ Richardson, J. S., Morgan, R. F., & Fleener, C. E. (2012). *Reading to learn in the content areas.* Belmont, CA: Wadsworth Cengage.

Using computers as tools for writing is not just for advanced writers or older students. Students in Grades 4 through 8 can benefit from using technology to access, store, and draft information as they use the writing process to work through a report of research. Various technology tools and means of producing writing provide different kinds of opportunities for students to develop and enhance their writing skills and use of strategies.

2 Developing Students' Awareness of Their Strengths as Writers With an I-Can! Chart

Joanne Durham

This chapter discusses how students can record positive aspects of their writing on a chart in their writing folders. These aspects include both authors' craft (techniques writers use to make their writing interesting and effective) and conventions of written language (grammar, spelling, punctuation, and capitalization). The chart functions as a personalized reference tool that students can add to; it serves as a reference to help them recall what craft and conventions they have already employed and can apply again in future pieces.

Specifically, using an I-Can! chart helps students

- build awareness of their strengths as writers,
- transfer those strengths from one piece of writing to another, and
- develop confidence in their writing capabilities,

WHY THIS STRATEGY IS IMPORTANT

Experts who teach students to write emphasize the following: *Accentuate the positive. Notice and build from students' strengths.* I couldn't agree more, and as a teacher and coach of writing in Grades 4 through 8, I have tried constantly to keep this mantra in the forefront of my instruction.

Teachers often keep their own checklists or conference notes on students' burgeoning strengths as writers. As I taught writing workshop, I began to understand it's not enough for the *teacher* to recognize students' capabilities.

Rather, it's when *students* recognize and believe in their own strengths that success is more likely to follow.

Research on the relationship of students' writing to metacognition (Harris, Graham, Brindle, & Sandmel, 2009) and motivation (Strickland, Ganske, & Monroe, 2002) confirms that helping students become cognizant of their strengths helps them develop as writers. The I-Can! chart puts this line of thinking into practice in a simple process for students to use. The very name of the strategy reflects metacognitive thinking and motivation—I Can!

The I-Can! strategy differentiates by its nature. It is a personal list of writing accomplishments—specifically, ideas for improving one's writing craft and conventions—that each student has selected as noteworthy. There is no expectation that every student will have the same list. In fact, the chart displays a variety of crafts and conventions that helps students look to one another for ideas and builds a community of support. The charts also serve as a handy reference for me when I confer with individual students about their writing. I can see patterns and determine aspects of writing that are missing. I can also use previous strengths as segues for teaching new techniques.

THE MINI-LESSON

Materials Needed

- Copies of I-Can! charts for students to put into their writing folder (Figure 2.1)
- Chart paper or a projector to model the strategy
- A piece of writing prepared for display to use as a model
- A copy of the I-Can! chart (Figure 2.1) enlarged for display to use as a model during the lesson
- (Figures 2.4 and 2.5 show part of a completed example)

I situate this lesson within our first cycle of the year on revision in writing workshop. Students by now have examined several published texts as examples of the genre we are studying. They have noticed a variety of writers' craft authors employ, and we have posted these on authors' craft charts in the classroom.

Model the Strategy

To begin, I ask students to assemble with drafts they need to revise and complete. I use the following type of dialogue when we meet.

Teacher: An exciting part of writing is to recognize how much we have learned about being writers by paying attention to mentor texts. This process helps us as writers to keep track of the craft we have used effectively in our own pieces. Just like we write to capture our ideas, feelings, and experiences so we will have them forever, we keep track of the writers' craft we have used well so we can remember to try the same approaches another time.

Figure 2.1 Reproducible I-Can! Chart

Name _____

I Can!			
		I Can . . .	
Date	Title	Craft	Conventions

Then, I show students a copy of an I-Can! chart.

> **Teacher:** I will give each of you a chart like this to keep in your writing folders for the rest of the year. We will use the chart to record elements of craft we have used in our own writing and think we can continue to use in the future. Let me show you how I'm going to choose the craft I can put on my I-Can! chart from the writing I have been working on with you. Later, you will begin to do the same thing on your own charts.

I begin modeling by sharing on the projector a piece of my own writing. I choose a piece that students will recognize from a previous drafting or revising lesson. I point out to students how I have tried to make specific parts of my writing effective. I choose two craft elements: one we have worked on in mini-lessons and one I have not taught. Since I usually start the year with personal narratives, I often use excerpts from a piece I wrote about the day my 5-year-old son got lost in the park.

My choice of craft elements varies with the grade and sophistication of the writers in my classroom. In the following example, I work with a group of fourth graders who do not have much experience with writing workshop. Since we have been focusing on using dialogue in our writing, I've chosen the following passage, which contains some lines of dialogue:

I saw some people who had been behind us come walking up. "Did you see a little boy?" I asked. "Wearing a red shirt and brown shorts?"

"No," they replied. "That little boy who was with you?"

"Yes. We can't find him." I could see the fear in my eyes reflected in theirs.

"Lee! LEE!" I called out, as loudly as I could. But my voice rang hollow—no one was there.

After sharing the passage, I ask students to share with a peer how they think the dialogue helps the story. I circulate and listen to their ideas. One student talks about how the dialogue helps pull the reader into the story. Another says that it draws out a part that is important. I refer specifically to those students' comments as I explain how I think the dialogue contributes to the story. It develops the part where I am searching for my son, so my panic can be felt more fully by the reader. I tell them I think I could use dialogue again in another piece of writing. Then I show students how I could record this information on my I-Can! chart (see Figure 2.2).

For my second example, I choose a slightly more sophisticated craft element we have not discussed in a mini-lesson. I want to encourage students not only to choose the elements we have studied but also to discover other craft on their own. This way, we wind up with a wide variety of craft, and students are motivated to try various crafts because their peers did.

Figure 2.2   I-Can! Chart Sample 1

		I Can!	
		I Can . . .	
Date	Title	Craft	Conventions
9:20	"Lost in the Park"	Use dialogue to bring my reader into the story.	

In this case, I decide to share the following lines, which appear in an earlier section of my personal narrative:

We paused at the tennis courts, again at the soccer field, and finally took a real rest at the snow cone vendor. Lee, his face now purple and his hands sticky, ran ahead of us back toward the parking lot.

Then I use the following type of language as I speak with students.

Teacher: In these two sentences, I summed up what actually occurred over an hour. Since I wanted my story to focus on Lee being lost and how I felt while it was happening, I didn't want to spend a lot of time writing about everything we did in the park. I didn't think I needed to tell readers how we ordered our snow cones: Lee chose a raspberry one, and he got it all over himself. As a writer, I can manipulate time, making it go slower or faster than it really did, depending on what I want my reader to notice. I made this part go fast, including just enough details to let the reader know we did a lot of fun things in the park, and then Lee was running in front of us. I think it helped my story to manipulate time to go quickly over unimportant events. I will add that to my I-Can! chart, too.

I show the students how I use ditto marks to signal I am repeating the same date and title, and then I enter "make time go fast over unimportant events" (see Figure 2.3).

Figure 2.3   I-Can! Chart Sample 2

		I Can!	
		I Can . . .	
Date	Title	Craft	Conventions
9:20	"Lost in the Park"	Use dialogue to bring my reader into the story.	
"	"	Make time go fast over unimportant events.	

Students Practice the Strategy

At this point in the lesson, we briefly revisit the craft charts posted in the classroom that show the elements we have studied and include examples from authors we have read. Then I ask students to look over their own narratives. I tell them to put a star beside places where they think they have effectively used a craft element we studied or where they think they have done something else "writerly" that might be worth doing again another time. I tell them to be ready to explain their choices.

I circulate among students and support them as needed. Then I have them turn and talk with a partner to share their examples and discuss how their craft helps their stories, just like we did when I shared my examples. I circulate again, listening for who has an idea and looking for students who have chosen clear examples that will help the group. If I think some students need more examples, I call on one or two of the students with strong choices to read the part of their narrative that contains their craft element. If it is a craft we already have on the chart, I may have the student call on other students to name the craft and discuss how it contributes to the story.

I keep this part as short as possible but developed enough to be sure that a significant number of students will be able to identify something to put on their I-Can! charts. I don't worry if everyone isn't ready to do this. There will be time for me to confer with individuals and more days of writing and revising for everyone to find something to add.

Independent Writing

When we've finished our discussion, I tell students that if they have identified something they feel is worthy of adding to their I-Can! chart, they may add it when they go to work independently. I ask them to leave their folders open to their charts so I can confer with them about what they have added. Then, I release them to write. Some work to complete their drafts, others work on revisions, and some confer with peers to help figure out what they need to do next.

When I come around to confer, I check to see if a student has added something to his I-Can! chart. If that is the case, I ask him to show me the reference in his writing and explain how the craft contributed to his piece. I congratulate students on recognizing their strengths and suggest they use the I-Can! chart to remember to use that technique again in another piece.

If a student has not identified anything for her I-Can! chart, I may look over the writing with the student, ask her to read me a selected part, and then ask if there is anything in that part that uses a craft element we have studied. However, I don't require students to add something to their charts on the first day I have introduced a new dimension of writing. Sometimes it is more productive for me to read their work later, make my own notes or put a sticky note on their writing, and then work with them another time.

If students use a craft we have not yet studied, I may help them name what they have accomplished. I congratulate them for discovering, all by themselves, a writer's technique. For example, I see that one fourth-grader has written, "Let me warn you about someone who lives with my grandma. Maria Grisella is her name." The story goes on about the misadventures of Maria Grisella. I explain how her words "Let me warn you" make the reader realize ahead of time that something bad but maybe also funny is probably going to happen regarding Maria Grisella. I note that authors do this a lot to get us interested, and I label it for her: *foreshadowing.* I then ask the student to write "foreshadowing" on her I-Can! chart and share it with the class during our group share.

Student Reflection

When we reassemble to share, I choose students who have added appropriate strategies to their I-Can! charts. I ask them to read the applicable parts, and we discuss what craft they have used and its effect on their writing. I then begin a large class I-Can! chart that I will display in the room. I use their examples and credit them by name (see Figure 2.4).

I close the lesson by explaining that students are building their own personal lists of craft elements that they know they can use over and over in their writing. I suggest they refer to their I-Can! lists and the large class chart when they are stuck for ways to improve their writing. They and their peers can be their own best teachers.

In later lessons, when we begin proofreading our pieces in preparation for publishing, I do another short mini-lesson with the I-Can! chart. This time I add to the conventions column of my own chart and encourage students to find conventions they can add to their own charts as well. I create a large class conventions I-Can! chart and post it near the class craft chart (see Figure 2.5).

Figure 2.4 I-Can! Class Chart: Author's Craft

Author's Craft	Our Examples	Author
Use a "power" word.	We also saw the lizards *camouflaged* by the trees.	Duane
Make interesting language choices.	The horse runs so fast it gives you wind when you ride it.	Ellyn
Choose a lead that makes the reader curious to read on.	When I first went skateboarding down a steep hill, I thought it was going to be easy.	Adam

Figure 2.5 I-Can! Class Chart: Conventions

Conventions	Our Examples	Author
Use complete sentences.	There were 4 seconds left on the clock.	Trevon
Correct spelling mistakes.	turble to terrible; socker to soccer	Leyla
Combine short sentences effectively into a longer sentence.	I did not know anything about this school, so the other kids helped me.	Kendra

We continue to add to the I-Can! charts after completing all published work as well as during drafting, revising, and proofreading throughout the year. I encourage students to add to the charts on their own. They keep their charts in their writing folders for easy referral. We look at them together when we confer about a piece of writing. We check to see if they have added new elements to their charts. We also note if they actually use elements of writing they have previously listed. In this way, they are accountable for their past performances, and they add to their writing repertoires. Figure 2.6 shows one student's chart at the end of a personal narrative study.

Figure 2.6   Sample I-Can! Chart Following a Personal Narrative Study

		I Can!	
		I Can . . .	
Date	Title	Craft	Conventions
9:25	"I Got My Shot"	Choose an ending that wraps up my story.	
10:12	"The Game We Won"	Make my writing more exciting by stretching out time.	
10:20	"The Game We Won"	Use strong verbs.	
10:22	"The Game We Won"		Indent every paragraph.

MODIFYING THE MINI-LESSON

Adaptations for Writers Who Struggle

Strickland et al. (2002) emphasize how important it is for struggling writers to experience success. They suggest that these students "need to be viewed as learners who can achieve . . . need instruction that emphasizes self-monitoring and control over their own learning . . . and need special efforts at motivation" (pp. 12–13). Because the I-Can! process supports all these needs, it is especially useful for struggling writers.

If my whole-class mini-lesson has not provided sufficient modeling, I might pull a small group or give more examples when I individually confer. Because struggling writers often do not recognize anything positive in their work, at first I may need to identify strengths for their charts. For example, let's say that a student has written, "When I got to the balls, I dove in." In this case, I would point out that the student has used a strong verb (*dove*), which enhanced the reader's picture of the action. As I point out and praise this writing and note that it's worthy of inclusion on the I-Can! chart, the student becomes aware of a capability he had not recognized.

Recording this achievement on the chart also serves two purposes for the student:

1. It builds his confidence.

2. It increases the likelihood that he will try to use a strong verb again.

This process develops students' metacognition, the "deliberate, conscious use of a writing or self-regulating strategy" (Harris et al., 2009, p. 140), which the same authors note as a characteristic of higher-achieving writers.

As struggling writers make small revisions, sometimes based on mini-lessons, they often generate material that can be added to their I-Can! charts. For example, a seventh-grader who revises the title of her personal narrative from "Birthday Party" to "Party of Chaos" shows she understands how a title might draw the reader into wanting to read the story. This could become an example not only for her I-Can! chart but also for sharing with the whole class, which is another way to build the confidence of a struggling writer.

When we find and focus on these specific strengths in students' work rather than on evaluating the whole piece, we give all writers, no matter how much they struggle, a way to shine. We also remind ourselves that every student has competencies. While it can be tempting to focus on everything that is wrong in a student's writing, we must remind ourselves, as Regie Routman (2005) writes, "Until the student thinks of himself as a writer, no real improvement is possible" (p. 80). The I-Can! chart can help us remember that one of our most important functions as teachers is to help struggling writers see that they are, indeed, writers.

Adaptations for English Language Learners

Many of the adaptations for struggling writers apply to beginning English language learners. It is important to build their writing confidence and awareness of their writing strengths by finding small but meaningful advances in their writing for them to record on their I-Can! charts. With these students, I may hold group conferences and identify strengths for their charts as we work on any part of the writing process. I encourage students who are not yet able to write in English to write in their native language and to record their craft on their I-Can! charts in their own language as well. In this way, they learn to look for and use craft elements in their native language. Later, this skill can transfer to English.

Adaptations for Advanced Writers

There are two reasons I include in my modeling a craft element we have not studied:

1. To open the door wide enough that all students can find something in their work to put on the I-Can! chart

2. To motivate students to try new techniques

Advanced writers often respond to this challenge to experiment. Sometimes I specifically suggest a new craft element for them to try. Also, when they are not aware that something they have done is, in fact, a technique good writers often use, I point it out to them and then ask them to share with the class. I monitor their charts carefully to be sure I challenge advanced writers sufficiently to discover how and when to use more sophisticated writing techniques.

EXTENDING THE STRATEGY ACROSS THE CONTENT AREAS

Students continue to use their I-Can! charts as they move into other nonfiction genres, such as essays, feature articles, opinion pieces, or research reports. They may note that they can use text features such as maps, charts, or graphs to help their readers understand the information they present, or they may note that they can support their opinions with evidence. By recognizing the characteristics of various types of nonfiction writing and noticing how they can use these in their own pieces, students become more capable of producing meaningful written work in content areas such as science and social studies.

RESOURCES FOR FURTHER READING

➤ Harris, K., Graham, S., Brindle, M., & Sandmel, K. (2009). Metacognition and children's writing. In D. J. Hacker, J. Dunloskey, & A. Graesson (Eds.), *Handbook of metacognition in education* (pp. 131–153). Abingdon, Oxon, UK: Routledge.

   The authors trace the history of studies that have documented the importance of metacognition in students' writing since the 1980s. They discuss the significance found in numerous studies of students having knowledge of their own abilities, including specific components they have accomplished successfully.

➤ Routman, R. (2005). *Writing essentials: Raising expectations and results while simplifying teaching.* Portsmouth, NH: Heinemann.

   Regie Routman helps us as teachers to recognize the importance of seeing the positive in students' writing. She proposes,

   > As teachers, we need to view children's writing through a nurturing, positive lens and notice all the small and big things kids do well. Too often, we teachers are unable to "see" what children have accomplished. When we cannot, we lose them as writers. We have to let children in on the secret of how powerfully they write. (p. 39)

➤ Strickland, D., Ganske, K., & Monroe, J. K. (2002). *Supporting struggling readers and writers: Strategies for classroom intervention 3–6.* Portland, ME: Stenhouse.

   In their chapter on the factors placing students at risk for failure, the authors discuss how researchers on motivation "stress the need for students to feel both competent and in control" (p. 14). They include "mildly disabled students" who qualify for special education services among those whose capabilities increase when they "learn to be strategic in their use of skills" (p. 13).

3 Using a Blueprint Graphic Organizer to Build a Story

Jennifer A. Fontenot

This strategy helps students learn how to develop an exemplary story using the Blueprint Graphic Organizer. The Blueprint alerts students to look for elements and structures that students and professional authors use in their stories. Once students have selected a topic for their story, this strategy helps them begin by introducing characters and a setting, a problem situation, and a conclusion where the problem is resolved or a lesson is learned. Students use their completed Blueprint Graphic Organizer to share their stories with a group of peers and, if necessary, use feedback from the group to modify their Blueprints. They are then ready to write the first draft of their story.

WHY THIS STRATEGY IS IMPORTANT

National testing shows that a majority of students in the United States at all grade levels are below proficiency in high-stake tests in writing. Historically, there has never been an academic program for consistently teaching writing to all grade levels. It's no wonder that teachers in Grades 4 through 8 find writing to be one of the most difficult subjects to teach. Quite often when it's time to write a story, students will shrug their shoulders and say, "I don't know what to write about."

Over the years, I've noticed that students do minimal planning even when they are familiar with the writing process. They hem and haw about their individual writing topic and then begin to write a narrative story without adequate preparation. The result is a story with inadequate character development; little attention to setting; and no substantive plot where a problem situation should have been introduced, developed, and eventually resolved in the conclusion.

To me, when students ask, "How many paragraphs do I have to write?" it implies they do not like to write. I view this as a problem that has a cause-and-effect relationship. Students don't enjoy writing because they don't know how to do it. It's hard to compose interesting, proficient stories if you don't have an organized methodology to help guide you through the process.

To address these issues, I have developed the Blueprint Graphic Organizer (Fontenot & Carney, 2008; see Figure 3.1). The Blueprint, as my students come to call it, accomplishes the following:

- It draws together all the preliminary work required for students to understand the theme of the writing assignment.
- It prompts each student to select a personal topic for the assignment.
- It results in a student-prepared document that guides the rest of the writing process through to completion of a final publishable draft.

Just as a carpenter uses a blueprint to guide the building of a house, students use the Blueprint Graphic Organizer to build proficient, personalized, exciting narrative stories.

To determine which students would benefit from learning this strategy, I assess students' narrative stories according to story elements. I use a simple rubric (see Figure 3.2).

This Blueprint Graphic Organizer has the added advantage of being transferrable to all genres; however, I find that beginning with a personal narrative provides opportunities for students to relate their own individual, special story to the teacher and the class. After all, each student does indeed have a story to tell! My teaching goals are twofold:

1. Motivate students to understand and write various types of narrative selections

2. Teach students to develop narrative stories using all the required components

The following mini-lesson shows how to use the Blueprint Graphic Organizer to enable students to self-regulate the writing process.

THE MINI-LESSON

Materials Needed

- Chart paper or a projector to model the strategy. To include as much appropriate technology as possible to capture students' attention, I choose a digital projector, a computer that has Internet accessibility, or a SMART Board.

(Continued)

(Continued)

- Thought-stimulating videos or pictures. It is easy to find short video clips for streaming that add excitement to lessons. To model my personal story I use a short video stream related to my personal topic—flying in an airplane during a thunderstorm. One website I found appropriate to my scary experience is www.flightlevel350.com/. When I don't have technology available, I use magazine pictures glued to cardboard to instill visual literacy and capture students' attention.
- A large, blank copy of the Blueprint Graphic Organizer (Figure 3.1) to display during modeling.
- Colored folders. I like to pass out folders and ask students to write their names and the date on them. Students keep all writing material for the current project in this folder: pictures, charts, any data collected, and most important of all, the critical component used in modeling this lesson, the Blueprint Graphic Organizer.
- One copy of a blank Blueprint Graphic Organizer for each student (Figure 3.1)

The first part of the Blueprint mini-lesson is critical because it draws students into the writing assignment. Here, I assign a universal theme. A highly motivating theme for students in Grades 4 through 8 might be something like this: "Write about a time when you were scared." Virtually all students have had frightening experiences they will remember for the rest of their lives. A universal theme such as this allows students to begin with a topic that relates to their personal experiences.

To begin, I tell my own story to help students generate their own ideas. In this example, I briefly talk about a time when I was in an airplane in a thunderstorm. Telling short bits of this story descriptively helps me draw students into my experience, and it also initiates their thinking about their own scary predicament. Once students begin to develop their own topic ideas, I prepare a class-generated list of topics and post them in the classroom. Figure 3.3 shows an example.

Notice that many students have similar topics. For example, Amy describes her scariest moment as playing in her first piano recital, while Justin's greatest fear was his first soccer game. This type of student topic connection is not atypical, nor should it be discouraged. Teacher-directed class discussions such as this one will generate great ideas for all students—no more "I don't know what to write about" complaints!

There are many benefits for this type of classroom discussion:

- Students generate individual student topics based on and directly related to the class writing themes.
- Students who have a difficult time coming up with original ideas can model the stories of their peers.
- This process motivates students to tell "their story."
- Students also relate to the stories of their peers, which helps to draw them into the writing assignment.

Figure 3.1   Reproducible Blueprint Graphic Organizer

Blueprint Graphic Organizer

Name _____   Date _____

Class Theme _____   Student Topic _____

Part 1: The Story Beginning

1. _____
2. _____

Include story beginning with setting and main characters.

Part 2: The Storyline Details With the Plot

1. _____
2. _____
3. _____
4. _____
5. _____
6. _____
7. _____
8. _____
9. _____
10. _____
11. _____

Include the storyline with the plot, using descriptive language.

Part 3: The Story Resolution With the Newly Learned Concept of Idea

1. _____
2. _____
3. _____

The plot is resolved, and the new concept is learned.

Figure 3.2   Reproducible Narrative Scoring Rubric

Student _____ Date _____

1. How well does the story descriptively develop the setting?

   1   2   3   4   5 (highest)

   Notes: _____
   _____

2. Are the story characters defined enough to allow the audience a clear
   visualization?

   1   2   3   4   5 (highest)

   Notes: _____
   _____

3. Is a sequential storyline developed?

   1   2   3   4   5 (highest)

   Notes: _____
   _____

4. Does the plot weave through the story to create audience interest?

   1   2   3   4   5 (highest)

   Notes: _____
   _____

5. Is the story plot resolved with a new concept communicated to the audience?

   1   2   3   4   5 (highest)

   Notes: _____
   _____

Figure 3.3   Sample List of Classroom Writing Ideas for a Scary-Time Theme

Student Name	Student Topic
Amy	Riding on the roller coaster at Cedar Point
Scott	Breaking my leg skateboarding
Andrew	Getting lost in the mall
LaTrisa	Going to the Haunted Castle
Shernia	Riding on the roller coaster at Cedar Point
Nadia	Falling off a minibike
Sherman	Getting lost hiking in the woods on vacation
Tyler	Jumping out of a boat and not being able to swim
Jessica	Breaking my leg jumping off the swing
Mohammad	Starting at a new school
Amy	Playing in my first piano recital
Justin	Playing in my first soccer game
Cameron	Getting lost walking to school
Lina	Coming to a new country to live
Jerry	Playing my fist baseball game
Anna	Getting a tooth pulled

Model the Strategy

Imitation is a powerful teaching technique, so now that students have a topic of their own in mind, I start to model the strategy by encouraging my students to imitate the format of my personal story. I begin by streaming a video onto the SMART Board of an airplane flying across the mountains in a thunderstorm. I ask the class to describe how they would feel if they were on this plane. I tell them, "I was on a plane just like this one over the holidays when another teacher and I were going skiing out West." After this introduction, I begin teaching the Blueprint Graphic Organizer using my own personal story as an example.

I post a large, blank copy of the Blueprint Graphic Organizer on a SMART Board or chart paper in front of the class and explain that each shape represents a different part of a story. The first shape, Part 1, is a medium-sized oval that represents the story beginning and introduces the key characters and the story setting. The second shape, Part 2, is a large square and represents the longest section of the Blueprint where a problem is introduced and developed. The third shape, Part 3, is a small rectangle where the problem is resolved and a lesson is learned. The Blueprint includes reminders on the side to prompt students to consider the appropriate story components. Here is an example of how I explain the form.

Teacher:	All stories must have three parts: a 1, a 2, and a 3. Part 1 tells where the story starts, sets the scene, describes the story setting, and introduces the characters.

Using my personal story as a model, I take notes in the oval shape of the Blueprint Graphic Organizer.

Teacher:	This story starts at the airport, where a teacher friend and I are about to leave on a ski trip during the holiday break. As we boarded the plane we had NO idea what we'd be in for!

As I identify the story topic, I write notes in Part 1 of the Blueprint (see Figure 3.4 for the completed sample). I reinforce the notion that this is Part 1 of the story by holding up my hand with the index finger extended.

Next, in Part 2 of the Blueprint Graphic Organizer, the large square, I model the plot where a problem is introduced and developed. I hold up my hand with my index and middle fingers extended to reinforce the notion that this is Part 2 of the story. I begin taking notes as I relate the storyline.

Teacher:	First, we boarded the aircraft, found our seats, and then we were soon on our way to our destination, Aspen, Colorado. After takeoff, we had 3.5 hours of uneventful flight time. Suddenly, everything changed! As we approached the destination runway, the plane stopped descending and accelerated back up into the sky like a rocket. Luggage came loose and sailed through the cabin. What in the world was happening? We got our answer when we heard the calm voice of the captain, "Cover your head and stay seated. Because of local conditions, we've aborted our landing at Aspen and are heading for the Denver Airport instead." When we arrived in Denver, we thought our adventure was over. No such luck. First, we waited 2 hours for a bus to Aspen. We loaded our luggage and climbed aboard the bus. Two hours later, there was an awful noise that came from the front of the bus. The bus had lost its transmission and had come to a dead stop. We were asked to wait next to the disabled bus until a rescue bus arrived. Another 2-hour wait! We transferred luggage and boarded the second bus. We arrived at the ski lodge nearly 6 hours late. Unfortunately, that was not the end of the story. The next day, we boarded a ski lift, and halfway up the mountain, it stopped. The ski lift had broken, and we were suspended in the air.

While telling this story to the class I continue taking notes in Part 2 of the Blueprint.

Finally, I model Part 3 of the Blueprint, the rectangle. I hold up my hand with three fingers extended to reinforce the notion that this is the third and final section of my story. I remind my class that the purpose of this section is to resolve the problem or relate the lessons learned. I begin taking notes as I conclude my story.

> **Teacher:** After hanging up in the air on the ski lift, we were rescued by the ski patrol. They threw a rope with a small seat over the ski lift cable and lowered us down from the lift one at a time. We thought that perhaps this trip wasn't such a great idea after all. We decided to give up on skiing and go shopping for the remainder of the trip.

After finishing the last section of my Blueprint Graphic Organizer, I ask my class to retell my story as I point to my notes on the SMART Board or the chart paper. Some students even embellish my story with sound effects. This retelling exercise cements Parts 1, 2, and 3 of a story so that students are prepared to begin their personal narrative.

Students Practice the Strategy

At this stage, each student has a topic. I give each student a colored folder in which to keep all the material for this project and ask students to write their names and the date on the folders. I then hand out copies of blank Blueprint Graphic Organizers. I also post my completed Blueprint in front of the room. I hold up a hand with the index finger extended and tell the class that it's time for them to begin their stories by taking notes in Part 1 of the Blueprint. I tell them to make sure they include all the elements that belong in the oval: the setting and characters. As they work, I walk around the classroom and ask them questions about their stories. This serves as a motivator because students like to share their stories. When Part 1 is completed, we repeat the process for Part 2 (where a problem is introduced and developed) and Part 3 (where the problem is resolved or a lesson is learned).

After students have completed their Blueprints, I ask for volunteers to share their Blueprint notes with the class. I use the SMART Board or chart paper to display these notes. I ask the class to identify Parts 1, 2, and 3 in the volunteers' stories. This encourages a dialogue between the class and the volunteers. Participating in this dialogue acts as a motivator because students take pride in their work.

Independent Writing

Once students have completed their taking notes and we have reviewed their work, they are ready to compose the rough draft of a story in full-sentence and paragraph form. After completing the rough draft, I continue the Blueprint process with an editing step that results in a finished selection that is ready for publication. Figure 3.5 is a student writing sample from a sixth-grade girl who is an English language learner (ELL). Our class thoroughly enjoyed her story, and I'm sure you will too!

Figure 3.4 My Sample Blueprint

Part 1: The Story Beginning

1. I went on a ski trip with a teacher friend out West over the holiday.
2. We were out to seek adventure but had no idea what we were in for.

Include story beginning with setting and main characters.

Part 2: The Storyline Details With the Plot

1. We got on the airplane pretty uneventfully.
2. We flew for 3.5 hours until we were almost there.
3. Suddenly the plane flew straight up in sky like a rocket.
4. All the luggage flew out into the cabin.
5. The captain came on the speaker and said we can't land.
6. We flew back to Denver and landed.
7. We got on a bus that would take us to Aspen.
8. The bus lost the transmission.
9. We waited for another bus and finally got to Aspen late.
10. We slept all night and got in the ski lift the next day.
11. The ski lift stopped, it was broken.

Include the storyline with the plot, using descriptive language.

Part 3: The Story Resolution With the Newly Learned Concept of Idea

1. We were suspended over the mountain, rocking on the lift, back and forth.
2. The ski patrol rescued us.
3. We decided it wasn't a smart thing to ski on this trip.

The plot is resolved, and the new concept is learned.

Student Reflection

I believe true learning becomes apparent when students are able to identify what they have learned about writing and when they can use these strategies without assistance to prepare quality written work again and again. At the conclusion of this lesson, I ask students to complete a Writing Reflection

Figure 3.5   Student Writing Sample

Lina's New Experience

Everything started at Easter Vacation. . . . I had just arrived back from England. I came back to 22C Unterberg, and that's where I call home. First of all, I went upstairs into my room and just looked at the familiar surroundings. Next, I got my suitcase and gave my family the presents I brought with me. Mom was thrilled about the typical British "black tea." After all the excitement we sat down for mom's award-winning spaghetti dinner.

Later on that very same day my best friend, Maxi, came over to hang out with me. We were sitting in my room talking about my trip and all the things I did over the past two weeks. Suddenly Dad called me downstairs. And I just thought, "Can't they just leave me and Maxi alone to talk? Why do parents always have to interrupt?"

We walked down the stairs onto the terrace where everyone was sitting at the table. Annoyed I asked why they called me. My dad replied, "Lina, we have something really important to tell you." My first thought was that someone had died. I was really scared!

It didn't sound good to me but I sensed happiness in my dad´s tone of voice. I wondered, "did someone die?" Hmm . . . I was still scared.

Daddy looked at me with a smile on his face like a big grin. I knew from his expression that it wasn't as bad as I thought it was. But what else could it be?

OMG! Dad pulled out a huge book hidden under the table and threw it onto the table. "What is that suppose to mean?" I asked in a confused way. I had totally no idea what was going on. Mom started crying buckets full of tears. Then I got even more confused. I thought to myself, "So if nobody died or nothing bad happened, why is mom crying then?" After making all these suggestions, I came to the GREAT idea to look at the book's title. It said United States! What does that mean?

I looked at Dad with this look, like a baby reaching for milk. I needed to know what was going on. NOW! I felt everyone knew about it except me! I felt left out. Someone tell me!

"You know when I was eighteen years I visited America, Daddy started to say slowly, and I really enjoyed my time."

I said, "But what does that have to do with us now?" I could not follow. I felt like someone tripped me and I fell. "I went to a private school and met lots of nice people there. I learned a lot and visited lots of interesting places throughout the U.S.," Dad continued. The book got opened and the smell of new pages was in the air.

After all these exciting minutes that nearly killed me my mom told me we are going on a long trip out of the country. I was overwhelmed with happiness but also sadness and at the same time really scared. I had to leave home and family for two whole years. But on the other hand excitement was there for something new. In comparison to me, Maxi started crying and grandpa too. My brothers' faces lit up like sunshine.

After that day everything changed. My friends and I spent lots of time together and while Mom and Dad went to our new country to pick house and school, my grandpa took care of us while Mommy and Daddy were gone. After a week they came back and told us they found a great school and a small but cozy home for us all. Then the real world started, which was packing. After everything was set and done we finally sat in the plane to America. We arrived safely but tired after our seven-hour journey over the big ocean. Even though our house was selected, it wasn't ready for us to move in. So we moved in the Sheraton Hotel while we put finishing touches on our soon to be Northville home. We were scared our furniture got dropped in the ocean, because of the long lasting six week wait. We were very relieved when everything arrived six weeks later intact.

The rest of our summer vacation we spent learning Michigan through our travels up North. It took a little while to get used to everything but now things are just perfect and I realized that I didn't have anything to be scared about. Now that we are "home" I hope the two years never end.

Questionnaire (Figure 3.6). Specifically, I ask them to identify key points about writing narrative stories. Invariably, they tell me they understand Parts 1, 2, and 3 of story writing—and that without these components, a story is not complete!

MODIFYING THE MINI-LESSON

Adaptations for Writers Who Struggle

Struggling writers frequently have difficulty due to an inability to spell, a lack of understanding of appropriate grammar and conventions, and an inability to think of a theme-based topic to write about. Each step of the overall Blueprint process writing strategy includes adaptations to support struggling writers in coping with these issues. My specific adaptations for the Blueprint Graphic Organizer strategy include the following:

1. I encourage students to draw pictures in the Blueprint Graphic Organizer showing Parts 1, 2, and 3 of a narrative story before they write any words. I also support students' use of cutouts and other story artifacts to embellish the Blueprint.

2. I then ask struggling writers to use the pictorial blueprint to verbally present their stories to the class or to a small group. This enables them to select specific words to go with their pictorial representation.

3. Once the struggling students have internalized their story with actual words, I choose a peer editor to help them fill out a new Blueprint with words. A completed Blueprint enables the struggling writer to complete a rough draft in complete sentences with only limited assistance.

The very nature of the Blueprint Graphic Organizer helps struggling writers formulate a story more easily. They begin to understand the required story components and what they must include in their own personal stories to transform them into an acceptable personal narrative. After struggling writers understand Parts 1, 2, and 3 of a story, they can make use of additional assistance such as an electronic speller to help them spell words or a computer with a spelling and grammar checker to assist with writing conventions.

Adaptations for English Language Learners

Many ELLs have difficulty with writing instruction because oftentimes the school curriculum doesn't connect with their background experiences (see National Center to Improve the Tools of Educators, 2001). I find that selecting universal themes helps ELLs find an individual topic for a writing assignment. The theme used as an example in this chapter is a good one—being really scared. Frightening experiences transcend borders and languages.

English language learners may also be reluctant to participate in whole-classroom discussions because of their lack of communication skills. They are

Figure 3.6 Reproducible Writing Reflection Questionnaire

Name _____ Genre_____

Date _____

1. What is different about using the Blueprint Graphic Organizer during the writing process?

_____

_____

_____

_____

_____

2. Can you name and now describe the three parts of a narrative story?

_____

_____

_____

_____

_____

3. How can you use this strategy again by yourself?

_____

_____

_____

_____

_____

more apt to ask questions and work on writing in small groups, which also promotes social interaction. I encourage ELLs to work in groups of three or four students to record their Blueprint notes and compose their stories.

Adaptations for Advanced Writers

Advanced writers usually have sufficient vocabulary to include more complex writing concepts in their assignments. Therefore, I ask advanced writers questions about their stories and attempt to get them to add more visualization to their writing selections. To accomplish this, I encourage them to use metaphors and similes and other techniques to enhance their writing selections. Also, these are the students I use as peer editors to assist struggling writers to advance from a pictorial Blueprint to a written Blueprint.

EXTENDING THE STRATEGY ACROSS THE CONTENT AREAS

The Blueprint Graphic Organizer can be used across the curriculum when narrative writing is required. For example, in a history class, teachers might ask students to tell about an event from a historical participant's viewpoint. Students could also use the Blueprint Graphic Organizer to write stories about important historical figures such as Galileo or Newton in science class. Teachers can also extend its applicability in English language arts by using it to teach genre-specific narratives such as mysteries, fables, fantasies, or folktales, to name only a few. Specific elements change, but each of these narrative forms has an underlying structure of Part 1, 2, and 3.

RESOURCES FOR FURTHER READING

➤ National Center to Improve the Tools of Educators. See Idea.uoregon/edu/-ncite

This study by the National Center to Improve the Tools of Educators analyzed research and identified principles for accommodating instruction for diverse learners that will level the playing field in classrooms. The first principle is the Principle of Big Ideas. Specifically, the Big Idea on which Blueprint for Exceptional Writing is based is that writing can be taught as a process that when followed will produce proficient writing selections. When Parts 1, 2, and 3 of writing are taught and modeled and when students repeat and execute these strategies, all students can produce proficient writing selections.

➤ Kam'enui, E. J., Carnine D. W., Dixon, D. C., Simmons, D. C., & Coyne, M. D. (2002). *Strategies for teaching students that accommodate diverse learners.* Columbus, OH: Merrill.

Blueprint for Exceptional Writing (Fontenot & Carney, 2008) takes advantage of all the strategies described in the book, *Strategies for Teaching Students*

That Accommodate Diverse Learners. The particular principle stated in this chapter, Using a Blueprint Graphic Organizer to Build a Story, is the Principle of Mediated Scaffolding. The Blueprint Graphic Organizer, with associated narrative teaching strategies, provides a specific example of mediated scaffolding.

➢ Marzano, R. J., Pickering, D. J., & Pollock, J. E. (2004). *Classroom instruction that works: Research-based strategies for increasing student achievement.* Alexandria, VA: Association for Supervision and Curriculum Development.

Robert Marzano, a leading researcher, has conducted research studies that identify nine essential instructional strategies that promote student learning across all content areas and grades. Marzano's Strategy 2, Summarizing and Note Taking, is taught when using the Blueprint Graphic Organizer. I model note taking and summarizing for my students before they begin to take notes themselves. This skill is at the heart of teaching the Blueprint. In addition, Marzano's Strategy 9, Cues, Questions, and Advance Organizers, is also well represented in these teaching strategies. The Blueprint Graphic Organizer is a specific example of an advanced organizer. Students develop a pattern for writing narrative stories, and they eventually internalize it. In addition, I ask questions and encourage other students in the class to ask questions about classmates' stories. These elements provide evidence that these strategies are necessary elements in teaching and implementing process writing.

4 Using Genre Charts to Guide Planning and Writing

Gabriel C. Horn and Susan D. Martin

Many students have limited exposure to genres of writing. However, they are expected to craft persuasive papers, biographies, procedural pieces, business letters, narratives, poetry, and several other types of writing. As each written genre contains unique purposes and features, developing genre knowledge is one of the major challenges in learning to write (Coker, 2007). We have found that development and use of a genre chart that lists purposes, formats, characteristics, and audiences for written formats provides students with a tool that helps them plan knowledgeably and independently.

WHY THIS STRATEGY IS IMPORTANT

Writers use many genres for communicating or learning. Chapman (1997) lists more than 200 forms of writing that elementary students can learn and use—ranging from acrostics to zigzag books. As Chapman notes, developing a repertoire of genres

- can be exciting,
- allows more choices in open-ended activities, and
- promotes success for more learners.

We have noticed, however, that students struggle with writing when they have little understanding of characteristics or purposes of particular genres. This lack of familiarity with written formats can hamper their ability to plan and create strong products. Students need to develop a repertoire of genres and knowledge so that they know when and how to use this information.

This strategy is not the same as using formulaic scripts for particular written formats. Instead, it draws on mentor texts (Dorfman & Cappelli, 2007) and student inquiry as a means to help students understand key features of a particular genre. When students learn and apply this strategy, they become familiar with various aspects of a specific type of writing: They are better able to plan and write an effective piece of writing within that genre.

THE MINI-LESSON

Materials Needed

- Common, everyday tools (spatula, screwdriver, pencil, notebook)
- A genre chart for each student (Figure 4.1)
- A recipe checklist for each student (Figure 4.2)
- An overhead or electronic version of the genre chart and recipe checklist to use while modeling
- Transparencies or electronic versions of two recipes
- Recipes from a cookbook for each group of students as mentor texts (Dorfman & Cappelli, 2007). We use databases such as the one at www.lib.muohio .edu/pictbks/ to find appropriate mentor texts for specific genres.

Before we work with the students to begin the construction of the genre chart, we engage them in a demonstration and discussion regarding the role of genre as a tool used for writing processes. In his classroom, Gabe asks for a volunteer to sit in the front of the room. After the student is situated, he informs the group that he is going to pretend that the student is at a salon or barber shop to get a haircut. Gabe explains that he is the beautician and that he is about to begin working on the student's hair. Then he grabs several everyday items, such as a spatula, screwdriver, pencil, and notebook, and pretends to attempt to give the student a haircut. As students laugh at this ridiculous situation, he explains that it is important for people to plan out tasks to ensure successful completion. This is what the ensuing conversation among Gabe and his students usually sounds like.

Teacher: That was pretty silly, but it teaches us that we always need to be prepared for whatever job we're going to try to do. What tools do I need to be a successful beautician?

Daysha: You would need scissors, some clippers, and a comb.

Trevor: You could also use a spray bottle.

Teacher: So I need to be prepared with the right tools. Writers also have tools that they use in planning and drafting their products. We will learn about several tools and strategies this year. One of these tools writers use involves being prepared before creating a piece of writing by knowing about the characteristics and purposes of the type of writing you are going to do. How many of you have ever been expected to write

	something but you didn't know what that type of writing was supposed to look like?
Maya:	That has happened to me before when I had to write a biography in third grade. I didn't know what a biography was.
Ryan:	I remember that. We also had to write all different kinds of poems, and I would always get confused about them.
Teacher:	That can be really frustrating for you when you don't know what a type of writing is supposed to look like. All those different types of writing that you have done are called *genres.* How many of you like rock music? How about country music? What about hip-hop? [Students respond after each question.] Each of those types of music is called a genre. There are all different types, or genres, of writing as well. If I asked the class to write a persuasive business letter, could you do it? How are you supposed to write a persuasive business letter if you don't know that much about it?
Ryan:	I don't know. I think we would just have to guess and hope we get it right.
Teacher:	I would like to show you a tool that we will develop and use that can help you know exactly how to write different genres. We will be writing in a lot of genres this year, and it is important for you to know a lot about each genre before you begin writing. Does anybody know what an audience is?
Emry:	It is like the people at a concert that are watching it.
Teacher:	Exactly. As writers, you need to know about your audience—the people who will be reading what you've written. This will help you know what kind of words to use. Another important thing to consider is that different genres have different purposes. Why would you write a recipe?
Stephen:	To show somebody how to cook something.
Teacher:	OK. What about a fictional story? Why would you write one of those?
Daysha:	So somebody would have fun reading it.
Ryan:	Or maybe to scare somebody, too.
Teacher:	Yes. When you write in a specific genre, you have different purposes.

Gabe then continues the conversation and discusses that different genres of writing have different types of words. For example, poetry might have strong verbs or similes, whereas procedural writing would have facts and transition words such as *first, next,* and *then.* The discussion includes the idea that different genres are organized in very different ways as well. Gabe explains that each genre has important features that make it unique and that it is important to know these features before attempting to write in that specific genre. He displays the genre chart and gives them a couple of minutes to examine it (see Figure 4.1). Next, he tells the students that they will be using this chart to help them become familiar with different genres of writing

Figure 4.1 Reproducible Genre Chart

Name _____

Genre Chart: A Writing Tool			
Genre	*Purposes*	*Characteristics*	*Format and Other Information*

Figure 4.2   Reproducible Checklist for Recipe Writing

Name:_____

Checklist for Recipe Writing

❏ I have a title at the top.

❏ I have included an ingredients list with amounts of food needed. The reader would know what to use.

❏ I have listed all the procedures in order. The reader would know what to do.

❏ I have checked to make sure there aren't any run-on sentences. My sentences are mostly short and to the point

❏ When necessary, I have included transition words at the beginning of sentences.

❏ I have included action verbs at the beginning of sentences.

throughout the year. They will keep it in their writing notebook, and it will become a valuable tool for them to plan their writing.

Model the Strategy

When Gabe begins modeling how to use the genre chart (typically the next day), he reviews the importance of being prepared with the right tools. He explains why developing a chart and using it strategically can be helpful for writers.

To begin the modeling, Gabe passes out a copy of the genre chart to the students and two recipes for cakes. The students will use the genre chart with many different genres throughout the year, but here we will discuss the genre of recipe writing to model the purposes and procedures of the chart. Gabe displays the chart on the overhead projector. The following dialogue offers a view of what a typical classroom conversation sounds like during this modeling.

Teacher:	You will notice that you have a genre chart and two examples of writing on your desks. Is anyone familiar with this type or genre of writing? What is it called?
Several voices:	Recipes.
Teacher:	Yes. These are recipes from this book, *Joy of Cooking*, by Irma Rombauer, Marion Becker, and Ethan Becker (2006). How many of you are familiar with recipes? Today we are going to discuss what you know about recipes and investigate them further. We are going to use this chart to help us in this investigation. The purpose of the chart is to help you familiarize yourself with different types of writing. We will add to it over the year. Some of the genres we will write in will be unfamiliar to you and more complex than recipes. You will use this chart to help you plan, draft, revise, and edit. Are there any questions?
	You'll notice on this chart that we have four different columns where we will write information about types of writing. The first column is labeled *genre*. Does anybody remember what a genre is?
Maya:	It's like a kind of writing. It's just like you have different kinds of music—hip-hop, rock, and country. A genre is the kind of writing you're doing.
Teacher:	So I'm going to write the type of writing down in the genre column. I'm going to write *recipe*. The next column on our chart is the *purpose* column. Does anybody know what an author's purpose is?
Emry:	Isn't it the reason somebody writes something? A purpose is the reason you do something, so an author's purpose is like the reason an author writes.
Teacher:	An author usually wants the reader to get something out of reading his or her book or story. Some genres are mainly to communicate with others—maybe to entertain readers or teach them facts about topics. Other genres are focused on ourselves and are meant to help us think,

learn, and remember. Keeping a personal journal and taking notes are examples of genres that are meant to help us think, learn, and remember. What do you think these authors' purpose is for writing these recipes in their cookbook?

Steven: I think they want to tell us how to make cakes.

Teacher: Any other ideas?

Stacy: They want to show us what ingredients to use and how to mix them together.

Teacher: Great! Recipes are a type of procedural writing. The purpose of this type of writing is to tell the reader how to do something step-by-step. Can anybody think of anything else that you could read that tells you how to do something?

Daysha: When my Dad was putting together our swing set, he read the directions.

Ryan: When I put together Legos, I follow the instructions. I can build different buildings and stuff.

Teacher: Those are great examples of procedural writing. I'm going to write those ideas in the purpose column. [See completed sample genre chart in Figure 4.3.] What does it say at the top of the next column?

Several voices: Characteristics

Teacher: Yes. So if I were going to describe the characteristics of my 3-year-old son, I would say he is about three and a half feet tall, has blond hair and green eyes, and is very playful, usually generous, and intelligent. So who wants to share what you think characteristics of something are?

Trevor: Are characteristics kind of what makes you a person? Is it what describes you—how you're made up?

Teacher: You're on the right track. Characteristics are things that would describe you and make you unique. Each genre of writing has characteristics that make that genre unique. Take a look at these recipes, think about other recipes you have used, and think about the characteristics of this genre. Turn to your table partner and see if you can come up with at least three characteristics that these recipes have in common.

As students note characteristics of the recipes, Gabe writes them on the genre chart. He also uses think-aloud to model elements that students may not have noted in one recipe. For example, he points out that most of the sentences begin with a transition word such as *first, then,* and *next.* The sentences seem to be very short and to the point. The author uses a lot of action verbs such as *mix, place, preheat,* and *bake.*

In a similar interactive manner, Gabe and the students investigate the format of these particular recipes. He continues to fill out the *format* or *organization* column. They discuss that format or organization is how a piece of writing is laid out and arranged—how it looks on the page.

Figure 4.3 Sample Completed Genre Chart for Procedural Writing

Genre	Purposes	Characteristics	Format and Other Information
Procedural writing Examples: recipes and directions	To give directions and instructions	Title Measurements Ingredient or materials list How many people it will serve Most sentences begin with a transition word such as *first, then,* and *next.* Sentences seem to be very short and to the point. The author uses a lot of action verbs.	Title at the top Ingredient or materials list near the top Paragraph with step-by-step instructions in the middle to the bottom A picture at the bottom with a caption

Once they have the class chart completed, Gabe models for the students how he could use the chart as a tool to aid him in planning and drafting. Using think aloud, he demonstrates composing a recipe for making scrambled eggs. Referring to the chart, he decides to create a simple planning organizer—listing the ingredients and then the procedures. He also models how to create a genre checklist from the chart and how to use it as a tool for reviewing his rough draft recipe (see Figure 4.2 for an example of a recipe checklist).

When Gabe has completed these processes, the class debriefs how and when he used the chart in his writing processes.

Students Practice the Strategy

This strategy is multifaceted, so Gabe has students practice two distinct elements:

1. Learning to gather the genre information

2. Using the chart to aid in planning and drafting

To practice gathering the data to complete their charts, students work in pairs to fill out their individual genre charts. Students have about 30 minutes to first scrutinize recipes that are placed at their tables and then complete their charts. They can also use the class model as a reference.

Once students complete their charts and Gabe checks them, they practice using the chart as a planning/writing aid for composing their own recipes. Because the learning focus is on the genre and not the topic, Gabe asks students to make recipes from their own experiences or create a silly recipe. In other words, he does not expect students to gather topic information for these pieces.

Since Gabe is concerned with the development of students' self-regulation of writing processes, he also asks that students work individually or together to create an appropriate organizer and/or checklist for recipes based on their genre charts. If this is too difficult for students, he reviews the organizer he made as a teacher, explaining again its links to the genre chart, and has students use it for guidance.

Independent Writing

Students add to their genre charts each time they are introduced to and expected to write in a new genre. Eventually, the goal is for them to self-select from a set of genres and add to and/or use their genre charts in their writing processes.

We seek to help the students develop as self-regulated writers and to move toward independence in identifying genre characteristics and formats. We have found that student-created organizers and checklists, specific to each genre, help students see links between the genre characteristics, formats, purposes, and their writing processes.

Student Reflection

Students need opportunities to reflect on both the usefulness of the genre chart and the specific genres about which they are learning. We find Think, Pair, Share is a wonderful informal way to encourage students to reflect on their learning and get further practice with concepts and vocabulary. Whole-class sharing provides opportunities for us to build on understandings and correct any misconceptions. Following are some useful prompts:

- How did using the chart help you to plan, draft, revise, edit, and publish?
- What did you learn about _____ (fill in genre)?
- What items should be included in _____ (fill in genre)?

Our students can gain awareness of their learning by responding to prompts through writing as well (yet another genre!). Entry slips for pieces for their writing portfolio pieces work well (Figure 4.4). Similarly, the use of pre- and postprompts with either a unit of study or the school year allows students to compare recent responses with earlier ones. For example, if the students have studied biographies, we ask specific questions such as these:

- Why would somebody write a biography?
- What items should be included in a biography?
- How is a biography organized?

Pre- and post-whole-year prompts can include the following:

- What do you know about written genres, their purposes, characteristics, and formats?
- How do writers use genre as a tool to plan, draft, revise, edit, and publish?

Figure 4.4   Reproducible Portfolio Entry Slip

Name: _____

Title of piece: _____

Genre: _____

What did I learn about this genre from creating this piece?

Who was my intended audience?

This piece shows that I am learning how to . . .

What I like best about this piece is . . .

MODIFYING THE MINI-LESSON

Adaptations for Writers Who Struggle

During the practice and independent phases of the lesson, we have found it important to meet with a small group of struggling writers and assist them as they analyze pieces of writing, fill out their genre charts, and create planning organizers and checklists. We continue to check in with students when they are revising and editing to ensure they are using their genre-specific checklist to guide them toward a more coherent, proficient piece of writing.

We also have found success with encouraging peer interaction during writing. Talking with other students during all stages of writing aids in scaffolding writing in important ways. Some students prefer to ask a peer for help instead of the teacher. In addition, we are not always able to get to students as quickly as we would like to provide assistance.

Adaptations for English Language Learners

Students who are English language learners (ELLs) need various supports to ensure success while they plan and draft. We have found that vocabulary in the genre chart may be difficult for ELLs to comprehend. Our encouragement of discussion between students in the writing environment has been particularly helpful for ELLs. If necessary, teachers can provide students with a handout that includes definitions of the terms that are used in the genre chart (Figure 4.5).

Adaptations for Advanced Writers

We suggest several adaptations for advanced writers, including abbreviated practice times with a quick transfer into inductive identification of other genre

Figure 4.5 Definitions for Genre Chart Terms

Purpose: The reason an author writes. Authors write for many reasons. An author may give information or facts about a subject. Some authors write fiction stories, which are stories that are not true. They may write these stories to entertain readers. Other authors may write to persuade or to try to get readers to do something or think a certain way about a topic.

Characteristic: Something that helps you identify or recognize a person or thing. A characteristic makes a person or thing different from other people or things. For example, the characteristics of a baseball are round, about 3 inches across, smooth white texture with bumpy red stitches, and weighs about 5 ounces. These characteristics help us identify a baseball.

Format: How your ideas, words, sentences, and paragraphs are put together or organized on the page. The format is what your writing looks like. Different genres of writing are formatted in special ways.

Genre: A type of writing. Examples of genres include fiction stories, poetry, and biography.

purposes, characteristics, and formats on their own. We also expect advanced writers to create graphic organizers and checklists independently that suit the genre and their own needs. In addition, we challenge them to create other types of recipes, such as recipes for life (e.g., recipes for friendship, love, or diversity) to provide challenge and independent practice. We have advanced writers view mentor texts independently or in small groups, and we ask them to meet with one another to corroborate information.

EXTENDING THE STRATEGY ACROSS THE CONTENT AREAS

This strategy lends itself well to writing projects across the content areas. Many subject-specific genres are complex and demanding of writers. Intermediate students are expected to write in various genres for projects in social studies and science. For instance, Gabe's fourth-grade students study the journey along the Oregon Trail. The genre chart is used to familiarize students with the genre of diaries when students write entries from the perspective of travelers along the Oregon Trail. Some other projects in social studies for which students can use genre charts are brochures, different poetry forms, biographies, persuasive essays, and time lines.

In fifth-grade science, students can use the genre charts to persuade readers which system of the body is more important. Some other writing projects where the genre chart may be used in science are comparison papers, descriptive essays, alphabet books, and letters to the editor.

RESOURCES FOR FURTHER READING

➤ Chapman, M. (1997). *Weaving webs of meaning: Writing in the elementary school*. Toronto, Ontario, Canada: ITP Nelson.

In the chapter titled "Expanding Young Writers' Repertoires of Genres and Forms of Representation," Chapman discusses issues related to teaching written genres and suggestions for teaching particular genres. Importantly, she also explores the connections between process and genre approaches for teaching writing in language art and across the curriculum. Few studies have investigated instructional support for writing in a variety of genres. But she draws on research and perspectives about the nature and functions of literacy as communicative and personal representations. Genres are flexible and fluid "*social actions* that occur in particular types of situations within a discourse community" (p. 217, author's emphasis).

Chapman proposes we think of genre as a process in which we "integrate process and genre in a complementary fashion" (p. 218). From this foundation, the genre chart strategy is designed to enable students to understand specifics of written forms and processes as written products unfold within particular genres or written forms.

➤ Englert, C. S., Mariage, T. V., & Dunsmore, K. (2006). Tenets of sociocultural theory in writing instruction. In C. A. MacArthur, S. Graham, & J. Fitzgerald (Eds.), *Handbook of writing research* (pp. 208–221). New York: Guilford.

Englert, Mariage, and Dunsmore draw on sociocultural theories, as well as their prior classroom investigations, to discuss the importance of procedural facilitation and tools in support of cognitive performance of students in advance of independent performance. This means that scaffolding composition performance with cognitive tools and strategies aids students in planning and monitoring their texts. The use of genre charts, along with modeling, think-alouds, and discussion in this strategy, aids students in gaining "access to writing actions and processes that deepen their participation and social position as competent language users in the broader sociocultural community" (p. 213).

Reciprocal Text Structure Mapping for Expository Writing

5

Joyce C. Fine

This strategy offers opportunities for students to apply their knowledge about mentor texts to their own writing. Relying on authors as writing mentors motivates students to look more closely at text structure. They map the structure of a text onto a graphic organizer that matches the specific text genre. Then, right below the graphic organizer or "map," they create a parallel, reciprocal map using the same type of genre-specific graphic organizer to plan the writing of their own ideas on the same or a different topic. This strategy mini-lesson focuses on the inventing process writers use to plan cause-and-effect expository texts. Additional reproducible reciprocal maps are provided to repeat this mini-lesson to teach four types of expository texts also.

WHY THIS STRATEGY IS IMPORTANT

When I teach expository text structure, I often find that either students do not see any meaningful connections to the content or else they make the text into a story. They sometimes think people in exposition are story characters with problems and they want to supply resolutions to these problems. I tell students the definition of expository text and how this type of text offers real information. In expository text, there are few, if any, resolutions to situations. I also explain how authors structure their writing. However, students often do not understand when teachers just tell information. More important, they do not recognize that expository texts can have multiple patterns or structures within one text. For example, an informative newspaper article might contain elements of both cause-and-effect and compare-and-contrast statements. The key to understanding and writing exposition is to know and recognize its internal structural composition. This mini-lesson helps students do just that.

THE MINI-LESSON

Materials Needed

- A fictionalized biography book, such as *The Story of Ruby Bridges* by Robert Coles (1995)
- Some short texts that have clear cause-and-effect text structure, such as *The Reason for a Flower* by Ruth Heller (1999)
- Text examples of each of the types of expository writing, which are useful for the introduction of each of the patterns. I often get good examples from short newspaper articles; you might find good examples in the social studies texts, as well.
- Blank copies of the cause-and-effect reciprocal map (Figure 5.1). See Figures 5.2 through 5.5 for reproducible reciprocal maps to repeat this mini-lesson when you are ready to teach these other common patterns of expository text: descriptive, sequence, compare and contrast, and problem and solution (Meyer & Freedle, 1984).
- The reciprocal maps constructed on a SMART Board or other digital device to model the strategy (chart paper could also be used)

To begin the mini-lesson, I sit with my group of students. I hold up the book, *The Story of Ruby Bridges* by Robert Coles (1995). I read the book aloud and then ask questions.

Teacher:	Can someone please retell the story? [A student volunteers.] Nice work. Now, who can tell me if there is a real Ruby Bridges?
Several students:	Yes!
Teacher:	So is she a fictitious character?
Several students:	No!
Teacher:	That's right. Ruby Bridges is a real person. OK so now let's look at the dedication from Robert Coles. His dedication says: "To Ruby Bridges Hall and to all who did as she did for the United States." Can someone please explain what he meant by "To all who did as she did"?

We take a few minutes to discuss that there were other brave students who helped to integrate United States schools.

Teacher:	The title says that it is a story. What do you think that means?

Figure 5.1 Reproducible Cause-and-Effect Reciprocal Map

Cause-and-Effect Reciprocal Map

Name _____ Date _____

Mapping a Mentor Text

Cause: _____ (signal word)

_____

_____ → [Effect]

Mapping My Personal Experience

Cause: _____ (signal word)

_____

_____ → [Effect]

Figure 5.2 Reproducible Descriptive Reciprocal Map

Descriptive Reciprocal Map

Name _____ Date _____

Mapping a Mentor Text

Signal word: _____

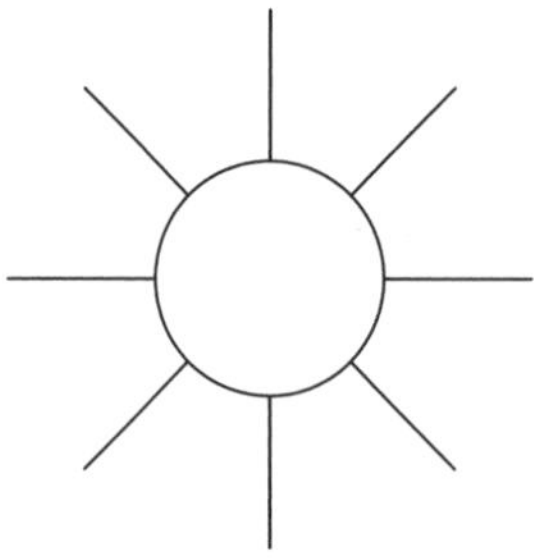

Mapping My Personal Experience

Signal word: _____

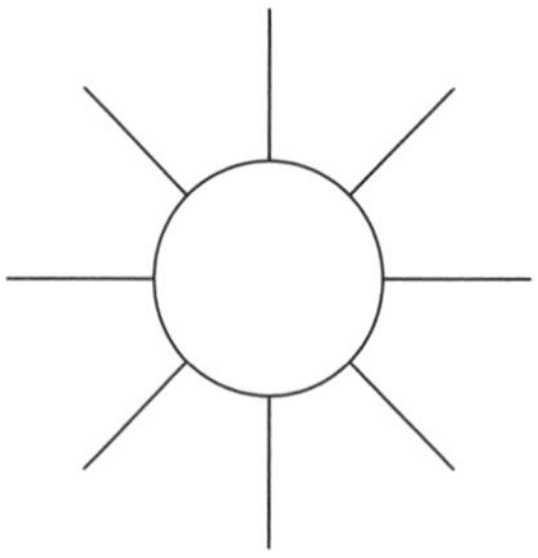

Figure 5.3   Reproducible Sequence Reciprocal Map

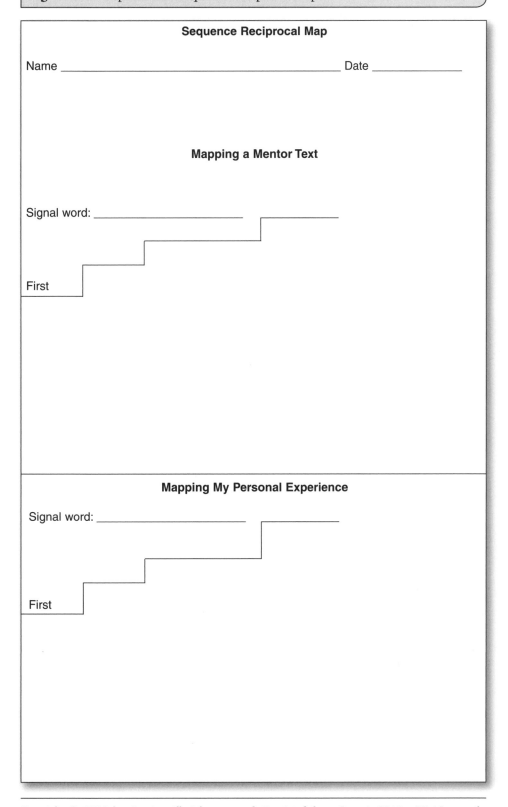

Figure 5.4   Reproducible Compare-and-Contrast Reciprocal Map

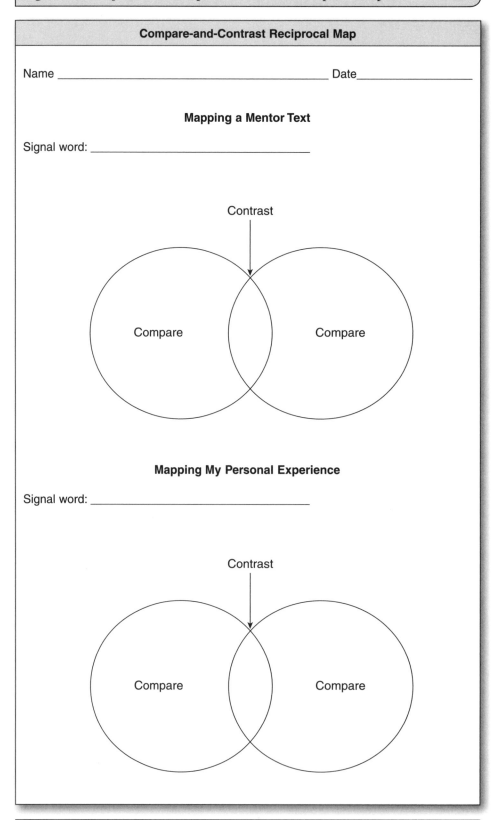

Figure 5.5 Reproducible Problem-and-Solution Reciprocal Map

Problem-and-Solution Reciprocal Map

Name _____ Date _____

Mapping a Mentor Text

Problem: _____ (signal word) → Solution:

Mapping My Personal Experience

Problem: _____ (signal word) → Solution:

Together we discuss the difference between stories and nonfiction.

Teacher:	So Robert Coles wrote for students about a real person's experience. By creating dialogue, he fictionalized a moment in history, telling about the situation as if it were a story. OK, so now that we've looked at the difference between narrative and expository text, we are going to study how there are different structures for expository text. Over the next couple of weeks, we will talk about and use reciprocal maps to show the differences in the patterns of expository text.

Model the Strategy

To model this strategy, I display the cause-and-effect reciprocal map on the SMART Board (see Figure 5.1).

Teacher:	Let's take a look at a cause-and-effect reciprocal map. You know this type of cause-and-effect thinking from your everyday experiences. For instance, you know that if you put your hand on a hot stove, you get burned. What happens if you put a pin in a balloon?
Students:	It pops!
Teacher:	Exactly. Those are two good examples of cause-and-effect.

I then read to the group a short newspaper article or a trade book, such as *The Reason for a Flower* by Ruth Heller (1999) and ask them to follow along with me. I emphasize the relationship or signal words, such as *because, as a result, the reason for, thus, so,* and *therefore* (see Figure 5.6; you can ask students to add to this list as they read). We reread the mentor text and place the signal word *because* on the map because it signals the cause-and-effect text structure (Figure 5.7). We also place the ideas on the map.

When students are comfortable with the cause-and-effect text pattern, I give them each a copy of the cause-and-effect reciprocal map. I also give them another piece of text with the cause-and-effect text structure to read. We fill in the top part of the map together. I ask them to think of a similar circumstance in their lives when they experienced a cause-and-effect situation. They fill in an experience of their own that demonstrates cause and effect in the bottom part to complete the map (Figure 5.8). I repeat this type of explicit instruction for each of the expository text patterns over the course of several mini-lessons.

Students Practice the Strategy

When students are ready to identify the text structure themselves, they choose a reciprocal map that matches the pattern they have identified in the text. Then, they go back to reread the text, map the mentor text, and map their personal experience. Finally, they use the pattern to write an original composition following the same text pattern.

Figure 5.6   Reproducible Chart of Signal Words for Expository Texts

Common Expository Text Patterns	Possible Signal Words
Description	characteristics are, for example, for instance
Sequence	first, second, third, next, then, finally
Cause and effect	reasons why, the reason for, as a result, therefore, because, thus, so, if . . . then
Compare and contrast	different, in contrast, alike, same as, on the other hand
Problem and solution or question and answer	the problem is, the puzzle is, solve, question . . . answer

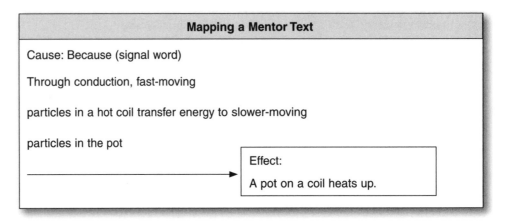

Figure 5.7 Cause-and-Effect Reciprocal Map, Sample

Mapping a Mentor Text

Cause: Because (signal word)

Through conduction, fast-moving

particles in a hot coil transfer energy to slower-moving

particles in the pot

Effect:
A pot on a coil heats up.

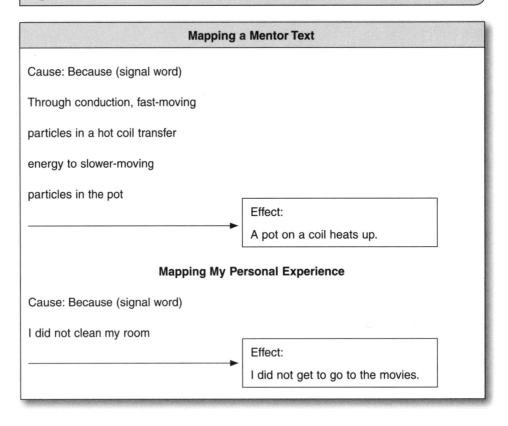

Figure 5.8 Cause-and-Effect Reciprocal Map, Sample 2

Mapping a Mentor Text

Cause: Because (signal word)

Through conduction, fast-moving

particles in a hot coil transfer

energy to slower-moving

particles in the pot

Effect:
A pot on a coil heats up.

Mapping My Personal Experience

Cause: Because (signal word)

I did not clean my room

Effect:
I did not get to go to the movies.

Independent Writing

When students are ready to write expository texts on their own, they examine mentor texts. They may see that the author used multiple types of text patterns to represent what is written. On their reciprocal map, they think of ways to parallel the text structure in their writing by examining the text very closely. They reread and make a mental note of how the author has used the type of text structure or structures. Then they select the reciprocal map that matches the text structure or structures.

This process provides opportunities for students to self-regulate the use of the different structures. At this point, students will also benefit from learning the Structure strategy presented in Chapter 12, "Applying the Structure Strategy to Write Persuasive Texts."

Student Reflection

After completing their reciprocal mapping plan using the same structure, students pair to share what they have written. Students give feedback to their classmates about whether the reciprocal map and their writing match the correct structure. The groups share their examples.

MODIFYING THE MINI-LESSON

Adaptations for Writers Who Struggle

I ask students who struggle to highlight the signal words in text, and I check whether or not they have matched the right ones to the right text structures. If they have not, then I ask these students to go back to the text and see what signal words the author has used. I also use paragraph frames to structure their writing. Paragraph frames give the beginning of sentences for the writer to identify the structure of the overall paragraph (Reutzel & Cooter, 2009).

Adaptations for English Language Learners

English language learners may draw pictures of the actions on the maps. I pair students with other students to discuss the details from the text. They also look at their peers' examples to see how the elements relate. In addition, they can use Inspiration software to illustrate the graphic organizer with clipart. This software can be accessed at www.inspiration.com/freetrial.

Adaptations for Advanced Writers

I ask advanced writers to read sample articles from the newspaper and map them. Articles often use different patterns for each paragraph. These students also write newspaper articles about the events in their textbooks. When they write the reciprocal parts, they write as if they were participants in the events.

EXTENDING THE STRATEGY ACROSS THE CONTENT AREAS

This strategy may be used to graph text structure across all the content areas. By looking closely at the ways authors construct meaning, students see the organization of ideas in science, math, and English, as well as in social studies. I have purposely introduced different topics across the content areas so that students see the applicability of studying text structure in all subjects.

RESOURCES FOR FURTHER READING

➤ Schleppegrell, M. J. (2004). Characterizing the language of schooling. In *The language of schooling: A functional linguistics perspective* (pp. 1–20). Mahwah, NJ: Erlbaum.

This text states that teachers' choice of tasks or ways to scaffold students helps to ease the cognitive demands of learning from text. These tasks actually are the determinants of students' development.

➤ Fine, J. C. (2004). Reciprocal mapping: Scaffolding students' literacy to higher levels. In A. Rogers & E. M. Rogers (Eds.), *Scaffolding literacy instruction: Strategies for K–4 Classrooms* (pp. 88–104). Portsmouth, NH: Heinemann.

This chapter gives details about the process of reciprocal mapping using narrative text structure with elementary students. It explains that there are leading activities from a neo-Vygotskian perspective that help students gain control over writing techniques.

Thanks for the Memories! 6

Using a Sensory-Details Chart to Prepare to Write

Sandra Gandy and Mariah Kraus

The Common Core State Standards (2011) state that students in Grades 4 through 8 should be able to write narratives that use "well chosen details to convey real or imaginary experiences" (p. 42). The Thanks for the Memories! strategy is designed to help students focus on concrete sensory details and organize their memories, or mental images of people and events, in preparation for writing about them. Including sensory details in personal narratives can lead to more realistic and interesting characters and settings.

WHY THIS STRATEGY IS IMPORTANT

My fourth-grade students often have difficulty including details in their writing. Although they write from their own personal experiences, as recommended by Fletcher and Portalupi (2007), their writing lacks the concrete details that the authors mention as vital to making a text come alive. Their personal narratives are especially abbreviated because they include few details about the characters involved. They assume readers know the story characters as well as they do. Therefore, readers have to rely on their own experiences or knowledge of people to fill in the missing gaps.

Before students can incorporate sensory details into their own writing, they must first learn to identify such details in texts they read or hear read to them. Since poetry often includes many concrete details, this genre is helpful to teach the use of sensory details (Oczkus, Baura, Murray, & Berry, 2006). Spandel (2008) also recommends using passages from children's literature to help students recognize sensory details in a text. Such passages should include all the senses, not just sight, which is the one most often used in student writing. Once students are proficient at identifying details, a sensory-details chart can guide them to include the details in their own writing (see Steve Peha's website, Teaching That Makes Sense at http://ttms.org).

THE MINI-LESSON

Materials Needed

- A copy of *The Bellmaker* by Brian Jacques (1994)
- A draft of an essay to use for modeling, prepared for display on chart paper or a SMART board
- Chart board or a SMART Board
- A computer (optional)
- Copies of the sensory chart for all students (Figure 6.1)

To start this lesson, I call a group of students to a small table to talk about what makes a story interesting and how details can make a story more appealing. I remind students of the five senses and ask them for examples of descriptive words for each sense. Then I read excerpts from *The Bellmaker* (Jacques, 1994), which I use as a read-aloud after lunch. Although Jacques often uses details that involve more than one of the senses, I select passages that focus on a specific sense. Following are the pages I focus on for each sense in *The Bellmaker*:

Senses	Pages of Selected Passages in *The Bellmaker*
Sight	24–25, 94–95
Sound	26–27, 51–52
Touch	63–64, 123–124
Taste and smell	44–47, 388–389
Feelings and movement	30, 66–67

As I read, I ask students to name the senses described, to imagine the scene, and to consider how the author's choice of details helps the reader enjoy the story. Finally, I encourage students to choose one of the senses and share some details about it.

Model the Strategy

During the modeling phase, I read an essay that I wrote about my once-in-a-lifetime ride on the American Eagle roller coaster at Great America in Gurnee, Illinois. I start by discussing my writing goal.

Figure 6.1   Reproducible Sensory-Details Chart

Sensory-Details Chart

Name: _____   Date: _____

Future Paper Topic: _____

Sights	Sounds	Taste and Smells	Feelings

Partner's Name: _____

Directions: Circle any sensory details below that you experienced when reading the details.

See	Feel	Hear	Taste	Smell

Teacher: Over the holidays, I visited my husband's family. They live near Gurnee, Illinois. As we traveled on the highway, I could see the American Eagle roller coaster in the distance. My mind roamed to the first (and only!) time I rode this behemoth over 30 years ago. Surprisingly, as I remembered different aspects of the experience, it wasn't just the facts I recalled, but how I felt, what I saw, what I heard, and what I tasted or smelled. I decided that I would like to write about this unique experience from my memories.

When we think of a memory we want to write about, we don't just think about the essentials, although that is important. We also think about the sounds and the smells we noticed at the event. We recall how we felt and how we reacted to what was said or done. These the sensory details help our readers connect with our experience or the characters involved in the event or memory. Helping readers make connections is the goal for a good writer.

Next, I explain how a sensory-details chart works and how it helped me when I was writing about my roller coaster ride.

Teacher: My memories of my ride on the American Eagle are old and somewhat jumbled. I wanted to organize some of the sensory details before I actually began writing about my ride. As it happens, I came across this graphic organizer that I think will help me to organize the sensory details I remember about the event or a person I am writing about.

A sensory-details chart is a prewriting device that helps us organize and remember sensory information about a topic we may want to write about. The topic for this sensory chart is the American Eagle. What I will do today is write down some sensory details I remember about my roller coaster ride on the American Eagle.

Figure 6.2 Sample Sensory-Details Chart

Future Paper Topic: My roller coaster ride on the American Eagle

Sights	Sounds	Tastes and Smells	Feelings
American Eagle was a skyscraper towering over the park.	Deafening screams of the riders as they began their sharp descent down the metal tracks	Tantalizing smell of freshly popped buttery popcorn	Fear rumbling upward from my stomach like an erupting volcano
People forming lines like a meandering snake	Thunder of the cars whipping around the sharp turns of the track	My mouth became a desert—it was too dry to swallow.	My nervous sweat became a flood.
Riders waving their arms like bare tree branches in the wind	Riders squealing with delight	Sweet smell of cotton candy wafting on the breeze	Tensing of my muscles seconds before the first plunge
			Paralyzed with fear

At this point, I ask students to help me record my memories on the sensory chart (Figure 6.2). As the following dialogue shows, we also discuss the definitions of metaphors, similes, and descriptive adjectives. Although students have previously received instruction about these literary devices, they do not often use them in their writing. I find this review helps students think about ways to use literary devices in their own work.

Teacher:	Before I begin sharing my memories, I want you to know I had no intention of ever riding a roller coaster. I always thought they were too dangerous. However, my husband, who is a huge fan of daring rides, had another idea. He began persuading me that the roller coaster ride was safe and exciting. The exhilaration I could believe, just listening to the deafening screams of the riders as they began the sharp descent down the metal tracks. In which column should I write this detail?
Michael:	Sounds!
Teacher:	Yes, I will write this detail under the *sounds* column. As my husband and I got closer to the roller coaster, I strained my neck to see the top of the ride. The American Eagle was a skyscraper towering over the park. Where shall I write this description of the American Eagle?
Travis:	Sights!
Teacher:	Yes, I will write it under *sights*. In this detail, I have compared the American Eagle to a skyscraper. What do we call this type of comparison?
Annie:	A metaphor!
Teacher:	Yes, it is a metaphor. As I stared at the ride, my fear began rumbling up from my stomach like an erupting volcano. I will write this detail under *feelings*, because fear is an emotion. In this detail, I wrote that the fear rumbling in my stomach was like an erupting volcano. What do we call this type of comparison?
Sujeong:	A simile!
Teacher:	Yes, this is a simile! As I listened to my husband's arguments for riding the roller coaster, I decided I would risk my life and take a ride on the roller coaster!
	We joined the people in the line. That detail does not appear very descriptive to me. What if I wrote, "We joined the people who had formed a line like a snake"? That seems better! What if I add the word *meandering* in front of the word *snake?* Meandering means winding. That's what the line was like. I will write this detail under *sights.* As we waited, the tantalizing smell of freshly popped buttery popcorn made me wish that I had purchased some before getting into the line. I will

add this detail to the *tastes and smells* column. I like that I used more than one modifier to describe the popcorn. As we moved closer to the front of the line, my nervous sweat became a flood. I will write this detail under the column *feelings*.

At last, ladies and gentlemen, the moment of truth arrived. We were on the platform waiting to board the roller coaster. My mouth became a desert—it was too dry to swallow. This detail will be added under *tastes and smells*. I stood debating with myself about which side of the car would be safer if the roller coaster flew off the tracks. When I decided it didn't matter, I stepped in, sat down, and grabbed the bar. The roller coaster climbed to the top of the first hill, and I felt my muscles tense seconds before the first plunge. I will write this detail under *feelings*. I was both paralyzed with fear and relieved to have survived the first drop. This is another *feeling* detail. As the roller coaster began its second ascent, I was amazed to see the people in front of me waving their arms like bare tree branches in the wind. I will write this detail under *sights*. I squeezed my eyes shut for the duration of the ride. The thunder of the cars whipping around the sharp turns of the track was deafening. I will write this detail under *sounds*. I thought the ride would never end as the riders in front of me were yelling with delight. I wonder if I can find a better word than *yelling*. I like the word *squealing* because to me squealing means someone is having a good time! I will write this detail under *sounds*. After the ride ended, I relaxed on a nearby bench and enjoyed the sweet smell of cotton candy wafting on the breeze as my husband rode the American Eagle again! I will write this last detail under *smells*.

I think my sensory-detail chart has recorded the sights, sounds, tastes, smells, and feelings of my only experience on the American Eagle. But what is most important is whether you can visualize my experience in your mind's eye? What do you think?

Weston: That ride sounds really cool!

Shawna: I would like some cotton candy right now!

Teacher: If you can visualize the experience, even without all the remaining details I will add later, then I have done a good job of completing my sensory-detail chart.

Students Practice the Strategy

For the practice phase of the strategy, I ask students to think about a memory they would like to write about and to use their copy of the sensory-details chart to record details they want to include in their writing. In late fall, I usually suggest that students write about a Thanksgiving dinner that was memorable or a similar holiday meal. I leave my completed sensory-details chart up for the students to use as a reference. As they begin to write,

I talk with each of them individually to discuss their progress, answer any questions they might have, and offer suggestions for those who might be stuck. I encourage students to include at least one metaphor or simile on their sensory-details chart.

When students have completed the chart, they exchange papers with a partner and together they assess the number and kind of sensory details. If some sensory details are missing, students continue working on the assignment. Students who want to share some of their details with the class are encouraged to do so.

Independent Writing

To scaffold automaticity and to prompt students to practice self-regulation as they use sensory details in their writing, I distribute prewriting rubrics (Figure 6.3). When students have completed their sensory-details chart, they use the prewriting rubric to expand their charts as they prepare to draft their narratives. It is easy for students to tally the number of details in each sensory category to apply the prewriting rubric. At this point, peer partners often work together to extend each other's thinking and vocabulary, adding to the charts collaboratively.

As students begin to work on their narrative, they use the sensory-details chart to help them include details. In teacher–student conferences during writer's workshop, we work together (with the rubric as a guide) to articulate the details that will enhance their writing. I find this feedback helps students, and the amount of scaffolding required is reduced and eventually eliminated.

After students write their first drafts, they peer-edit each other's writing. Working with markers or colored pencils, peer editors use a different color to underline details used for each sense, checking off details from the sensory-details chart as they find them within the narrative. Finally, peers provide feedback and suggestions for revision.

Student Reflection

I encourage my students to share their final writing product with their partners and the class. During all peer conferences, partners are expected to do the following:

- Affirm (make positive comments about what has been written)
- Ask for elaboration (point out what the reader would like to know more about)
- Seek clarification (share any confusion about what was written)

Negative or nonspecific comments are not allowed. The specificity of the peer conferencing structure allows student writers to view their product from a reader's perspective. Students also use the rubric to score and self-evaluate their writing.

Figure 6.3   Reproducible Prewriting Rubric for Sensory-Details Chart

Name _____   Date _____

Narrative Writing: Prewriting—Sensory-Details Chart

Category	4	3	2	1
The number of details	There is a minimum of one sensory detail in four of the senses columns.	There is a minimum of one sensory detail in three of the senses columns.	There is a minimum of one sensory detail in two of the senses columns.	There is a minimum of one sensory detail in one of the senses columns.
Figurative language	A simile or metaphor is used within a sensory detail for one detail in each of the four senses columns.	A simile or metaphor is used within a sensory detail for one detail in three of the four senses columns.	A simile or metaphor is used within a sensory detail for one detail in two of the four senses columns.	A simile or metaphor is used within a sensory detail for one detail in one of the four senses columns.
Modifiers	Two modifiers are used for a sensory detail in each of the four senses columns.	Two modifiers are used for a sensory detail in three of the senses columns.	Two modifiers are used for a sensory detail in two of the senses columns.	Two modifiers are used for a sensory detail in one of the senses columns.
Vocabulary levels	Descriptive language is above grade level.	Descriptive language is on grade level.	Descriptive language is one level below grade level.	Descriptive language is two or more levels below grade level.

MODIFYING THE MINI-LESSON

Adaptations for Writers Who Struggle

Struggling writers require exposure to a wide variety of good authors who use details to facilitate the visualization process of an experience or character. Authors such as Eve Bunting and Jane Yolen might be a great place to start.

Many students also benefit from recording the details on a chart during a teacher read-aloud of a mentor text. This process helps struggling students construct visuals of what another author has written

As students complete their individual sensory-details chart, I have the opportunity to review the details they have recorded and ascertain those they have overlooked. I also informally assess their comprehension of figurative language. These observations assist me in tailoring future instruction to meet my students' specific needs. Figurative language is a difficult area for some students (Norton, 2007); think-alouds and modeling help students understand the figures of speech and move from comprehension to including them in their own writing.

Adaptations for English Language Learners

The primary objective of using a sensory-details chart is to encourage the use of sensory details in the writing process. I keep this objective in mind when I work with my English language learners (ELLs). I am aware that vocabulary may impede ELL students when they lack the English words to describe the details they want to include in their writing. If students are more comfortable writing in their native language, I allow them to do so and then work with them to write an English version (Dworin, 2006). Writing about family events encourages ELL students to use their out-of-school knowledge and experiences. Collaborative work is culturally appropriate and less intimidating than independent, isolated work. The process of translating from one language to another facilitates knowledge of both languages. Publishing their finished work and sharing it with family members is also empowering for these students (Dworin, 2006). Other scaffolding can include additional models of descriptive writing like that mentioned for struggling writers. I also find that a teacher-created chart of the five senses is helpful for ELL students. Additional editing might be necessary to work on conventions.

Finally, students, perhaps especially Spanish-speaking students, often enjoy hearing and reading a book of poems edited by Lori Carlson (1995). The poems about her childhood as a Hispanic in the United States provide models for writing that students can follow.

Adaptations for Advanced Writers

I want to stretch the capabilities of my advanced writers. They can use the sensory-details chart to enhance descriptions of multiple characters and settings. I also encourage these students to include more metaphors, similes, and descriptive adjectives in their writing. These features are at the higher end of my expectations. The finished product of advanced writers is also expected to be longer since they tend to better organize information.

Advanced writers may also publish their work online. Several sites suitable for publishing student writing include www.kidsbookshelf.com, www.cyberkids .com, and www.kidpub.org/kidpub.

EXTENDING THE STRATEGY ACROSS THE CONTENT AREA

I modify the use of the sensory-details chart to enhance my students' understanding of social studies. For example, when students are learning about the Battle at Valley Forge, they use the sensory-details chart to imagine what the conditions were like for the colonialists who fought during this historical event. I also use modified versions of the sensory-details chart to teach other writing genres (e.g., expository, persuasive, etc.) and literature genres (e.g., biographies, autobiographies, and historical fiction).

A study of fruits and vegetables offers another opportunity for students to record sensory details. A favorite activity my students enjoy is to invent their own fruit and describe it using descriptive words and all five senses.

Geography is another subject in which the sensory-details chart can be used. Sights, sounds, and smells in the tropical rain forest can be recorded for a student essay, along with the taste of fruit that grows there and the feel and sounds of animals that inhabit the rain forest.

RESOURCES FOR FURTHER READING

➢ Gambrell, L. B. (1982, December). *Induced mental imagery and the written expression of young children.* Paper presented at International Reading Conference, Clearwater Beach, FL. Retrieved from ERIC database. (ED 228632)

This study researched the impact of mental imagery on the quality of written expression. The participants were 28 students randomly divided into two groups. The experimental group received explicit instruction on how to induce mental imagery from what they read. The control group was told to "think about" what they read. Students read a section of a story and wrote their predictions about what would happen next. The researchers measured four parameters: thought units, facts, predictions, and number of words. The results demonstrated that there were no significant differences in the number of thoughts, facts, and predictions. However, there was a significant difference in the number of descriptive words in the written expressions of the students in the experimental group. The control group used 44 words. The experimental group used 66 words. The author concluded that inducing mental imagery was a viable method of improving written expression.

➢ Patel, P., & Laud, L. (2009). Helping students to add detail and flair to their stories. *Preventing School Failure*, 54(1), 2–9.

To help three middle school learning-disabled students who struggled with writing, the researchers used visualizing as a reading strategy and verbalizing as a writing strategy. The students were taught a mnemonic and asked to visualize details such as color, shape, mood, and other details. Results showed increases in the number of words and in the number of images included in student writing. Other measures, such as organization and conventions, showed little or no increase.

7 Organizing an Expository Essay

Using Big Idea Checklists to Support Writers

Allison Stone and Joyce C. Fine

The Big Idea strategy is useful as students invent, draft, edit, and revise a first-draft expository piece. Organization and well-developed ideas are paramount before students can move on to other aspects that help make an exemplary piece of writing. Students use a planning sheet to invent a response to a prompt, and then they develop two key reasons and a thesis statement. As they draft their writing, they continually revisit the planning sheet to self-check for focus and organization.

Two Big Idea checklists also include questions to guide students as they revise and edit. These questions prompt them to review their planning and check the organization and focus of the rough draft.

WHY THIS STRATEGY IS IMPORTANT

At the beginning of each year, we ask students to write an expository essay. This allows us to evaluate their strengths and identify areas for growth in writing expository text. I've noticed that regardless of grade level, their writing often tends to lack focus and organization. Not only does it have a tendency to drift off topic, but the sentences in their individual paragraphs do not center on the topic idea.

Generally, in Grades 4 through 8, teachers introduce students to the different types of writing, with moderate (in fourth grade) to extensive (in eighth grade) exposure to expository writing. The Big Idea strategy gives students guidance and direction as they think of support for their thesis. It can serve as a template for expository writing because students can use it as a formula to construct a focused and well-organized piece of writing.

THE MINI-LESSON

Materials Needed

- Big Idea Planning Sheet, one for each student (Figure 7.1)
- Big Idea Checklist for Planning Sheets, one for each student (Figure 7.2)
- Big Idea Checklist for Essays, one for each student (Figure 7.3)
- Lined paper, two pieces per student
- A Promethean Board, SMART Board, or overhead projector (chart paper can also be used)
- The Big Idea Planning Sheet and the checklists prepared for display to use while modeling
- A sample essay prepared for display to use while modeling

I begin the mini-lesson by giving students these deliberately confusing and ambiguous directions.

Teacher:	I need you to follow a few directions. Make sure you keep your eyes on your own paper. As you follow my directions, I am going to follow them as well. Here we go. Listen carefully. First, draw two circles with a dot inside each at the top of your paper. Dots remind me of raindrops. Next, draw a triangle underneath. My triangle looks just like a piece from a puzzle that I have. It is blue. Then, draw half a circle. Finally, draw a squiggly line on each side of the paper. Now, let's hold up our drawings and share them. Does your drawing look like the face of a lion the way mine does?

Then, I explain the importance of staying on topic, being focused, and saying precisely what you mean to ensure that your listener or reader is able to follow exactly what you mean.

Teacher:	The directions I gave you were confusing because I gave you unnecessary information and I wasn't clear, precise, and focused about what I wanted you to draw. What information was not important?
Dhriti:	The raindrop!
Mason:	The parts about your puzzle!
Teacher:	What kind of information could I have given you instead?
Antonia:	Where to draw each shape.
Dylan:	How big each shape should be.

Giving students directions that contain unclear and irrelevant information offers opportunities for them to feel dissonance and confusion. Therefore, I

Figure 7.1   Reproducible Big Idea Planning Sheet

Name _____ Date _____

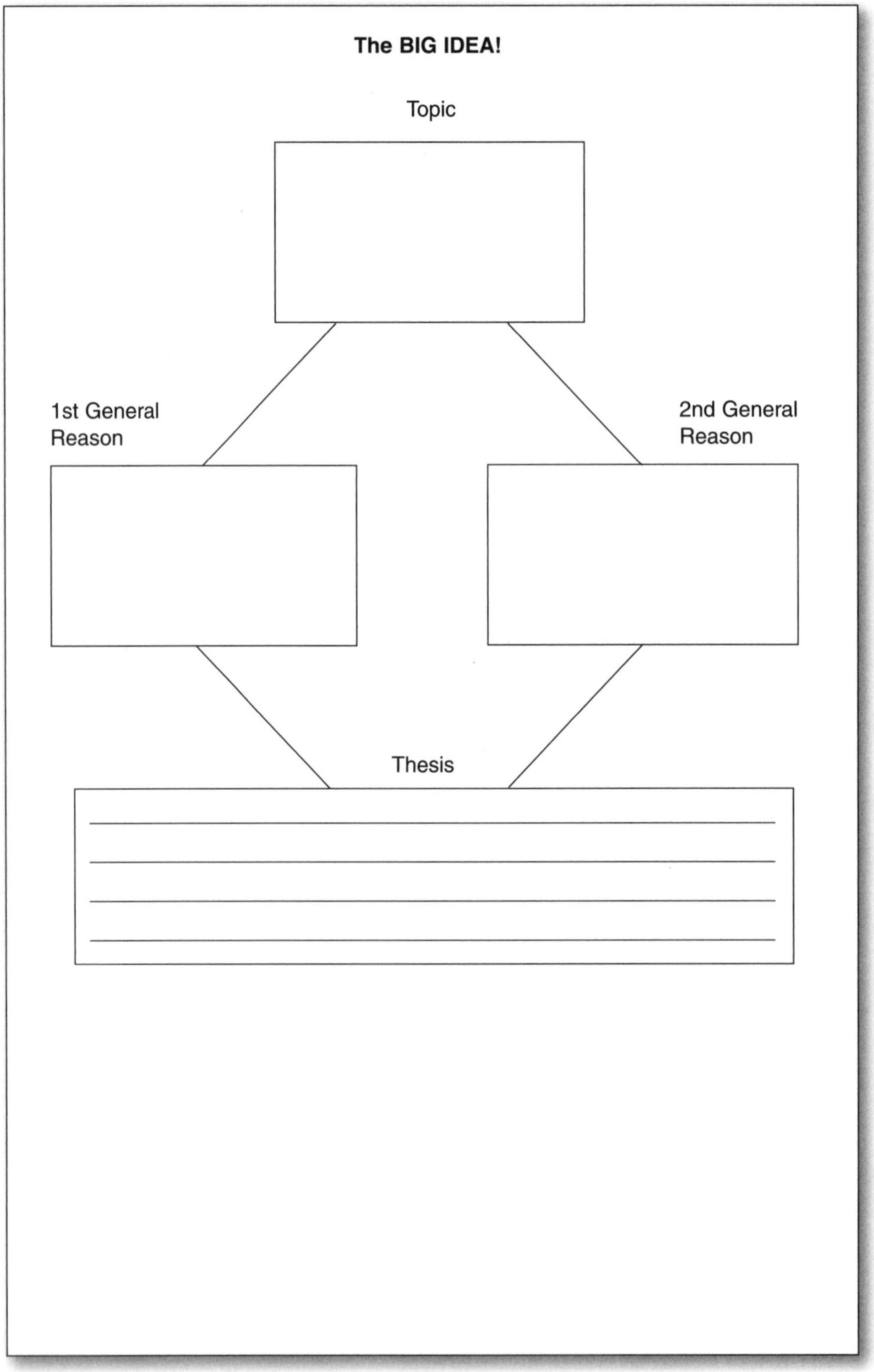

The BIG IDEA!

Topic

1st General
Reason

2nd General
Reason

Thesis

_____

_____

_____

_____

Figure 7.2 Reproducible Big Idea Checklist for Planning Sheets

Name _____ Date _____

Big Idea Checklist for Planning Sheets		
Questions	Yes	No
Did I respond to the prompt in a minimal amount of words and write it in the topic box (black)?		
Did I write a first general reason that supports the topic?		
Did I write a second general reason that supports the topic?		
Did I write a one- or two-sentence thesis statement that includes words from the prompt, the topic, and the first and second reasons?		

Figure 7.3 Reproducible Big Idea Checklist for Essays

Name _____ Date _____

Big Idea Checklist for Essays		
Questions	Yes	No
First Paragraph		
Did I include my complete thesis statement from the planning sheet?		
Did I keep all of my sentences about the general topic and not go into detail about my first and second reasons?		
Second Paragraph		
Did I create a main idea sentence based on the topic and first general reason?		
Is my second sentence about the topic and first general reason?		
Is my third sentence about the topic and first general reason?		
Is my fourth sentence about the topic and first general reason?		
Third Paragraph		
Did I create a main idea sentence based on the topic and second general reason?		
Is my second sentence about the topic and second general reason?		
Is my third sentence about the topic and second general reason?		
Is my fourth sentence about the topic and second general reason?		
Conclusion		
Did I restate my thesis statement using similar words?		
Did I confirm my point of the essay?		

facilitate a discussion about their feelings when they received my confusing directions and their reaction when they realized their drawing did not look like mine. I also ask, "What did this exercise show us about how we need to write?" This discussion helps them remember the importance of organization, precision, and focus.

Next, I have students read the first expository essay they wrote this year to determine if and where they lost the focus of that piece. Sometimes they are able to identify the points of digression—places where they strayed off the topic—and sometimes they cannot. Either way, they are ready to continue learning how to plan so they can maintain focus while writing.

Model the Strategy

I explicitly teach and model for my students how to use the Big Idea Planning Sheet along with the two checklists so that eventually they can use the strategy independently (see Figures 7.1 through 7.3). I explain that before they begin a piece of expository writing, they can use the sheet to invent a response to a prompt and then develop two key reasons and a thesis statement. I project the Big Idea Planning Sheet at the front of the class and then complete a demonstration of the entire process as I think aloud.

> **Teacher:** This is a specific type of planning sheet that you will use for your expository writing. It's called the Big Idea Planning Sheet. I'll be using it to help me stay focused and organized as I invent, draft, edit, and revise.
>
> I'm going to complete the Big Idea Planning Sheet so you can see exactly how it's done. I'm going to use this expository prompt to show you how it works.

I show them the following prompt and read it aloud:

Everyone has a favorite classroom job. Think about your favorite classroom job and write to explain why it is your favorite.

> **Teacher:** After I determine that this prompt requires an expository response, I get my planning sheet. In as few words as possible I'll respond to the prompt and write it in the topic box. The prompt asks me to decide what my favorite classroom job is. My favorite job is being line leader, so I'm going to fill it in the topic box. [See Figure 7.4 for a completed sample planning sheet for this example.]
>
> Next, I need my first general reason that tells why being the line leader is my favorite job. It needs to be something general because I'm going to have to write an entire paragraph about it. The first reason why I like being line leader is because I get to be first. Now I need a second reason. It also needs to be something I can write a paragraph about. The

second reason why I like to be line leader is because everyone has to follow me. I'm going to write both reasons in the separate boxes.

The last step of the Big Idea Planning Sheet is to create a thesis statement. A thesis statement is just the main idea of the entire essay. It tells the reader what the entire paper is about. When writing the thesis statement, I will use words directly from the prompt, the topic box, and the first and second general reasons. My thesis statement is going to include this information: my favorite classroom job is being the line leader, I get to be first, and everyone has to follow me. This sentence will prepare readers for reading my essay. It will help them predict what the essay is about and will guide their comprehension of the essay. You can see how important a well-written thesis statement is! I'm going to construct a thesis statement with that information and fill it in the thesis box.

Figure 7.4 Sample of a Big Idea Planning Sheet Completed for the Line Leader Essay

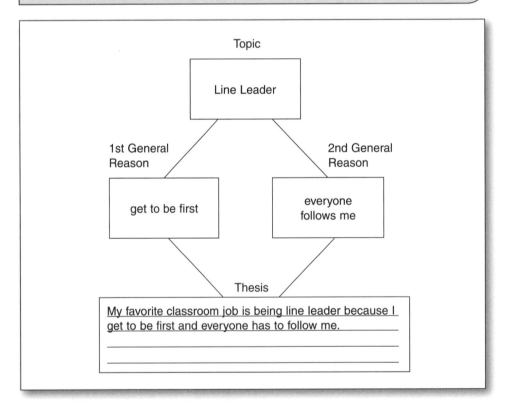

Teacher continues: Now that I have finished the Big Idea Planning Sheet, I will complete the first part of the Big Idea Checklist for Planning Sheets before I begin to write my essay. I'll read the questions and make sure every answer is "yes" before I begin writing.

I read each question on the checklist and ask students to help me review my planning sheet to answer the questions. After we've gone through each question, checking the "yes" box for all, I continue the demonstration.

Teacher: Awesome, I'm ready to write my essay. If any of the answers had been no, I would have had to make corrections on my planning sheet before I wrote.

Now, it's time to write the first draft of my essay. The thesis statement will go in the first paragraph. The first general reason is the topic for the second paragraph, so the second paragraph should be all about being first. The second general reason is the topic for the third paragraph, so the third paragraph should be all about how everyone follows me. As I write my second and third paragraphs, it is very important that I go sentence by sentence and make sure I stick to the topic. Now that I have completed the Big Idea Planning Sheet and the Big Idea Checklist for Planning Sheets, I'm two steps closer to writing a focused and organized essay.

I pass out a copy of the prewritten line leader essay (Figure 7.5) as well as a blank Big Idea Checklist for Essays so students can follow along.

Teacher: Here is a sample essay that I have already written. Place the papers side by side and follow along.

Figure 7.5 Sample Line Leader Rough Draft

Swoosh, as I race out of my seat to the door. Being line leader is my favorite classroom job because I get to be first and everyone follows me. I wish I could have this classroom job forever, but unfortunately classroom jobs change. Being line leader is as powerful as a lion.

One superb factor about being line leader is you always get to be first. That means I get to be the first one to walk into the cafeteria and begin enjoying my delicious lunch. At 3:05pm I get to be the first one to feel the sun's golden rays on my face. However, my favorite time to be first is when I'm walking under the PE shed and it's student choice day. As line leader, I get to walk everywhere and be everywhere before anyone else in my class.

Another reason being line leader is the best classroom job is because the class has to follow me. Since they have to walk where I lead them, I feel incredibly powerful. Knowing it is my decision which hall to walk down is a big responsibility. My teacher allows me to be line leader because she trusts that I will lead the class correctly. I make sure to always set a good example so that I can continue to be line leader.

There isn't another classroom job that even compares to being line leader. It is the only job that lets you be first and makes everyone follow you. Being door holder is great, but the opportunity to be line leader is phenomenal. Tick, Tick, Tick! The classroom job wheel is being spun. I hope my name lands on line leader again.

Teacher continues:	Just as I completed the Big Idea Checklist for the Planning Sheets, I'm going to do the same thing for the essay using the Big Idea Checklist for Essays [see Figure 7.3]. This time I'll go question by question, locate the sentence in the essay, read it, and determine if it should get a check in the "yes" column or the "no" column. I'll know that if I have any extra sentences in my essay that aren't identified in my checklist, I must have gone off topic. The checklist will help me determine if I've digressed or gone off topic.
	Let's take a look at the first question under the heading First Paragraph. Did I include my complete thesis statement from the planning sheet? Let me read the first paragraph and locate the sentence where I included the thesis statement. There it is: it's the second sentence. I can place a check in the "yes" column.

We go through each question and sentence in the essay.

Teacher:	If my answer was "no" for any of the questions, that would mean there was a sentence that did not belong in that paragraph or that did not belong in the essay at all. At that point I would need to rewrite that sentence and revisit the checklist.

Students Practice the Strategy

Now that I have modeled how to use the Big Idea Planning Sheet and the checklists, students need to practice using this strategy to become familiar with the process. I give each student a copy of the Big Idea Planning Sheet, two pieces of lined paper, and the Big Idea Checklist for Planning Sheets. Next, I write the prompt on the board.

What if your teacher told you that you could have any animal as your classroom pet? Think about what animal you would choose. Write to explain why you would choose this animal.

We complete the Big Idea Planning Sheet together. I constantly think aloud to remind students what type of information belongs in each box, and I call for student volunteers to give me the ideas and wording. Our completed Big Idea Planning Sheet might look like Figure 7.6.

Once the planning sheet is complete, we need to fill out the Big Idea Checklist for Planning Sheets before we write the essay. I read each question out loud and call on students to answer. Before accepting their answer, I ask for an explanation. This helps clarify the process for any student who is having difficulty. Then, we construct the essay together. I probe and prompt students to give sentences that are both on topic and age appropriate.

After we have written a collaborative class essay, we use the Big Idea Checklist for Essays together to verify that the essay is focused, organized, and on topic. I ask questions from the checklist out loud and students volunteer to locate the sentence and answer the question. Before accepting their answer and

Figure 7.6   Sample Big Idea Planning Sheet Completed for Monkeys Topic

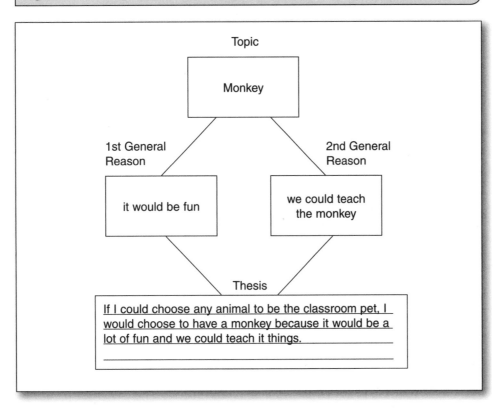

placing a check mark, I ask for an explanation. Again, this helps clarify the process for any student who is having difficulty.

Independent Writing

Now that I have modeled the process for students and completed the strategy with them, they are ready to execute the process independently. To support them, I will have these steps on the board:

1. Complete the Big Idea Planning Sheet.

2. Use the Big Idea Checklist for Planning Sheets.

3. Write your expository essay using the planning sheet as your guide.

4. Use the Big Idea Checklist for Essays to verify that your essay is focused, on topic, and organized.

5. Edit and revise any sentences you found that didn't correspond to the checklist questions.

Student Reflection

When students become familiar with the strategy and can see an improvement in their writing, we have a discussion about our new writing skills. I facilitate conversation among students in which they note changes they perceive in their writing as a result of the strategy. I ask them to write an expository essay where the strategy is the prompt, such as the following:

> *Describe the most recent writing strategy you have learned. Explain how it helps you to write a focused and organized essay.*

Students share their compositions.

MODIFYING THE MINI-LESSON

Adaptations for Writers Who Struggle

When a student is struggling, I assign another student to serve as a mentor. The student mentor uses more examples from life to demonstrate the process. For instance, the student mentor might choose a topic such as being ready for school. Then, with the struggling student, the mentor will brainstorm supporting ideas, such as waking up, getting dressed, and walking to school. The familiarity of the ideas helps to make the concepts clearer, and it gives students additional practice identifying and developing supporting ideas.

Adaptations for English Language Learners

I also use the mentor system to provide assistance to English language learners (ELLs). Specifically, I pair students who can write well in English (L1) with those whose English is still being developed (L2). This allows the L1 student to use the academic language of topic, explain that *topic* is the BIG IDEA, and share his own examples. I also teach mentors to explain that details are the little ideas that support the BIG IDEA, just as a table top (BIG IDEA) is supported by its legs (details); together, they make the whole table (thesis). When ELLs are ready, I encourage them to write their planning sheet in their first language.

Adaptations for Advanced Writers

I encourage students who are advanced writers to look carefully at the microstructure of their work to determine if each paragraph relates to the previous paragraphs. I also help students use subheadings to ensure smooth transitions throughout the piece.

EXTENDING THE STRATEGY ACROSS THE CONTENT AREAS

The Big Idea strategy easily extends across all content areas—social studies, science, English, and even mathematics. Students choose or are assigned a topic and then use the planning sheet and checklists to write an expository text about it.

RESOURCES FOR FURTHER READING

➢ Applebee, A., & Langer, J. A. (1987). *How writing shapes thinking: A study of teaching and learning.* Urbana, IL: National Council of Teachers of English.

Applebee and Langer say that when we specifically teach writing, we help improve the quality of thinking of children. When students see the logical thinking that writers use, they are likely to begin to internalize the clarity of thinking in other areas as well. Children need to understand that writing is communication between the author and the reader.

➢ Fletcher, R. (1993). *What a writer needs.* Portsmouth, NH: Heinemann.

Fletcher tells teachers to allow students to take risks. While this strategy helps to focus student's writing, it does not limit students' creativity. Students get to write their own ideas.

Section II

Strategic Drafting

Putting Ideas on Paper

O nce students have activated their prior knowledge about a topic, gathered some new information they have discovered that they need to write knowledgeably, and considered how they will structure and organize their writing, they are ready to set ideas, knowledge, experiences, and eventually, words to paper. They are ready to draft.

When we think of the writing process, we typically envision that students will compose a "rough" draft of their thoughts after they have practiced some form of inventing (see Section I). Simply put, the drafting process involves writing. If they've put time and effort into the inventing process, their first draft will have some structure and coherency. However, we don't expect the first draft to be polished or highly developed. We tell our students that drafting is all about spilling their ideas out on paper as an initial effort. We encourage them to think of writing as the beginning of a process that allows writers to continuously revisit and rethink concepts and storylines.

Drafting can be compared to the sketches Michelangelo toiled over before he started painting on the ceiling of the Sistine Chapel. Drafts contain raw material, and writers don't expect the first draft to be a masterpiece. However, when we work with students as they draft their writing, we want them to start with raw material that is of the highest quality they can produce. We've all heard the phrase "garbage in, garbage out." To a large degree, we can think of drafting like that. We don't want to tell students to write simply anything when they are drafting. Drafting is different from freewriting, after all. For example, Michelangelo's sketches weren't stick figures! They were detailed, creative conceptualizations that richly and solidly supported his eventual painting—the masterpiece. When our students draft, we want them to put time and effort into the composing process to support the masterpiece that their final draft will eventually be.

Each of the strategy mini-lessons presented in this section is designed to help students put words to paper in a thoughtful, meaningful, and skillful way. The strategies will help students produce the rich, raw material that they will continue to mold and refine as they develop a piece of writing. The strategies also show writers what they still need to know and include in their writing. Some chapters provide reproducible outlines to prompt students to organize their writing. Some use popular culture to help students make connections between what they know and new strategies. Other chapters provide practice in constructing strong sentences. Each chapter offers a mini-lesson to foster students' self-regulated use of drafting strategies as a way to produce high-quality drafts.

Take some time to review each strategy in this section. Read the opening paragraphs, skim through the modeling section, and get a feel for what the strategy involves and how your students would benefit from learning it. Note what students would benefit from each of the mini-lessons.

The best way to start integrating these strategies into your students' writing is simply to start teaching them. Soon, you will hear students using the strategies by name as they draft their compositions and reports.

Quilting Together an Expository Paper in Four Steps

8

Cynthia A. Lassonde

As students learn to write research papers based on their developing writing abilities, they need a structure and a system to help them synthesize information from several resources into a first draft. This strategy shows them how to accomplish this goal in four steps:

Step 1: Tell the Story

Step 2: Retell the Story

Step 3: Let the Notes Tell the Story

Step 4: Quilt the Story Together

These steps guide students as they create a writing frame to "quilt" together the concepts and information from multiple resources into a coherent piece of informative writing. The process not only promotes their writing abilities but also enhances their understanding of the research topic.

WHY THIS STRATEGY IS IMPORTANT

When I work with students as they create expository papers, I find that after the note-taking stage of their research they are left with a wide variety of information they have gathered from multiple resources. They know the next step is to organize their notes in some way, but typically they end up taking this route:

1. "Plopping" information from one resource on the page.

2. Following that with information from another resource and then another, until they've used up all the notes they've taken.

3. Announcing, "Ta-dah! I'm finished! I've used up all my notes!"

The result is a lot of information strung together in no particular order.

All writing teachers want more from students' research efforts than a list of information. For example, I want the following:

- Evidence that they have critically analyzed and interpreted the information they've noted
- Indications that they have thought through multiple perspectives and have filled in their gaps of understanding about a topic

To ensure that this happens, I teach writing and thinking by encouraging students to explore and interpret as they actively construct meaning (Barnes, 1992; Newell, Koukis, & Boster, 2007). This is why I model the quilting strategy. Using the "quilting" process helps writers engage in piecing the information from various resources together into a quilt of understanding (i.e., the self-created writing frame).

THE MINI-LESSON

Materials Needed

- A quilt or a picture of a quilt
- A quilting frame or a picture of one
- A set of prepared notes to use as a model of how to create the writing frame (I create a set or use a set of a student's notes I've saved from a previous year)
- Poster paper to compose (and later display) the writing frame first draft
- Large sheets of unlined poster paper, one for each student (the size frees up space for revisions)
- A large poster that outlines the four quilting strategy steps
- Copies of the steps (Figure 8.1), one for each student's writing notebook
- A large supply of sticky notes in several sizes and colors readily available for students to use

To prepare students for their existence in a world of international commerce and communication, it is very important to introduce various perspectives on each content area topic. Therefore, I incorporate opportunities to examine global and diverse perspectives in everything I teach. For example, when we study history and current events, my students and I look at conflicts from all sides. We discuss how and why people have different opinions and views on a topic. In science and technology, we reflect on ethical and environmental concerns as they relate to what some researchers support as advancements. There are many opportunities to survey and assess students' ability to quilt together—orally and in writing—the ideas and information presented in various resources.

As we approach the research paper, students and I talk about where we get information or where we go to learn about something. Of course, the first responses are "the Internet" or "the library," but then they get more daring

Figure 8.1 Reproducible Poster of the Steps for Quilting Together an Expository Paper

The Quilting Strategy
How to Quilt Together an Expository Paper

Step 1: Tell the Story

I tell a friend a story about all I've learned about my topic through my reading and note taking. I use story language to pull together everything I've learned from all of my sources.

Step 2: Retell the Story

I work alone now and retell the story using my notes. I use the sticky notes to record the main components of the structure of the report on large poster paper.

Step 3: Let the Notes Tell the Story

As I tell my story, I write the main points of my report on other sticky notes. I organize them on my poster paper under the main components, leaving room between each one to write my story.

Step 4: Quilt the Story Together

From these sticky notes, I create a writing frame and begin to quilt the story together into an expository paper or report.

when I say I learn from my parents and television. We generate a whole list of resources. Then, I ask the question, "If I were writing a report for school, which of these resources would be the best, most trusted ones I could use?" That opens the discussion to issues of reliability (consistency) and validity (accuracy) at an appropriate developmental level of understanding. I observe and note how students respond to the idea that various resources will offer different perspectives and information that readers have to piece together to get the full story. Then, I tell them the stories that follow. In between stories, I ask them what we know so far and how the additional stories add to what we understand about the story.

Story 1

The other day I was walking down the street and I saw a man with a hoodie pulled up over his head running out of the bank with a bag. I screamed, "Help! Police, there's been a robbery!" The police officer standing on the corner started chasing the running man, hollering, "Stop. Police."

Story 2

The other day I went shopping. With my arms full of shopping bags, I walked into the bank to take care of some business. I set my things on the counter as I handed my deposit to the teller. A few minutes later, with my transaction completed, I left the bank. I was surprised when all of a sudden I heard someone behind me yelling about a robbery and saw a man and a police officer running toward me.

Story 3

The other day I was in the bank. As I was leaving, I noticed the lady at the next teller station had left one of her shopping bags on the counter. I grabbed it and hurriedly, trying to catch her before she disappeared into the crowded street, ran out to return her bag to her. Before I knew it, there were people screaming and a police officer was chasing me.

We discuss who is telling each story, why the storyteller interpreted the action the way he or she did, and what the full story most likely is. I introduce and define the term *synthesize,* and I converse with them about how we synthesized the three stories or resources into a retelling that makes sense to us. I listen to their oral responses and then ask them to write a short story that quilts together all the information given and makes sense. I assess their ability to incorporate the details from all three stories to construct their logical interpretation of the event into a meaningful report. I look to see that they have included details from all three stories, such as the hoodie, the yelling, the running, the crowded street, and the bag. The assessment reveals which students retell each story separately rather than synthesize and interpret the event based on the information given—these are the students who will benefit most from learning the quilting strategy.

Model the Strategy

I begin direct instruction of the strategy by modeling the quilting strategy. If students are not familiar with the quilting process, I show them a quilt and a quilting frame and explain how the process works. Then I start with Step 1: Tell the Story. I think aloud as I model.

> **Teacher:** I have all these wonderful notes for my report. [I show them a set of notes that I've either saved from a student's report the previous year or that I've created myself.] The first thing I do is pretend I'm a storyteller and tell a friend a story about all I've learned through my reading and note taking. Step 1 is Tell the Story. I say . . .

Here I insert a story that synthesizes the notes. I truly make it sound like a story by

- developing characters,
- using story language (e.g., once upon a time),
- sequencing events in a beginning, middle, ending structure,
- expressing characters' motivation,
- changing my voice to be expressive, and
- incorporating other story features as needed.

> **Teacher:** Telling the story of what I've learned helps me review what I've learned and helps me quilt together all my notes from all my resources into one story—*my* story. I'm going to organize what I've learned from my readings and from taking my notes in a way that will tell the story of what I've learned so it teaches my readers about my topic. To do this, I'm going to use the quilting strategy to help me synthesize the ideas from my notes.
>
> I've already told my story to a friend in Step 1, so now I'm going to move on to Step 2, which is Retell the Story. I go off on my own with some sticky notes and retell the story to myself. As I retell the story, I'm going to listen for the big things I've learned.

Here is where I customize my think-aloud and modeling to match the structure of the report students are writing. For example, they may be writing a report that has a beginning, middle, and ending to it—such as sharing an event in history or a mathematical or scientific process—or they may be using a cause-and-effect or a cyclical structure. Sometimes students report about various characteristics of a topic, such as writing about the geography, history, and resources of a state. Whatever the structure of the report, I guide my students to use the sticky notes to record the main components of the structure—such as "geography," "history," and "resources" for the state report.

> **Teacher:** I write the main parts of my report on the sticky notes. I place them on my poster paper, leaving room between each one to write my story.
>
> For Step 3, Let the Notes Tell the Story, I start retelling my story to myself again. As I do, this time I place my notes on the chart under the sticky note that identifies the main part where the note belongs. For example...

I read one of the notes and place it under the appropriate sticky note. I do this for several of the notes. For this section, it is best if notes have been originally written on index cards; however, I tell students they can cut their notes apart as needed as long as they keep track of the source of each note. We discuss how to go about this step based on the method we've used for taking notes.

> **Teacher:** Now that I have my notes laid out to tell my story on the poster paper, I quilt the story together by making a writing frame. I think of the writing frame as my quilting frame. The frame will end up displaying all the wonderful things I've learned about my topic, just like a quilt shows all the beautiful variety of colors and patterns in the materials a quilter uses. I'm going to take another piece of poster paper now to compose my writing frame. A writing frame helps writers outline the structure of a piece of writing. Today we're going to make our own writing, or quilting, frames by following the structure of the story we told about our topic.
>
> For Step 4, Quilt the Story Together, I'm going to start with the first main part of my report. [I point to the first sticky note.] I am going to start the first sentence of this paragraph by saying...

I write the beginning of a main idea sentence about the first part of the report. For a state report, I might write, "The geography of New York State is" leaving the rest of the sentence to be filled in later.

> **Teacher:** Now I review my notes and think about my story. What do I want to say next about this part? [Students respond.]

For a state report, I might want to write, "The main rivers in New York State are" again leaving blank space. I continue to write just the frame of my report—that is, just the beginnings of sentences and paragraphs—that I will fill in later after I have told the whole story about my topic.

> **Teacher:** Did you see how I really thought about how I wanted to tell my story based on everything I'd learned? I didn't worry about just copying my notes into a report. Did I? No. Before I even looked at my notes, I told my story. That helped me quilt all the things I learned from all the books, websites, interviews, and maps or whatever resources I used

> together so I could understand what I learned instead of just copying my notes. That's what I want you to do. Think of your report as if you are putting together a bunch of stories from your resources (like the bank stories we started with) to make your own special story that will teach your readers about your topic.

As I model the steps of quilting the resources together, I provide examples of how one resource might fit with another to provide a full picture. Or I might show an example of how two resources contradict each other and talk through how I might handle that. To be most effective, my think-aloud modeling has to be adapted to the content area and the type of report students are writing.

Students Practice the Strategy

As students begin to practice the strategy, I scaffold their efforts by asking them to quilt together a small sample of notes I have prepared for them. I hand each student a copy of Figure 8.1, Reproducible Poster of the Steps for Quilting Together an Expository Paper, to insert into their writing notebook. I walk through the four steps with them, guiding their progress and supporting them as needed. I often place students together with a partner to tell the story; this helps them put the notes into their own words and take ownership of their writing piece.

Once students have started the process, I help them organize the main parts of the report and place the note cards under the appropriate sticky note. As they begin to construct the writing frame, I support them by asking them first to express orally what they want to write. I remind them not to write whole sentences but just to frame their report by writing sentence and paragraph beginnings. Gradually, as students become confident and competent using the strategy, I allow them to practice the new strategy independently and provide feedback on their finished work.

Independent Writing

I encourage students to apply the strategy independently with notes they have gathered for their research report. I provide the materials and allow them to self-regulate their use of the quilting strategy.

Student Reflection

As students complete each step of the strategy, I ask them to share what they have accomplished and how it is working for them. We both reflect on how the strategy is helping them or how it could be adapted to be more helpful for them. This process allows me to assess what is working and what is not working for individual students so they don't waste time applying the strategy ineffectively.

MODIFYING THE MINI-LESSON

Adaptations for Writers Who Struggle

This strategy helps students who struggle with writing to write coherent reports because they are physically moving things around to organize the knowledge they've accumulated. It is a hands-on approach. Often, however, students who struggle with writing are intimidated by writing lengthier pieces that they perceive as complex. Also, if students aren't given a choice as to what topic to research, they can be unmotivated to put much effort into it.

I have found that providing an authentic purpose for research and report writing can motivate these writers to engage in the process. In our school, for example, when the state reports are completed, students share their work by participating in a State Fair Day. Advertisement posters go up in advance; we send out invitations to other classes, teachers, and all staff, and the entire student body waits for the day. Students represent their state by dressing up and decorating their desk; displaying maps, artifacts, and pictures; and reading their favorite part of their report throughout the day. As guests visit, students answer questions about their state and tell their story. It's a joyous, anticipated event.

Adaptations for English Language Learners

If the purpose for assigning research reports is to encourage students to learn about a topic by reading, taking notes, and writing about it, then it is important to help English language learners focus on constructing content-related meaning from the assignment (Fitzgerald & Amendum, 2007). Therefore, I adapt this strategy by encouraging students to write notes and the writing frames in their native language to ensure they comprehend the topic they are researching. Then, I have them tell me the synthesizing story in English to see where their gaps of understanding are. I help them fill in the gaps by directing them to appropriate resources.

Adaptations for Advanced Writers

I guide advanced writers to use the strategy with concepts and topics that are advanced in complexity and that involve more demanding skill in interpreting an author's perspective. Advanced writers developing technology abilities can learn how to use graphic software to organize their notes.

EXTENDING THE STRATEGY ACROSS THE CONTENT AREAS

The quilting strategy can be used across the content areas any time students inquire about a concept and want to research and write about it. Whether they are writing biographies of famous mathematicians and scientists or news reports for a class newscast, students can apply this strategy to help them pull together information from a variety of resources to construct knowledge and understanding.

RESOURCES FOR FURTHER READING

➤ Graham, S., & Harris, K. R. (2007). Best practices in teaching planning. In S. Graham, C. A. MacArthur, & J. Fitzgerald (Eds.), *Best practices in writing instruction* (pp. 119–140). New York, NY: Guilford Press.

Graham and Harris tell us that writing strategies are more than just procedural knowledge for doing something or accomplishing a goal. They say that "intentions and know-how have to be paired with will and effort for writing strategies to be effective" (p. 127). The quilting strategy provides both. Not only does it break down the process into four manageable steps that are easy to remember, it involves peer interaction, hands-on manipulation and placement of noted ideas, and storytelling as approaches to motivate students to extend the effort needed to complete a complex assignment such as a research report.

➤ Kolln, M. (1999). Cohesion and coherence. In C. R. Cooper & L. Odell (Eds.), *Evaluating writing: The role of teachers' knowledge about text, learning, and culture* (pp. 93–113). Urbana, IL: National Council of Teachers of English.

Kolln defines the term *coherence* as "cohesion on a global scale" (p. 94). In other words, students write coherently when their writing produces a unified text in which sentences and ideas are arranged into paragraphs and other genre-specific structures that help authors fulfill the expectations readers bring with them to the text. Writing that is coherent flows for the reader. Concepts are explained and sentences gel together into a comprehendible message. The quilting strategy aims to improve the coherence in students' writing.

9 Team Writing to Foster Students' Motivation to Write

Moving From Group Work to Independence

Janet C. Richards

This strategy provides opportunities for students to write collaboratively in small groups, which fosters their motivation and enthusiasm to write. It promotes a reading–writing connection, and it helps students compose stories that contain the essential elements of characters, settings, problems, and solutions. In addition, the strategy helps students review content material and engage in social learning tasks. As students become proficient in the strategy, they write with partners and then compose independently.

WHY THIS STRATEGY IS IMPORTANT

Many of my graduate education majors (teachers) are concerned because their English language arts students are unmotivated writers. These students tend to write quickly and minimally, and they give up easily on writing tasks. They say writing is boring, and they confide they don't like to write because they are poor writers. These students have difficulty passing annual standardized writing tests. Research indicates that students who are reluctant, unmotivated writers often decide to omit stages of the writing process and neglect to self-regulate their writing (Troia, Shankland, & Wolbers, 2012).

Conversely, strong motivation is tied to students' engagement in writing and their successful writing performance (Troia et al., 2012). Motivated writers believe in their abilities to effectively complete a writing assignment. Therefore, they stick to a writing task because they know they will do well if they persevere (see Baker & Wigfield, 1999).

To help my graduate students motivate their unenthusiastic writers, I developed a strategy I titled Team Writing. The Team Writing strategy provides opportunities for students to write in small, collaborative groups. This experience fosters their motivation to write because the strategy is enjoyable, is socially constructed, and provides opportunities for students to write in a risk-free environment. At the same time, students who engage in Team Writing can connect the reading and writing processes and review both story structure and content material. The strategy also offers opportunities for students to learn how other students write, and it exposes them to diverse points of view, knowledge, and life experiences. In these ways, the strategy connects to theories of learning that indicate that the social environment provides opportunities for students to observe and develop higher levels of cognitive processing (Vygotsky, 1978).

THE MINI-LESSON

Materials Needed

- Writing paper
- Pencils
- A SMART Board or other tool (e.g., chart paper) to display examples

I begin this first phase of the lesson by going over two terms pertinent to the strategy: *collaborate* and *team writing.* I use both of these terms in complete sentences and ask for student volunteers to also use these terms in complete sentences. Here are a few examples:

- When people collaborate they work together to finish a task.
- In the Team Writing strategy, students take turns writing a sentence to complete a story or a content passage, such for as history, mathematics, science, or English.

I also explain the benefits of Team Writing to students:

- Students can write in a risk-free environment.
- Team Writing is a fun way to write.
- Team Writing helps students practice reading and writing.
- When students engage in Team Writing, they can compose stories, poetry, content text, and other types of writing genre in an enjoyable way.
- Students can also observe how others write.

Before I model the strategy, I take time to review with students the important elements of all good stories: characters, settings, problems, and solutions. As we review, I demonstrate on my SMART Board (chart paper can also be used) how these elements relate to one another.

Model the Strategy

After we review story elements, I model how the Team Writing strategy works. To begin, I ask for four student volunteers. We form a circle, with two students on either side of me, and I start to explain the process.

Teacher:	I am going to write one sentence of a short story on the top of my paper, like this.

I write, "Sam is a good dog." I display my sentence to all of the students.

Teacher:	Now I will pass my paper to the person on my right, Janice, who will silently read the sentence I wrote and then write an appropriate second sentence to the story.

The class watches as Janice does this.

Teacher:	Janice will now pass the paper to the next student on her right, Juan. Juan will read the two sentences on the paper and add a third appropriate sentence that continues the story.

I continue to provide these directions and remind students of the four major parts to a story (characters, settings, problems, and solutions) until all four students have read and responded to the sentences. At this point I receive my original paper back; it now contains five sentences of a completed story. I ask for a student volunteer to read our Team Writing story aloud. Students usually are amused and pleased by the creativity in their Team Writing efforts and eagerly volunteer to read the story. This is how the story of "Sam Was a Good Dog" turned out.

1. Sam was a good dog.
2. He always walked nicely on a leash when he was outside.
3. But one day Sam dashed after a cat.
4. His owner had to run after him.
5. From then on Sam had to wear a strong collar when his owner took him for a walk.

This strategy can also serve as an assessment of the students' knowledge of story structure. In this case, the five-line story contains characters, a setting, a problem, and a solution.

Students Practice the Strategy

Once I am certain students know how to execute the strategy, I organize them into small groups of five. Each student in the group writes a first sentence on a piece of paper. Then all students pass their papers to the student on their right. Thus, each group of five students completes five short stories. As students write, I circulate among the teams and offer suggestions if necessary. When students have developed proficiency with the strategy, depending on their writing skills, I encourage six to eight students to join a Team Writing group. Their input makes the story longer and more complicated, and the strategy becomes more complex.

When students develop expertise collaborating in Team Writing stories, I extend the strategy to include content and informational subjects. Since many students find it more difficult to write informational text than to write narrative and fiction, I model attributes of informational text using passages from students' textbooks:

- Superordinate statements (e.g., a strong beginning statement) followed by subordinate statements (e.g., facts and details)
- Enumeration (e.g., cats, dogs, and mice)
- Time order (e.g., first, second, third)
- Compare and contrast (e.g., He is short, but she is tall)
- Cause and effect (e.g., He ate too much and felt sick)

I also speak with the students and their content teachers to learn what specific topics and concepts they are studying. Then I ask students to write a first sentence that focuses on a specific content or informational subject. For example, here's what I might say to a group of fifth-grade students.

> **Teacher:** I know you are currently studying about the Declaration of Independence. Write a beginning superordinate informational sentence on the top of your paper about the Declaration of Independence like I did on my paper.

I show students my sentence: "Many men authored the Declaration of Independence; it was a group-writing project."

> **Teacher:** When you have completed your first sentence, pass your papers to the student on your right, who will write a second sentence of a content informational passage about the Declaration of Independence. Continue reading, writing, and passing your papers until you all receive your original paper back. Remember, informational text has a different structure than narrative stories. Using this structure, authors begin with a strong opening statement followed by supporting facts and details.

When all groups have completed their Team Writing informational passage, students volunteer to read their collaborative work. Students always remark that writing informational text is more difficult than writing stories. We often discover that some papers contain incorrect or minimal content information. This discovery provides opportunities for students to review content material, and it alerts me and content teachers about students' need to review content information. In addition, Team Writing illuminates difficulties some students have with content vocabulary pertinent to informational text.

When these problems are identified, I ask students to write in their writing notebooks what dimensions of informational text they understand and what dimensions they need to strengthen and to provide examples of each. For example, "I need to learn the signal words, or connectives, that authors use to write in a cause-effect pattern, such as *because, since, therefore,* and *consequently,*" and "I know the differences between superordinate and subordinate information." I also remind students to refer to their notebook entries when they engage in independent writing of informational text in their content classes.

Independent Writing

I encourage students who understand the Team Writing strategy to begin their journey toward independent writing by engaging in Partner Writing. In Partner Writing, two students collaborate on a writing project. This approach provides opportunities for students to continue to connect with another writer in meaningful, supportive, social interactions about writing. Then, I encourage students to write independently. However, I continue to remind them that they always have a buddy to turn to when they need writing support and encouragement.

Student Reflection

Reflection helps students review and process new learning. I form small groups of students and ask them to identify ways that Team Writing helps them with their writing. I often use their responses to rethink and revamp my writing strategy lessons. Here are some reflections that students recently shared with me:

"I learned a lot from what other students knew and wrote."

"I felt comfortable writing with my team because the pressure was not just on me to write a perfect paper."

"The group writing made me think that writing can be fun, and I also got to understand some writing tips that I entered in my writing notebook."

"I learned the different patterns in stories and informational text."

MODIFYING THE MINI-LESSON

Adaptations for Writers Who Struggle

I take the middle position in a group of writers who struggle and become one of the Team Writing participants so I can offer support and structure the group's work passage if necessary. This type of participation also allows me to see what extra help students need in specific areas of writing. When struggling writers begin to demonstrate proficiency in their Team Writing efforts, I gradually release responsibilities to the members of the group.

Adaptations for English Language Learners

I have found it beneficial to sit next to an English language learner (ELL) as he or she participates in the group so I can take dictation. The ELL student can observe me writing English, and I whisper as I write so the student can hear and see English words concurrently. At the end of the lesson, I help ELLs record some of these English words in their personal dictionaries. I also encourage ELL students to write in their first language until they feel more confident writing in English.

Adaptations for Advanced Writers

I extend this strategy for advanced writers by helping them learn how to write an entire paragraph before passing their papers to a student on their right. We begin by writing stories and then move on to informational text. Writing entire paragraphs that focus on informational text is no easy task for students. Therefore, I work with advanced writers in their groups until they can complete an informational text proficiently.

EXTENDING THE STRATEGY ACROSS THE CONTENT AREAS

The Team Writing strategy works well in all content areas. One requirement is that content teachers must recognize and be able to help students with the structure and attributes of content text.

RESOURCES FOR FURTHER READING

➢ Strong, R., Silver, H., & Robinson, A. (1995). What do students want (and what really motivates them)? *Educational Leadership, 53*(1), 8–12. Retrieved from http://www.ascd.org/publications/educational-leadership/sept95/vol53/num01/Strengthening-Student-Engagement@-What-Do-Students-Want.aspx

These authors posit that teachers can motivate middle school students by considering four areas that middle school students perceive as important and are basic needs of middle school students: success (the need for mastery), curiosity (the need for understanding), originality (the need for self-expression), and relationships (the need for involvement with others).

➢ Troia, G. (2007). Introduction: Research on writing-knowledge development, effective interventions, and assessment. *Reading and Writing Quarterly, 23*, 203–207.

Troia notes that we know a great deal about the efficacy of specific writing strategies. However, scholars and practitioners know less about the emergence of typical and struggling writers' knowledge about the forms, purposes of different writing genre. In particular, Troia argues we need to know more about how best to teach students informational text structure organization.

10 Use Your Own Words

Learning to Paraphrase

Janet C. Richards

Students' ability to paraphrase is listed as a key research and writing skill for students in Grades 4 through 8 on numerous English language arts core standards. The strategy presented in this chapter helps students at these levels learn how to paraphrase information an author has previously stated. The strategy also reminds students to give credit to authors when they quote from a direct source and also when they paraphrase material originally composed by another author.

WHY THIS STRATEGY IS IMPORTANT

When I teach expository writing lessons, I notice that students usually include too many direct quotations in their final drafts. Scholars state that only 10 percent of a final copy should contain directly quoted material. Writers "should use direct quotations sparingly, choosing them carefully to make an impression. A paper composed mostly of quotations from other authors runs [into] the plagiarism risk called 'patchworking'" (*Cornwell's Writing Guide*, 2008–2009, p. 2). Students also neglect to provide appropriate reference documentation for the quotations they insert in their work, which is illegal.

Many students also fail to paraphrase information. When writers are able to paraphrase, they understand material well enough to put it in their own words without changing the meaning of the original information. However, even when writers paraphrase material, they must give credit to the source by citing the author(s) of the material. When students learn to independently paraphrase information and give credit to the original source, they acquire a skill they will continue to refine and use as they compose expository text in high school and postsecondary education.

THE MINI-LESSON

Materials Needed

- A SMART Board and a computer (chart paper may also be used)
- Pencils
- Students' writing notebooks (or blank paper)
- Grade-level thesauruses (such as the Scholastic *Pocket Thesaurus*)
- Copies of the Checklist for Using Direct Quotations and Paraphrased Material, one for each student (see Figure 10.1)
- Glue or a stapler

I begin the lesson by discussing the difference between expressing direct quotes and paraphrasing. Then, I ask students to sing or tell the beginning lines of a current popular song. I explain that if we wanted to write the song as a direct quote in our essays, we would have to supply the name of the author and the date of the original publication, plus the page number on which the song was printed, and the publisher. However, we might want to paraphrase this song.

Then, I ask students to listen carefully as I state some of the lyrics in my own words. Next, we discuss how the two versions of the song differ. Then I discuss documentation.

Teacher: Even though I used my own words in the second version of the song, I still have to give credit to the original author, and I have to supply the date of the publication.

When writers paraphrase, they restate in their own words information another author has already written. Let's try to paraphrase together. Pretend that I wrote an informational essay that presents facts about snails and I included the sentence "Snails like to eat leaves" in my writing. Then, imagine you also want to write about snails and you want to explain what they like to eat. It is illegal and dishonest to copy my exact words unless you give me credit. You can also paraphrase my sentence by restating it in your own words, but you still have to give me credit for writing the original information. You might paraphrase the sentence "Snails like to eat leaves" like this: "Snails enjoy eating the foliage of shrubberies and plants." Let's try paraphrasing the snail sentence using your own words. Remember, when you paraphrase you cannot change the meaning of the sentence written by the original author.

Next, I scaffold students' efforts as they offer their paraphrased versions of the sentence "Snails like to eat leaves." They come up with lines such as "Snails think plants are an appetizing snack," and "Snails really like to eat plant foliage." Then we discuss how writers' knowledge of vocabulary enhances their ability to paraphrase and how a thesaurus is helpful to writers who want

Figure 10.1   Reproducible Checklist for Using Direct Quotations and
Paraphrased Material

Name _____ Date _____

Checklist for Using Direct Quotations and Paraphrased Material in My Writing
1. I used _____ (how many?) direct quotes in my paper to explain or support my statements. _____
2. I identified the author of the original quotation, and I provided a complete citation at the appropriate place in my paper. _____
3. I paraphrased material _____ (how many times?), and I read the original material. I paraphrased several times so that I understood the information. _____
4. I rewrote the material in my own words without looking at the original source. _____
5. I checked my paraphrased rewrite against the original source. _____
6. I made sure my paraphrased version contains the same information as the original source, but I used my own words. _____
7. I remembered to identify who wrote the original information. I referred to an outside source in the body of my paper, and I provided a complete citation at the appropriate place in my paper. _____

to paraphrase material. I close this part of the lesson by explaining to students how the strategy Use Your Own Words: Paraphrase will help them monitor their use of direct quotations and their ability to paraphrase material.

Model the Strategy

I begin the modeling phase of the lesson by typing on the computer "Today is Monday." I display this three-word simple sentence on the SMART Board, and we read it aloud as a group. Then I explain how to paraphrase.

> **Teacher:**   I am going to paraphrase this sentence. I have to use different words, and I cannot change the meaning of the sentence. That means I cannot take away, add, or change the information in the sentence. For example, I cannot write, "Today is not Monday" or "Tomorrow is Monday." But I can write, "This day is the day before Tuesday." I can also write, "This is the day after Sunday."

I type and display these sentences as I speak. Then I ask a student volunteer to dictate a sentence of her choice (e.g., "Ice cream is delicious"), and I model ways the sentence might be paraphrased (e.g., "Frozen dessert made with milk, sugar, and flavoring tastes fabulous").

Once students demonstrate an understanding of how to paraphrase short sentences in subsequent lessons, we move on to longer connected discourse. For example, I model how to paraphrase short paragraphs taken directly from students' textbooks and from other reference material.

Students Practice the Strategy

When I am certain students have developed an understanding about how to paraphrase, I refer them to their thesauruses, and we take a few minutes to review how to use this useful paraphrasing reference tool. Then students take out their pencils, open their writing notebooks, and date a new page they title Paraphrasing. I dictate a sentence twice and ask students to write the sentence in their notebooks. (e.g., "We like to learn how to write"). Next, students work individually or in pairs to paraphrase the sentence. We share all our efforts (e.g., "Our group enjoys gaining knowledge about how to compose," and "This group is fond of studying about composing"). We discuss if any of the paraphrased sentences have added or subtracted information or have changed the meaning of the dictated sentence. I carefully monitor students' abilities to paraphrase and determine how many practice sessions we need before we are ready to continue to the next part of our practice phase, which focuses on independently paraphrasing short paragraphs.

Independent Writing

At this stage, I supply students with the checklist of statements shown in Figure 10.1. I ask them to glue or staple these statements in their writing notebook and refer and respond to them whenever they have completed a first draft of an expository paper. Responding to the statements helps students self-regulate their writing as they revisit their work and fine-tune their composition before turning in their papers for a grade. As students move through executing the writing process, I remind them that paraphrasing information means using your words to restate an idea and that paraphrased material can be longer or shorter than the original passage as long as the meaning of the passage remains the same. I say, "Always remember to *use your words: paraphrase.*"

Since learning is a social activity, I urge students to work with a partner or in small groups to share ideas as they carefully revise and edit their work. Partners help each other make sure that if they included direct quotations, they also supplied appropriate documentation and that if they paraphrased information they also included appropriate citations. Here again, I continue to monitor students' understanding of the strategy, and I note which students need additional help. I continuously remind them, "Use your words: paraphrase."

Student Reflection

I ask students to share in small groups what still confuses them about using direct quotations and about paraphrasing and to also communicate what they think are the most important concepts learned in our paraphrase mini-lesson. Then I ask volunteers to share their thoughts with the entire class. As students share, I am able to pinpoint and resolve any misconceptions they have about the strategy, about using direct quotes, or about paraphrasing material. In addition, sharing

- helps students take on the role of teacher,
- allows students to review the strategy, and
- provides an occasion for students to construct additional knowledge and understanding about the Use Your Own Words: Paraphrase strategy,

MODIFYING THE MINI-LESSON

Adaptations for Writers Who Struggle

Struggling writers are a diverse group of students with different reasons for their writing difficulties. Therefore, as a precursor to adapting the Use Your Own Words: Paraphrase strategy for writers who struggle, I try to determine the type of problem each student experiences.

Understanding the nature of struggling writers' difficulties serves as a starting point for me and helps me move forward as a focused learning helper (see Page-Voth, 2010). Once I figure out the problem(s) encountered by individual students, I create differentiated mini-lessons designed to provide each writer with success. For example, some students may have initially discounted or disregarded the strategy mini-lesson. Therefore, they might need a review of the entire Use Your own Words: Paraphrase strategy. Others may need to be reminded to use their thesaurus, or they may need to learn how to use their thesaurus correctly.

For some writers who struggle with paraphrasing, the problem may reside with inadequate vocabulary. These students need considerable language expansion activities. In addition, writers who struggle generally underuse writing strategies (Chalk, Hagen-Burke, & Burke, 2005). As teachers, we must recognize that "students learning how to apply a strategy does not guarantee that the students will use it when an opportunity arises or be able to adapt it to new but appropriate situations" (Graham & Harris, 2005, pp. 26–27). Therefore, I supply writers who struggle with the reminder sheet shown in Figure 10.2: How to Paraphrase: Choose, Change, and Whisper (C, C, and W). Students can paste it into their writing notebooks and refer to it as needed. The three sentences in this reminder serve to prompt students to use this structure to paraphrase successfully. Note that this checklist is tailored to fit the developing cognitive abilities and developmental stage of writers who struggle.

Adaptations for English Language Learners

English language learners (ELLs) especially need considerable support with paraphrasing. They often lack sufficient English language vocabulary necessary to paraphrase. In addition, they have difficulty manipulating the syntax (order of the words) in English language sentences. Syntactical changes usually occur when authors paraphrase. Therefore, I work often with ELLs and supply clear and systematic guidance. I modify the Use Your Words: Paraphrase strategy for ELLs by first concentrating on individual words (i.e., synonyms). I gather ELLs in a small circle, and we each take a turn paraphrasing familiar, frequently encountered words such as *funny* or *loud.* Then we move on to paraphrasing an adjective that precedes a noun, such as *happy* horse (*glad* horse, *joyful* horse, *cheerful* horse, *jovial* horse). Our long-term goal is to shift from paraphrasing one or two words to paraphrasing complete sentences and longer passages. Students record these original words and sentences and their paraphrased examples in their writing notebook so they can refer to them as they write independently.

Adaptations for Advanced Writers

Advanced writers possess exemplary thinking and writing abilities ("Writer's Workshop," 2012). They have a large store of advanced vocabulary, and their writing organizational skills are well developed. In addition, they are self-sufficient and can write independently. Moreover, they are confident about their writing proficiencies. Therefore, I expect advanced writers in Grades 4 through 8 to accept responsibility for turning in well-developed expository papers that contain a few direct quotes and also paraphrased information that support their statements. In addition, I assume advanced writers will accompany direct quotations and paraphrased material with appropriate citations. To communicate my expectations, I meet with advanced writers as necessary and go over our guidelines for embedding quotes and paraphrased material in exposition.

Figure 10.2 Reproducible Checklist of How to Paraphrase

How to Paraphrase: Choose, Change, and Whisper (C, C, and W)
1) **Choose (C)** a sentence or sentences from a book or other reference material that you want to paraphrase. _____
2) **Change (C)** as many words as you can in the sentence or sentences, but keep the meaning of the original material. _____
3) **Whisper** (W) the paraphrased sentence or sentences aloud, and make sure your paraphrased information states the same meaning of the original sentence. _____

EXTENDING THE STRATEGY ACROSS THE CONTENT AREAS

Students' ability to appropriately insert direct quotations and paraphrased material within the body of their papers applies to all content area writing. For example, students who know how to embed direct quotations in their essays about historical events show they can use evidence to support their assumptions and claims. Similarly, students who can paraphrase or restate mathematical or scientific terms and applications demonstrate their understanding of math and science concepts. Direct quotes and paraphrased material accompanied by author citations enhances students' abilities to write effectively in all content areas.

RESOURCES FOR FURTHER READING

Teaching paraphrasing improves reading comprehension. (n.d.). Retrieved from http://online.edfac.unimelb.edu.au/LiteracyResearch/pub/Projects/ MDaly.pdf

This study investigated the effectiveness of teaching paraphrasing, as an aid to improving reading comprehension. Participants were two male and two female ESL students in Year 3 of their schooling in Canada. The students had limited English language vocabulary and exhibited reading comprehension difficulties. Study results indicate paraphrasing practice had a positive effect on students' abilities to paraphrase independently. The investigation also showed improvement in students' English language vocabularies and gains in students' reading comprehension. Moreover, students showed an increase in confidence and enthusiasm for writing and reading comprehension.

➢ Keck, C. (2006). The use of paraphrase in summary writing: A comparison of L1 and L2 writers. *Journal of Second Language Writing, 15(4),* 261–278.

Paraphrasing is considered an important skill for academic writing. Scholars note that the teaching of paraphrasing might help students avoid copying from source texts. This study analyzed L1 ($n = 79$) and L2 ($n = 74$) writers' use of paraphrase within a summary task and developed a method for classifying these paraphrases into four major paraphrase types: near copy, minimal revision, moderate revision, and substantial revision. The researcher then compared the L1 and L2 writers' use of these paraphrase types within their summaries. Results indicate that although both groups used about five paraphrases per summary, L2 writers used significantly more near copies than did L1 writers. Conversely, the summaries of L1 writers contained significantly more moderate and substantial revisions than those of the L2 writers.

11 Creating Rounded Characters Through Cartoon Connections

Krishna Seunarinesingh

This strategy helps students who have difficulty creating well-rounded characters in their creative writing. Students reflect on the character traits and attributes of well-known pop culture cartoon characters with whom they are familiar and apply their observations to their own writing.

WHY THIS STRATEGY IS IMPORTANT

I often find my students' stories lack interest because the characters are "flat." Their story characters are not invested with emotions, feelings, or identifiable attributes. To assist students' ability to create better characters, I have devised a four-step instructional process I call Creating Rounded Characters Through Cartoon Connections. Students and I view episodes of *SpongeBob SquarePants* (Viacom, 2009) or other popular cartoons on television, we discuss some episodes, and we create a portrait of the protagonist (i.e., the main character) and his or her fellow characters in the show.

Research suggests that making connections between students' popular culture interests and their school-based literacy practices can be both entertaining and educational (Hoffner, Baker, & Quinn, 2008; Skinner & Hagood, 2008). Instead of resisting students' interest in television, this strategy immerses them in discussions and writing about favorite shows. It helps them create rounded characters that are plausible and recognizable.

THE MINI-LESSON

Materials Needed

- A poster of SpongeBob (or other character being studied)
- A poster of Squidward (or other character being studied)

- Large pieces of paper to create concept maps
- A large, deflated balloon with SpongeBob (or other character) sketched on it by tracing images printed from the Internet (see resource list)
- A poster of how to round characters (Figure 11.1)
- Copies of the Student-Friendly Rubric for Self-Regulated Learning, one for each student (Figure 11.2)

I begin the mini-lesson with a discussion of my students' favorite character from television. In this particular lesson, we focus on SpongeBob SquarePants. I mount a large poster of SpongeBob in our classroom to motivate our group discussion. Following is an example of what the discussion might sound like.

Teacher:	So does anybody here watch SpongeBob?
Chloe:	Yes!
Patrick:	Of course!
Teacher:	Great. Let's talk about him. Would someone like to start by describing what he looks and sounds like?
Grace:	He's yellow and square.
Angel:	He has large eyes.
Gil:	He has a funny laugh.

While they speak, I go to the poster and draw lines like spokes on a bicycle wheel radiating out from the picture of SpongeBob. I write the adjectives and adjectival phrases students generate.

Next, I engage students in conversation about SpongeBob's personality.

Teacher:	What kind of "person" is he? What are some of his characteristics?
Gil:	He is trusting.
Grace:	He's loyal to his friends.
Angel:	He isn't too smart.

I add these around the picture. If no one uses the word *naive*, I add it, circle it, and extend a line outward from it so I can verbalize a sentence and write the sentence with the word *naive* in it. Next, I ask students to volunteer to use the word *naive* in a sentence.

I then ask students about the character's relationships with other characters in the cartoon to get them to think about that aspect of the character's round personality.

Teacher:	What kind of relationship does he have with others?
Benny:	People like Mr. Krabs take advantage of him.
Yasmin:	Squidward thinks he is irritating.
Luke:	Patrick thinks he is a great pal, and Gary loves him.

Figure 11.1   Reproducible Poster of How to Make Rounded Characters

Name _____ Date _____

Answer each question by making a check in the appropriate column. Use the chart to revise your story so all checks end up in the "Yes" column in your final draft.

	Yes	A Little	No
Can readers "see" my character when they read my story?			
Do readers get to know my character by reading my story?			
Do readers know how my character gets along with the other characters in the story?			
Do I use a lot of good words to describe my character's looks, feelings, relationships, thoughts, and actions?			
Does my character feel round or just flat?			

Figure 11.2 Reproducible Student-Friendly Rubric for Self-Regulated Learning

Name _____ Date _____

Creating Rounded Characters Scoring Rubric			
Criterion	0–1 point	2–3 points	4–5 points
Description of physical characteristics	Description includes virtually no physical details, or just one detail presented in passing. Character is just a name.	Description includes some details, such as height and size, but we can't "see" the character.	Description is vivid. We "see" the character because many details, such as color, size, height, sound of voice are presented.
Description of traits	Description includes virtually no details of traits or may just hint at it by passing reference to the character's action.	Description includes at least one clearly recognizable trait, but it may be inadequately/ perfunctorily treated.	Recognizable traits, such as kindness, forbearance, persistence, are presented and illustrated briefly through reference to a specific incident in an episode.
Treatment of interpersonal relations	Description includes no details of relationships with other characters, or it is vaguely hinted at.	Description includes cursory treatment of inter-personal relations. It may include a statement or statements that are not supported with anecdotes.	Description consists of showing relationships instead of just telling about them. Use of appropriate adjectives to describe relationships. Narrator's attitude may be present.

I add "loyal to his friends," if no one offers it. I ask if anyone can use the word *loyal* in a sentence. If no one responds, I recount an event in which SpongeBob is loyal. I ask if someone would like to devise a sentence with the word *loyal* in it.

At this point, I turn the focus to Squidward, who is another character in the cartoon. He is a stark contrast to the hero of the show because he is morose, cynical, and pessimistic at heart. (His name conjures up for me the idea of a damp squid!) I introduce an open-ended question: "How much of a friend is he to SpongeBob?" This generates a range of reactions and creates opportunities for students to justify their opinions. The contrast also establishes a potential source of tension that I will use in the succeeding unit to teach about types of conflict. Students comment on the degree of friendship existing between both characters, and they offer examples from episodes they remember.

Our board now has two drawings or pictures side by side: SpongeBob and Squidward. Around each are descriptive words that evoke their characteristics, traits, and students' understandings of their interpersonal relations.

By conferring with students, I have learned what they know about the cartoon characters, the vocabulary they have available to think about character traits and attributes, and most important, what they know about character development.

Model the Strategy

I help students visualize what we mean when we talk about "rounded characters." I take out the deflated balloon that I have sketched with a picture of SpongeBob. I model as follows.

Teacher:	When we first started talking about SpongeBob, we didn't have much information up here about him. Did we? [I point to the concept map we created together previously.]
Students:	No.
Teacher:	But then we talked about him and described what he looks and sounds like. So we started to round him out. [I blow a couple of breaths into the balloon to inflate it a little.] Then, we talked about his personality and rounded him out a little more. [I add a few more breaths.] And finally, we talked about the relationships he has with other characters and rounded him out even MORE! [I finish inflating the balloon to its full size.] Now look how much we know about SpongeBob! He went from being flat to being rounded. Didn't he? That's what we want to do when we write stories. We don't want our characters to be flat like this. [I let the air out of the balloon.] That's dull and boring, that flat balloon just sitting there. Boooooring! We want our characters to be round so our readers know a lot about them. We want to fill them up by telling what?
Gil:	What they look and sound like.

Lukey:	What their personality is like.
Jamal:	What their relationships with other characters are like. [As students give me these answers, I puff breaths of air into the balloon again to visualize a rounded character.]
Teacher:	Yes, look at how round our character is now. We know so much about him. We created a rounded character, and that is what we want to do when we write. When we have rounded characters in our stories, they are much, much more interesting to our readers. We make our characters round by telling readers…let's say it together…
Teacher and students together:	What they look and sound like, what their personalities are like, and what their relationships with other characters are like.
Teacher:	Yes, and here is a poster to help us remember how to make characters round, not flat and boring. [I show them the poster in Figure 11.1.]

The next stage is an integrative one that pulls together what has been said about both characters and compares/contrasts them in a character sketch. This is a difficult stage because students eventually have to be able to transition independently from generating "points" and features to composing full sentences.

Teacher:	Let's look at what we have on the board. [I ask for volunteers to read aloud the descriptions around each character.] Remember, you said Squidward thinks SpongeBob is a nuisance. For the next few minutes, we are going to contrast these two employees of the Krusty Krab. Telling how the characters are different from each other is a good way to tell our readers about the characters. Here is an example of what we can say.

As I create the following narrative, I refer and point to the notes on the concept maps we constructed for each character. I speak as if I'm telling a story.

Teacher:	*SpongeBob is a square, yellow fellow, who lives in a pineapple under the sea. Squidward works with SpongeBob at the Krusty Krab Restaurant, but he looks very different. He is thin and tall and has long arms and legs. SpongeBob has a really silly laugh that sounds like a dolphin, but Squidward almost never laughs. When he does, it is because he is laughing at someone else.* Now let's put in something about how others feel about our characters. *SpongeBob is fun to be around, especially when he is trying to catch jellyfish, and he is very hardworking. On the other hand, Squidward hates his job, and is rude to others.* [I insert an example of this here by asking for suggestions from the class.] *He does*

> *not really care if he hurts SpongeBob's feelings. He is not much fun to be around, except maybe when he is trying to play the clarinet. When that happens, people cover their ears and run away. Unlike Patrick, Squidward is not SpongeBob's loyal friend. This does not bother SpongeBob, who remains cheerful and full of life almost all the time.*

Finally, I remind students of the main questions we used from the poster (see Figure 11.1). After this, I carefully point out to students how we created contrast by telling how the two characters look, sound, and act differently from each other. We identify contrast words, note where and how they were used, and determine what job they do for us as writers. At the end of the session, I ask students to bring to class either drawings or downloaded pictures of the characters about whom they propose to write.

Students Practice the Strategy

I scaffold students' efforts as they write about a pair of characters of their choice. I remind them to follow the steps we have used. I often place students together with a partner to talk about their characters; This helps them increase the vocabulary they will use to talk about the characters and broadens their knowledge of the character. Once writing begins, I help composers by asking them to say out loud what they want to express. They write what they talked through. I help them organize the information, combine sentences, and use descriptive vocabulary. When they have finished their draft, I remind them to review it by ascertaining that they have answered each of our questions. They read their story to a peer and then to me. When they are ready, they share with the entire class.

Independent Writing

To encourage students to use this strategy as they write independently and to become self-regulated at monitoring their progress with developing rounded characters, I give each student the Student-Friendly Rubric for Self-Regulated Learning (see Figure 11.2). First, we discuss each of the rows in the rubric and practice using it on a common piece of writing together. Then they try using it on their own to improve their writing. I stand by to facilitate their progress with this exercise in self-regulated learning.

Student Reflection

As students apply the strategy, I encourage them to share their stories with family members. I ask students to tell their family how to do the strategy. The next day in class, I ask them to share what family members said about their stories and how the Creating Rounded Characters Through Cartoon Connections strategy worked for the students.

MODIFYING THE MINI-LESSON

Adaptations for Writers Who Struggle

This strategy usually encourages students to want to write lengthier sentences because they are so motivated to tell about their characters. I help to alleviate the gap between motivation and skill by

1. having writers who struggle create a bulleted list of the details they generated,

2. modeling for them how to use selected coordinating conjunctions to chain the details together, and

3. modeling how to decide where a full stop (i.e., end punctuation) goes.

Adaptations for English Language Learners

Some English language learners (ELLs) already "know" English because their lexicon is English-based. This is the case, for example, of writers from the English-speaking Caribbean. Other ELLs' first language is very different from English. I have found that teaching them about formulaic sequences (Boers, Eyckmans, Kappel, Stengers, & Demecheleer, 2006; Wray, 2000, 2008) helps them build their characters' portraits. Some common examples from everyday speech are, "If the truth be told," "You're never going to believe this," and "I wouldn't do that if I were you." Specifically, I encourage them to

1. locate and snip out formulaic sequences from newspapers and magazines, and

2. experiment with formulaic sequences, like putting puzzle pieces together.

Adaptations for Advanced Writers

I present more challenging stimulus texts for advanced writers. For example, I read aloud the first chapter of an intriguing story, such as *The Homework Machine* (Gutman, 2007). In this story, four children use a homework machine named Belch to do their homework for them, and they attract the attention and suspicion of their teacher and their peers. I direct their attention in Chapter 1 to how Gutman deftly reveals details about each character and about their interpersonal relationships. Though the stimulus is not a visual one, like SpongeBob, we focus on the same questions and attempt to get answers from the text. I also teach them how to weave character details into the action of a story. Instead of presenting character information in a block, like writers who struggle, fluent writers reveal details as observed by other characters. For example, a writer who struggles might say, "Spiderman wears a blue and red body suit that shows his rippling muscles. His foe, Doc Ock, has metal tentacles for arms, and he wants to wreck the city." A fluent writer would learn to take a different perspective and write something like this: "Spiderman had to save the city from the menace of Doc Ock's metal tentacles. As he swung from the bridge in his blue and red suit, his rippling muscles ached from the last battle with his foe."

EXTENDING THE STRATEGY ACROSS THE CONTENT AREAS

What better way to learn history than through telling stories? I like to have students choose people from history to characterize based on what they did in history. For example, students can easily write a character description of Benjamin Franklin or George Washington. I have students create rounded characters out of real people from history, which involves reading, researching, and learning about them.

Another way I extend the strategy across the content areas is to have students characterize abstract concepts. In science and math I have them create rounded characters of *electricity* and *negative numbers.* They follow the same procedure of asking questions about how they'd describe the concept, what its personality might be like, and how it relates to other key concepts. Students explore their understandings of the concepts as they describe and contrast them.

RESOURCES FOR FURTHER READING

➤ Graves, D. H. (1994). *A fresh look at writing.* Portsmouth, NH: Heinemann.

In Chapter 18, Graves points out that children love to create fiction, but that it is the most difficult of all genres to produce. After making the telling observation, "Character is all" (p. 288), Graves points out that in the stories children write, characters "exist merely to serve plot" (p. 289). These young writers seem unaware that a character's nature propels what happens in stories. Graves speculates that part of the problem young fiction writers face is that they want to excite their readers, and they rely on the "high-action plots" they view in movies and cartoons. These tend to be full of high-speed chases and violence.

Graves's observations relate to the making cartoon connections strategy. They support the idea that children are developing composers of creative writing and need our guidance to understanding how to write rounded characters whose nature and attributes drive the story.

➤ Hong Xu, S. (2005). *Trading cards to comic strips: Popular culture texts and literacy learning in grades K–8.* Newark, Delaware: International Reading Association.

Using popular media such as cartoons, songs, comic strips, and Internet texts for classroom instructional purposes is a significant strategy for motivating young readers and writers to "engage in meaningful literacy practices"

(Hong Xu, 2005, p. 2). According to the author, the argument for using popular media is that it (a) bombards the youth of the 21st century, who spend significant time watching television and playing computer games and thus already enjoy engagement with the text, and (b) is an additional genre of text "that holds personal interests for students" (p. 2). That is, there is a match between instructional stimulus and learner interest. Teachers can capitalize on this to support students' literacy development. As an example, the authors introduce April, a teacher who experimented with using an episode of *Scooby Doo* and the book based on the show. The students were thrilled at the choice of teaching materials, and even struggling and reluctant writers participated in the writing process and evinced interest in their work.

This work supports the idea of making cartoon connections to develop rounded characters. When we incorporate cartoons as an instructional stimulus, students become highly interested in the writing process and creating interesting stories.

12 Applying the Structure Strategy to Write Persuasive Texts

Bonnie J. F. Meyer,
Jennifer Ireland, and Melissa Ray

Applying the Structure strategy helps students write persuasive texts independently. Students study how authors use text structures such as problem and solution, cause and effect, and comparison to organize nonfiction, and then they practice these techniques in their own writing. Their knowledge of the authors' craft also increases their own learning from texts (Meyer, Brandt, & Bluth, 1980). In this mini-lesson, students use the Structure strategy to recognize and understand an author's argument and to construct their own persuasive texts on the same topic.

This mini-lesson models a mentor text-mapping approach similar to the one presented with expository texts by Joyce C. Fine in Chapter 5, "Reciprocal Text Structure Mapping for Expository Writing." However, this mini-lesson moves beyond the inventing process to focus on the drafting process for writing persuasive texts. Students use an outline to draft the essay. For this mini-lesson, writers are invited to use and add to the signal words handout provided in Figure 5.6

WHY THIS STRATEGY IS IMPORTANT

Students often struggle with drafting persuasive essays. This difficulty likely arises because they have trouble generating and organizing ideas at the same time (Hammann & Stevens, 2003). Furthermore, an expository essay can contain elements of multiple patterns or structures. Strategic knowledge about text structures helps students remember important ideas, organize, write, and revise their persuasive writing as they construct and apply new understandings about the connections between reading and writing (Meyer, 1982).

Many students have told us they are frustrated writing persuasive essays. They say that although they are able to verbally communicate their ideas and select what information they want to include as evidence in their essays, their written essays don't come out the way they hope. Their ideas seem to get lost somewhere between the oral and written forms. This problem is due to the complex nature of organizing the structural components of expository texts.

The Structure strategy provides students with a framework for organizing their writing that is linked to how they interpret what they read. After learning to use text structure to better understand the content of persuasive text, students then have the opportunity to apply this same skill to their writing and become authors of well-developed and well-organized persuasive texts. The power of the Structure strategy in writing is that it supplies a skeleton of organization that helps students more easily flex the muscle of evidence they have researched, bringing their whole paper to life. With a confirmed structure, students are free to analyze information and draft their ideas. They no longer have to struggle with generating and organizing complex ideas and structures at the same time!

THE MINI-LESSON

Materials Needed

- Copies of the article (Figure 12.1), one for each student. We created this piece after reading several articles about the treasure pit (see Ansary, 1997; Nickell, 2000). It is written at an eighth-grade reading level.
- Highlighters
- Copies of the Chart of Signal Words for Expository Texts, one for each student (see Figure 5.6 in Chapter 5)
- Copies of the Reproducible Structure Strategy Outline (Figure 12.2), one for each student
- Pencils
- A document camera and a projector (chart paper could also be used)
- Notebook paper

Jennifer, a middle-school language arts teacher, begins the mini-lesson by discussing mysteries. She knows her students are familiar with mystery novels and television shows; they will be able to make connections between solving a mystery and solving a problem.

Teacher: Mysteries are problems that people try to solve. I've projected an article about a mysterious treasure pit. Here is a copy for each of you [Figure 12.1]. Please follow along as I read the article aloud.

OK, now please read the article again on your own and highlight the signal words you find within the article. Remember that sometimes an essay can contain more than one type of structure. For this article, you should look for and highlight problem-and-solution *and* compare-and-contrast signal words. Go ahead and refer to your signal words chart as a tool [see Figure 5.6].

Figure 12.1   The Treasure Pit Article

Puzzle of a Mysterious Treasure Pit

A mysterious and perplexing pit, long believed to be the location of hidden treasure, is located on a 140-acre island in eastern Canada. Treasure hunters have searched this location for over 200 years, hoping to unearth its mysterious contents. Former U.S. President Franklin D. Roosevelt had a company called Old Gold Salvage, which explored the treasure pit. He even joined the search in the summer and fall of 1909. Later, the actor John Wayne had a company that searched for the treasure. No one has found the treasure yet, but six people have died searching the pit. No one knows what type of treasure could be buried there. Some people have claimed it's pirates' gold. Others believed it could be the missing crown jewels of France. One odd theory proposes that the treasure was the original works of William Shakespeare.

The mysterious puzzle began in 1795 when three Canadian boys discovered an unusual dip in the ground by a large oak tree and thought that pirates' treasure had been buried at that spot. At that time, there were many stories about an infamous pirate, Captain William Kidd, burying valuable treasure on some island east of Boston. Some reports also have said that the boys found pulleys with a rope connected to the oak tree. The three teenagers cleared the area and started digging. At two feet down, they found a layer of flagstones; ten feet lower, they found a tier of oak logs. They dug 15 feet deeper and knew that they needed help to dig further in their quest for buried treasure.

The first solution posed to solve the puzzle of the treasure pit was further digging. The three original discoverers returned older, stronger, and with help in about 1804. They were members of a treasure-hunting company called the Onslow Company. As they dug deeper, they reported layers of oak platforms separated every 10 feet by dirt. At 90 feet deep, they reported finding a flat stone with a code translated as "forty feet below 2 million pounds are buried." Finally, at 98 feet deep, they hit a hard surface and thought they had finally arrived at the treasure. When they arrived to work the next day, instead of finding the hoped-for treasure chest, they found the pit was full of 60 feet of seawater. Did pirates build a booby trap of channels from the beach to protect their treasure? Now, how could the treasure hunters get to it without destroying the treasure or themselves first? The Onslow Company workers dug a new shaft 14 feet from the treasure pit and 100 feet in depth. Then, they started a horizontal tunnel toward the treasure pit. After digging 12 feet toward the treasure pit, water rushed in leaving both pits with 65 feet of water. After running out of money to fund the hunt, the discoverers and their company gave up their search for treasure.

A different solution was attempted in 1861. This solution focused on getting the seawater out of the treasure pit. These treasure hunters made a deal with the landowner to give him one-third of any treasure recovered. For several days, they tried bailing out the seawater with four 70-gallon buckets involving 63 men and 33 horses, but that had little success. As they were working, two big crashes were heard and the bottom level of the pit dropped 14 feet. Next, the treasure hunters tried to pump the water out of the pit using a cast-iron pump powered by a steam engine. When the boiler of the pump burst, one person was killed and several were injured. This group of treasure hunters ran out of money in 1864 and gave up on their idea to remove the seawater from the pit.

Figure 12.2   Reproducible Structure Strategy Outline

Using the Structure Strategy for Persuasive Writing

1. Identify and write the signal words.

2. What overall structures or structures are in the piece?

   _____ compare and contrast   _____ descriptive

   _____ problem and solution   _____ sequence

   _____ cause and effect

3. What is the problem?

4. What are the two solutions?

   a.

   b.

Hint 1: Instead of recalling the text, write a persuasive essay. You will be the author describing the problem and then trying to persuade your readers that you have a *better* solution than what you think is the best solution in the article.

---

5. Write a thesis (main idea = give the problem and the best solution from the article *plus* your solution):

6. Write a persuasive/position statement (State that your solution is better than the article's solution):

Hint 2: Examine the article and fill in notes about the problem that you want to include in your essay. Also, write notes in the second column about what you think is the best solution in the article. In the final column, write notes about your idea for a solution.

(Continued)

Figure 12.2 (Continued)

7. Prewrite: Fill in notes about the problem, the article's solution (Solution 1), and your solution (Solution 2) in the boxes.

Problem	Solution 1 (Best from article)	Solution 2 (Your idea)

Hint 3: Compare your notes to those of another eighth-grade student. If you get some ideas, add them to your notes. Next, using your notes, write in the spaces provided for each section of this four-paragraph persuasive essay. Read the reminders that tell you what to put in each space.

8. Write Paragraph 1.

    a. Topic sentence (e.g., "There was a mystery at the treasure pit.")

    b. Thesis (main idea: the problem and two solutions, the best from the article vs. your solution)

    c. Persuasive statement (that your solution is best)

_____

_____

_____

_____

_____

_____

_____

_____

9. Write Paragraph 2: Problem paragraph (3–5 sentences that give specific details from the article).

_____

_____

_____

_____

_____

_____

_____

_____

10. Write Paragraph 3: Solution 1 paragraph (3–5 sentences that give specific details about one of the article's solutions).

_____

_____

_____

_____

_____

_____

_____

11. Write Paragraph 4.

   a. Solution 2 paragraph (3–5 sentences with specific details about your solution to the treasure pit problem)

   b.   Explain and tell why Solution 2 is the best solution. _____

_____

_____

_____

_____

_____

_____

_____

Jennifer gives them reading and thinking time and then asks students to volunteer answers. If they struggle with the task, she offers a clue using signal words. She might say, "There are two signal words in the title and twelve other places where you can find signal words in the article." Then she hands out the Structure Strategy outline (Figure 12.2).

Teacher: This outline is going to walk us through drafting our persuasive essay. Over the next few days, it will help us write an essay that will persuade readers that our solution to a problem is the best solution available.

For students who might be overwhelmed by receiving a multiple-paged outline, she hands out a page or two each day. She reassures them that they will work on this together and that this outline will make the job easier, not more difficult. Together, the students identify all the signal words in the article. Jennifer steps in to provide help as needed, and students record the signal words on the outline under Question 1. Students also add them to their charts. Following are signal words students might find:

Compare-and-Contrast Signal Words	
instead, but, however, or, alternatively, whereas, on the other hand, while, compare, in comparison, in contrast, in opposition, not everyone, all but, have in common, similarities, share, resemble, the same as, just as, more than, longer than, less than, act like, look like, despite, although, difference, differentiate, different	
Problem-and-Solution Signal Words	
Problem: *problem, trouble, difficulty, hazard, need to prevent, threat, danger, puzzle, can hurt, not good, bad*	Solution: *to satisfy the problem, ways to reduce the problem, so solve these problems, protection from the problem, solution, in response, recommend, suggest, reply*

For Question 2, she asks students to think about the signal words they found and name the top-level or overall structure or structures that organize the paragraphs together. After they have checked off the structures, they identify the problem and solutions (Questions 3 and 4). As students write, Jennifer walks around and checks their thinking. The students discuss each answer as a class and make revisions as they go.

Model the Strategy

Now the class begins to actually draft the essay. Jennifer thinks aloud as she writes the thesis in Question 5.

> **Teacher:** We need to write the thesis or main idea of this article using the problem-and-solution Structure strategy. We have learned that a persuasive solution must reduce a problem by eliminating or reducing one of its causes [see Meyer et al., 2002; Meyer et al., 2010]. We may each write this a bit differently; however, we will all write down the most important information from what we read.

Using the document camera or chart paper to display her copy of the outline, Jennifer writes:

The problem is they can't get to the treasure. One solution was digging. Another solution is swimming down and drilling.

> **Teacher:** We are going to be writing a persuasive essay so we need to write a persuasive statement that states that the solution we came up with is the best solution. You may come up with any solution you think would work to retrieve the treasure from the pit.

For Question 6, she writes:

Swimming down and drilling is the best solution.

Students Practice the Strategy

Next, Jennifer has students follow the prompts on the outline and begin to fill in the details in the spaces provided on the outline. As they work, she circulates and monitors their answers, providing individual feedback. After the majority of students have filled in three to five details, she brings them back to the whole class and asks students to share what they have. During the reporting-out time, she also encourages students who have fewer examples in their boxes to consider some of the ideas they heard from others. If students are struggling, she offers her own examples to assist them in completing the boxes.

Independent Writing

After several students have had the opportunity to share, Jennifer asks students to move on to complete their outline by turning their lists (the notes from the boxes) into sentences under the respective headings. Each box becomes a paragraph.

Student Reflection

After students have had a chance to practice on their own, Jennifer pairs them and has them share their thesis, persuasive statement, and prewrite. Then she pulls all students back to the whole class and asks for volunteers to share their work. Sharing allows students to engage with each other in determining alternative solutions and writing a complete draft. It also allows Jennifer the chance to resolve any difficulties students might be having in writing this portion as well as to clear up any misconceptions or confusion students have regarding the implementation of the Structure strategy. Following this whole-class discussion, she moves students back to completing the outline on their own.

MODIFYING THE MINI-LESSON

Adaptations for Writers Who Struggle

To adapt the strategy for writers who struggle, Jennifer gives sentence stems for each paragraph, such as

- one problem is . . .
- another problem is . . .
- an additional aspect that would affect (the topic) is . . .
- a solution to this problem could include . . .
- another resource to solve this problem would be . . .

Another way she supports students who struggle with writing is to have them write about familiar topics. This option helps them concentrate on the steps of the strategy without having to focus their attention on new content ideas. Here's how one struggling writer used the Structure strategy to write a compare-and-contrast persuasive essay.

In this case, the prompt was *Compare two activities, topics, food groups, or ideas of your choice and persuade the reader which choice is best.* The student selected two familiar topics, which allowed him to use his background knowledge to support his ideas with examples. He applied the structure of comparison and then incorporated this structure to support a developed persuasive thesis. The student wrote,

> *Summer and winter recreational activities will be compared on the kinds of activities you can do, comfort, and how easy it is to enjoy the activities. I think summer is the best time for people to do recreational activities.*

He also provided specific details as evidence to support his position:

> *Different from winter, in summer it's easier to do sports and outdoor activities like camping. It's safer to get to the destination with no wet or slick streets.*

Adaptations for English Language Learners

To adapt the strategy for English language learners (ELLs), Jennifer encourages students to use bulleted lists to communicate their ideas regarding the problem and solutions. Depending on their level of proficiency, they may then be able to work on combining their ideas with the sentence stems listed in the Adaptations for Writers Who Struggle section.

Adaptations for Advanced Writers

To adapt the strategy for use with advanced writers, Jennifer has students include specific references and quotes from the text(s) they read as examples of the problem or solutions. In a further extension, she includes independent research for advanced students to find specific examples and quotes from other sources and to create an annotated bibliography to cite their sources. This incorporates the additional skill of evaluating sources, such as critical thinking and making inferences regarding those sources.

EXTENDING THE STRATEGY ACROSS THE CONTENT AREAS

The Structure strategy lends itself well to social studies and science texts, which often include a combination of the text structures. The English language arts class can pre-read the articles that are taught in the other content areas or find supporting articles that correspond to the concepts being taught. Further, content teachers usually find that by using the Structure strategy in their own classrooms, they can spend more time discussing concepts because their students understand more of what they read. During in-class discussions, social studies teachers and science teachers can frame students' ideas and examples with the prewrite or the boxes that students complete when reading an article.

The following example involves a nonfiction writing assignment that integrated a social studies topic. The assignment was to write about the function of the Underground Railroad, organizing ideas/content and correctly applying the problem-and-solution structure. After using the Structure strategy, Jennifer's student provided specific examples from the text to support the problem-and-solution structure:

> *The problem was African Americans were stuck in slavery. . . . Between the 1500s and 1800s the Portuguese, Spanish, British, and Dutch transported almost 10 million enslaved Africans. . . . The solution to slavery back then was an underground railroad. . . . An example of a conductor is John Fairfield. He didn't like slavery, so he helped guide the railroad and the people on it to safe and happy freedom.*

This response reflects the student's growth as a writer. It shows her ability to successfully apply the problem-and-solution text Structure strategy and include specific examples from the text.

After assessing this work, Jennifer decided to promote the student's growth as a writer by providing feedback through questions such as, "How could you explain why this mattered?" The student recrafted her essay, which was strong in text support, into a final product that provided a strong commentary to explain the significance of the facts to the topic:

> *These facts add to the problem because asking permission to do everything makes them feel unhuman, like an animal. . . . This also is a problem because even if you got out of slavery you couldn't help any of your family because it's illegal and could get you in trouble.*

Ultimately, the student learned to infuse her voice through an interpretation of the text to create a stronger piece of writing.

RESOURCES FOR FURTHER READING

➢ Hammann, L. A., & Stevens, R. J. (2003). Instructional approaches to improving students' writing of compare-contrast essays: An experimental study. *Journal of Literacy Research, 35*(2), 731–756. doi:10.1207/s15548430jlr3502_3

In this study, eighth-grade students learned to use text structure to write compare/contrast essays based on informational texts that they had read. Language arts classrooms were randomly assigned to one of three instructional groups: a summarization strategy group, a text Structure strategy group, and a combination group that taught both strategies. Structure strategy instruction proved to be more helpful than summary instruction in improving essay organization when readers wrote about unfamiliar topics. There was no difference between instructional groups when readers wrote about more familiar topics.

➢ Meyer, B. J. F., Middlemiss, W., Theodorou, Brezinski, K. L., McDougall, J., & Bartlett, B. J. (2002). Effects of structure strategy instruction delivered to fifth-grade children via the Internet with and without the aid of older adult tutors. *Journal of Educational Psychology, 94*, 486–519.

In this study, fifth-grade students were randomly assigned to one of two versions of Structure strategy instruction or a control (regular classroom reading activities). Students receiving Structure strategy instruction improved in reading comprehension more than the control group. Superiority in reading comprehension by students receiving Structure strategy instruction over the control group was found 2.5 months after training. The average reader receiving Structure strategy instruction had a total recall score equal to a reader in the control group who scored at the 81st percentile on the delayed posttest ($d = 0.92$).

Buddies Build It Stronger 13

A Sentence-Combining Strategy

Todd Sundeen

Many students find it difficult to construct complex and well-formed sentences. Sentence combining can help these writers improve their sentence structure. Students blend weak, kernel sentences into more complex and meaningful sentences. The Buddies Build It Stronger strategy combines a highly effective sentence-combining strategy with peer support.

WHY THIS STRATEGY IS IMPORTANT

The Common Core State Standards for English Language Arts requires students to demonstrate increasing complexity in their writing as they progress through grade levels (Common Core State Standards Initiative, 2011). Sentence combining—which prompts students to change short, choppy sentences into longer, more complex sentences—has long been recommended by linguists to effectively improve the writing of students with varied skill levels (Hillocks, 1986; Mellon, 1967; Strong, 1986; Vitale, King, Shontz, & Huntley, 1971; also see Graham & Perin, 2007b). When we teach students patterns for constructing more complex and longer sentences, their reading skills also improve (Hunt, 1965; Neville, 1985; O'Hare, 1973).

Research indicates that when students understand how larger units of text are used to make more meaningful sentences, they also write better-developed paragraphs (Graham & Perin, 2007a). Learning to write more maturely also helps students remember more of what they have read (Graham & Herbert, 2010). In fact, sentence combining has been included as part of the National Writing Project initiative, which trains more than 10,000 teachers annually (see http://www.nwp.org).

The Buddies Build It Stronger strategy mini-lesson incorporates a sentence-combining strategy that encourages student teams to develop weak, simple sentences into more complex structures. The struggling writers I have worked with in Grades 4 through 8 frequently produced sentences that were short and

137

syntactically simple. For example, a fifth-grade student once composed the following sentences: "The car is fast. The car has silver wheels." After teaching her the Buddies Build It Stronger strategy, she constructed these sentences: "The car with the silver wheels is fast" and "The silver-wheeled car is fast." I'm sure you agree that these sentences are stronger.

THE MINI-LESSON

Materials Needed

- Figure 13.1: Reproducible Writing Observation Checklist for Sentences and Paragraphs to use for assessment to plan the lesson
- Copies of sentence examples, one for each student
- Copies of practice sentences, one for each student (content may vary by group)
- The students' writing notebooks or pieces they are working on
- Sentence strips for additional scaffolding
- Paper
- Pencils

Prior to beginning the Buddies Build It Stronger mini-lesson, I use two forms of curriculum-based assessment to understand the skill levels of my writers. Initially, I ask students to write a short paper based on a general-knowledge prompt such as these:

- Describe your favorite pet.
- Tell about your favorite place in the world.
- What is your favorite food?

I use the checklist in Figure 13.1 to observe students as they plan and produce their essays; this set of data helps me identify their current writing proficiency. Specifically, I note whether students

- write in short, choppy sentences,
- create sentences connected by a series of *ands*, or
- write several sentences that begin in the same manner.

I also use the checklist to note whether a student takes extended time to complete his or her writing.

After I determine which students have difficulty developing syntactically complex (i.e., strong) sentences, we gather in small groups to discuss what makes a sentence strong. Students bring pieces they are working on. To begin, I ask them to listen to me say several short, simple (i.e., weak) sentences.

"My dog likes treats."

"My dog is brown."

"My dog's name is Rocky."

Figure 13.1 Reproducible Writing Observation Checklist for Sentences and Paragraphs

Student name: _____ Date: _____

Assignment: _____

Writing Observation Checklist for Sentences and Paragraphs

_____ Takes time to plan

    _____ min. (Approximate time spent planning)

_____ Organizes ideas using a graphic organizer

_____ Organization is smooth and effective

_____ Writes complex sentences

    _____ Vivid and descriptive words are used frequently

_____ Most sentences include a single descriptor (adjective, adverb, etc.)

    _____ Most sentences include multiple descriptors

    _____ Sentences demonstrate a variety of structures

_____ Includes rich detail

_____ Vocabulary is precise and appropriate

    _____ Uses appropriate word choices

    _____ Varies word choices

    _____ Uses transition words to link sentences or paragraphs

_____ Writing is compelling and engaging for the intended audience

_____ Writing conventions are mostly correct

_____ Proofreads writing

_____ Revises sentences independently

_____ Seems to enjoy writing

    _____ Stays engaged with the process

    _____ Writes more than the minimum

    _____ Shares work with other students

_____ Took extended time for completing the assignment

Then, I say,

"My dog Rocky is brown and likes treats."

I ask, "Does the last sentence contain all the information from the first three sentences?" When they agree that it does, I ask, "Which sounds stronger?"

Next, I ask students to look at their own piece of writing. I help them select and read aloud short, weak sentences that they could improve. They are often surprised by how different their short sentences sound when read aloud. I explain that we will be learning to write stronger sentences by using the words they have already written. The students usually appreciate that they will have a chance to use their original ideas rather than developing new ones.

After I have assessed and conferred with my students, I have a clear idea who would benefit from explicit teaching of the Buddies Build It Stronger strategy. One benefit to this strategy is that it can be tailored to specifically meet the needs of students at varying levels of writing competency. Another is that it can be used as a whole-class exercise or with specific groups of students who need additional help.

Model the Lesson

Before students do any writing during the mini-lesson, they observe me demonstrate each step of the strategy. To begin, I explain how important it is for writers to create good sentences that include enough information to tell readers what they really mean to say. I also tell them the Buddies Build It Stronger strategy will help them write better for their other content areas, including social studies and science.

The first step is to read and think out loud about several short sentences. I give each student a copy of the example sentences.

> **Teacher:** Let's think about birds. Read the first sentence on your handout quietly to yourselves while I read it out loud for you: "The bird landed." Now, read the second sentence as I say it out loud: "The bird was blue." I wonder how I might build a stronger sentence by putting these two sentences together. I know! "The bird landed." *Landed* is a clue word, so I'll underline that. I also know the bird was blue. *Blue* is a clue word that I want to be sure to include in my stronger sentence, so I'll underline that, too. Now, how can I combine these two sentences in a stronger sentence that will include both clue words? I think it would sound best to write: "The blue bird landed." See how this new sentence combines the two original sentences and both clue words? My writing sounds stronger when I combine the sentences. Doesn't it? And I'm saying the same things. I haven't changed my meaning at all.
>
> Remember, our new, combined sentence must have the same meaning as our original, simpler sentences. We are merely moving words or parts around to make the sentences sound stronger. The clue words will help you remember the important ideas as you combine the sentences to build stronger sentences.

I model this step by thinking aloud as I work with a buddy to underline clue words in several sentences.

> **Teacher:** To start, let's underline the clue words: the words or phrases we will put together into the new sentence. Clue words are often the adjectives, predicate adjectives, adverbs, or verbs. When you work with a buddy, you decide together what they think the important information is to include in the stronger sentence.

The student I've selected as my buddy helps me identify these words. As I think aloud, I ask myself and my buddy, "What are the important clues, information, or details we want to be sure our stronger sentence includes?"

I stress that there might be several possible sentences that we can make from our two or three original sentences, depending on how we combine them. My buddy and I each draft a strong sentence. Then we discuss them and decide which sentence we think is stronger and sounds better. We check that the final sentence includes all the information and clue words from the original sentences and that we haven't changed the meaning. If I think it would be helpful, I model using more examples.

After I'm satisfied that I've modeled the strategy adequately, I ask students what we did to combine the weak sentences into a strong sentence. I guide them to construct these steps:

1. Read the original weak sentences with your buddy.

2. Discuss and decide with your buddy what the important ideas in each sentence are.

3. Together, underline the clue words in each sentence.

4. Work separately from your buddy to draft a stronger sentence that combines the clue words and ideas from the weak sentences.

5. Read both sentences out loud with your buddy to confirm that they both make sense and that they both include all the same information and clue words as the original sentences.

6. Discuss and decide with your buddy which sentence sounds stronger and better.

7. Replace the weak sentences with the new, strong sentence.

I have buddies work together to write these steps in their writing notebooks for future use. I may also ask several students to work together to make a poster of the Buddies Build It Stronger strategy steps to display in the writing center.

Students Practice the Strategy

Practice involves two steps. First, I pair students with buddies and give each buddy a practice sheet with sets of two or three short sentences to be combined.

I often develop practice sheets specifically for their level of writing based on previous assessments and observation. Buddies use the practice sheet and their notes to combine and build stronger sentences together.

For the second practice step, I ask buddies to write sentences to describe a photo or picture or to respond to a prompt such as these:

- Describe the funniest thing that has ever happened to you.
- If you could become any animal, what would you be?
- Describe the best gift that you ever received.
- Tell about your best day ever.

Individually, students write two to four simple sentences, and then buddies work together to build them into more complex sentences. As I observe the buddy teams, I remain ready to support their progress with scaffolded instruction.

Independent Writing

After I determine that each buddy has grasped the strategy, I ask them to work individually to write a paragraph based on their prompt. I remind them to underline clue words and identify sentences they should combine. I encourage each student author to reread the combined sentences to see if they make sense. We often reread their sentences out loud to see if they sound correct.

Student Reflection

Finally, my students reflect on the final versions of their combined sentences. When they are done working individually, the buddies put their heads back together to read each other's work to see what needs to be improved. They share ideas and often combine additional sentences to create substantially more complex sentences. In this phase, they have a renewed sense of confidence about their writing. The buddies are enthusiastic about sharing their improved work with me and often ask to read their papers to the class.

MODIFYING THE MINI-LESSON

Adaptations for Writers Who Struggle

The Buddies Build It Stronger mini-lesson is an excellent strategy for students who struggle with composing sentences that are short and syntactically simple. Providing additional scaffolding for struggling writers encourages them to become more confident as they compose their sentences. I have found three learning scaffolds that are particularly helpful.

First, I provide a word bank of connecting words for my students to access as they build their stronger sentences (Figure 13.2).

Figure 13.2 Word Bank of Connecting Words

after	also	although
and	as	as if
as long as	as though	because
before	but	earlier
either	for	furthermore
how	if	indeed
instead	in case	in order
neither	nor	once
since	than	that
though	till	until
unless	when	whenever
where	wherever	whereas
while	who	which
what	whose	where
wherever	when	why

I provide a second layer of scaffolding by instructing students how to use sentence strips as manipulatives for building stronger sentences:

1. Students write out their sentences on strips of paper.

2. They identify clue words by highlighting subjects and predicates with different color markers.

3. They work with a buddy to cut the strips into individual words or phrases and practice assembling the words into stronger sentences.

4. They read each strong sentence out loud to see if it makes sense to them.

As a third scaffold, instead of asking students to write the sentences themselves, I provide base and modifying sentences. This scaffold is useful for students who have a particularly difficult time grasping the concept. I start by asking students to develop basic compound sentences and then progress by asking them to combine compound predicates. For example, I initially develop base sentences that can be easily combined with connecting words such as *and, for, nor, but, or, yet, however,* or *so* to build simple compound sentences. In this way, students can use the word *but* to combine the sentences

"Maria enjoys cake."

"Kevin likes ice cream."

into

"Maria enjoys cake, but Kevin likes ice cream."

Once my students have practiced and mastered building stronger compound sentences from two simple sentences, I ask them to combine compound predicates. For example, they can build

"Dominic ordered a hamburger. Dominic ordered a cola."

into the stronger sentence

"Dominic ordered a hamburger and a cola."

Adaptations for English Language Learners

Students who are English language learners (ELL) often benefit from participating in oral discussions prior to beginning writing. This provides them with vocabulary practice and support for organizing their ideas. I create extra opportunities for oral interactions as students work in their small group. In addition, when the students revise their work with their buddies, I pair them with cooperative students who will facilitate their understanding of correct spelling, grammar, and punctuation.

Adaptations for Advanced Writers

Advanced writers also benefit from the Buddies Build It Stronger mini-lesson. My advanced authors often write sentences that are long and complex. Sentence-combining strategies provide them with practice in controlling the syntax by rearranging the sentence elements. When they learn how to identify the basic syntactic kernels by underlining clue words, they are able to rewrite sentences that were overly complex or unclear. Rather than writing sentences that are longer, advanced students learn to produce more cohesive sentences that are strong.

EXTENDING THE STRATEGY ACROSS THE CONTENT AREAS

I encourage my students to write in all content areas. The Buddies Build It Stronger strategy helps students write extended responses to social studies and science assignments and questions. For example, when I ask my students to write a paragraph about the Pilgrims' trip to the New World, the buddies share their papers and make suggestions for combining the sentences. I also ask my students to write for science. After writing a short composition on the water cycle, for example, each buddy makes suggestions for writing more complex sentences that better convey the intended meaning. With practice, my students find that they can use the strategy to write better in all their content areas.

RESOURCES FOR FURTHER READING

➤ Saddler, B., & Asaro-Saddler, K. (2010). Writing better sentences: Sentence combining instruction in the classroom. *Preventing School Failure, 54*(3), 159–163.

Sentence combining has been shown to be an effective strategy for improving the compositions of young writers for more than 30 years. In this recent article, Saddler and Asaro-Saddler provide a research-based snapshot based on decades of research. This guide is useful for teachers who plan to use sentence combining in their own classrooms. It provides solid instruction and examples of using sentence combining for use by teachers in the late primary grades.

> ➢ Berninger, V. W., Nagy, W., & Beers, S. (2010). Child writers' construction and reconstruction of single sentences and construction of multi-sentence texts: Contributions of syntax and transcription to translation. *Reading and Writing, 24*, 151–182. doi:10.1007/s11145–010–9262-y

Virginia Berninger and her colleagues studied three cohorts of children as they progressed from elementary school to seventh grade. They found that sentence combining was effective for teaching students to use syntax for reconstructing more complex sentences. The sentence-combining strategy also provided a developmental foundation for translating single sentences into more intricate structures. Older students developed more complex and meaningful compositions.

Section III

Strategic Revising

Attending to Organization and Cohesiveness

Regardless of personal writing style, during the revision stage all good writers "adopt the persona of visual artists" (Richards & Miller, 2005, p. 128). They step back from their writing and scrutinize it using revision strategies they find most useful.

Revision does not simply involve fine-tuning words or attending to errors. Rather, revision requires authors to

- re-see what they have created,
- study their personal writing over and over,
- consider their audience,
- analyze the organization and cohesiveness of a composition, and
- delete, move, or add large chunks of text as needed.

There is no doubt that significant revision is rigorous and time-consuming. It takes intense concentration, and writers must be able to distance themselves from their writing. No wonder students often resist revising their work. Some think that what they have written is already "correct" and that if they revise it, they might make their writing less than perfect. Others experience revision as extremely hard work, or they do not understand its importance. Many students do not know how to revise because they have not learned revision strategies.

The strategies presented in this section help students independently revise their writing efforts. They guide students to become astute readers of their own work. They encourage students to identify areas for revision in their narrative and expository writing. They support students so they can bring organization to their messy drafts. The strategies are enjoyable, clever, and unique, and they fit the cognitive levels of writers in Grades 4 through 8.

Each of the revision strategies in this section has been field-tested in Grades 4 through 8 classrooms and they connect to the English Language Arts Common Core Standards. (Refer to the Common Core Standards Chart on the inside cover of the book.) We invite you to study your students' specific revision needs and then model and teach the revision strategies in this section that you think would benefit them. You and your students will appreciate how using these strategies helps writers alleviate their resistance to revision and enhances their strategic, independent writing efforts.

Deconstruct Then Reconstruct a First Draft

14

Cynthia A. Lassonde

The Deconstruct–Reconstruct strategy helps students restructure a first draft so their work reads fluently and is easily understood by readers. Students deconstruct or visually depict a first draft by creating an outline or graphic organizer that represents the structure of the draft as it currently is written. Then, they analyze the outlined structure of their draft by reviewing the outline. If they determine their draft needs to be reorganized, they reconstruct or rebuild their outline and composition to make the report flow better. Students also refer to and employ a list of transitional words they have previously compiled and recorded in their writing notebooks to help make their draft cohesive. Or you may distribute a list of transitional words. See list of materials in this chapter.

WHY THIS STRATEGY IS IMPORTANT

I consider writing to be a process, which is how I teach it to my students. Still, even though I encourage them to plan their writing first, I know that I don't always stick to my own outlined plan or concept map when I'm composing a first draft. For instance, sometimes while I'm drafting, I discover additional information I want to include in my report. At other times, new insights and thoughts become clear as I write a report; this also changes my understanding of a topic and the ideas I want to include. For various reasons, writing isn't static. My ideas evolve as I write. I don't always stick to my original plans or outline for a draft.

Students face the same issues. Sometimes they feel overwhelmed with the task of constructing a lengthy piece of writing out of piles of notes. As a result, they may throw chunks of information into a report in a disorderly, jumbled way. Other students discover that their original plan for their writing doesn't accommodate all the information they want to include. These students try to include so much information that the report becomes a list of disjointed facts—even though they followed their original plan.

The Deconstruct–Reconstruct strategy presented in this chapter addresses these types of dilemmas. Specifically, it helps students restructure their drafts so sentences and paragraphs flow into each other in a manner that is understandable, logical, and enjoyable to read.

THE MINI-LESSON

Materials Needed

- A list of transition terms for each student (good sources include www.virtualsalt.com/transits.htm; http://writing2.richmond.edu/writing/wweb/trans1.html; and for students with less-developed vocabularies, http://www.greenville.k12.sc.us/taylorse/Taylors%20Elementary%20Curriculum%20Information/elatrans.asp)
- Writing samples (see Figures 14.1 and 14.2)
- A SMART Board (or chart paper)
- A red marker
- A black marker
- Students' report drafts
- Students' writing notebooks
- Pens and pencils

Figure 14.1   The Life of Terry Fox

Terry Fox was diagnosed with bone cancer when he was only 18 years old. His leg was amputated to stop the spread of the cancer. But this didn't keep Terry down. He decided that to raise awareness and funding for cancer research, he would run across Canada. He wanted to help others.

Terry Fox was born in Winnipeg, Canada, in 1958. He loved sports, but he didn't have a very muscular physique. He had a hard time keeping up with the bigger kids in his school in competitive sports.

In high school, Terry wanted to be on the basketball team. Although he was much shorter than the other boys trying out for the team, he was determined to be a guard. His hard work paid off. By 10th grade, he was one of the best guards on the high school team.

Terry Fox began his marathon in 1980. He ran about 23 miles each day for 143 days. After running 3,339 miles, Terry had to stop. His cancer had spread to his lungs. He died at the age of 22.

If students have been composing on a computer, I teach the lesson at the computer center so they can work with the word processing program they have been using. I begin the lesson by reading to students my short sample report about Terry Fox (Figure 14.1). The report—my first draft—is informative but obviously scrambled and disjointed. To focus students' attention on the sequencing of the information, I ask them, "What can you say about the order

Figure 14.2 Reproducible Examples of Report Structure Patterns of Organization and Their Criteria

Categories—classifies items into parts or types of something. Example: explaining the various biological systems
Cause and effect—indicates results (effect or solution) from some action (cause or problem). Example: scientific or historic reports that ask "why?" and "with what results?"
Chronological order—a description of events as they occur over time. Example: biographies and historic events
Comparing and contrasting—a description of similarities and differences. Example: report on the governments of two countries
Definition and Example—explaining the meaning of a concept and providing illustrative examples. Example: Defining an abstract term such as *trust* and explaining it through examples
Listings—a presentation of information as a list. Example: descriptive listing of a category of items, events, reasons, places, or consequences
Order of importance—a presentation of information sorted from most to least important (or the reverse). Example: a persuasive essay that presents its arguments from most to least important
Process order—a description of a series of stages, steps, or changes needed to make or do something in proceeding to an end result. Example: directions on how to do something

of the information in this report?" We discuss how the time sequence is out of order and how we could easily fix this so readers will understand how devastating it was for Terry Fox, who was determined to play on his high school's basketball team as a teenager, to lose his leg. We conclude that a biography is best told as a story of the person's life from birth to present day or to the person's death. I propose that all reports have a certain order to them that makes the best sense. We review possible report structures as appropriate for their skill or grade level (see Figure 14.2). I remind them that as writers, we need to look for that order to help our readers comprehend.

Model the Strategy

The aim of this portion of the mini-lesson is to show students how to organize their thoughts and the information about a topic into a report that flows in a way that accurately represents the subject. This strategy will help students better understand the needs of their readers, a skill they will continue to hone as they become expert researchers through high school and beyond.

To begin, I show students another short report in which the order isn't as obvious as the time sequence order of the Terry Fox piece. I select a sample report that resembles whatever report structure (see Figure 14.2) they are working on at the time. We discuss the criteria this structure requires to be fluent and comprehendible. For example, if the report explains a process, have they accurately explained the procedures, stages, or changes necessary to do or make the end result occur?

As I read the report out loud, I insert the thoughts I have as a reader who is trying to negotiate the structure. For example, if I were reading a sample organized by categories of advantages and disadvantages, I might say the following:

> **Teacher:** Wait a minute! The writer was just listing the advantages but snuck in a disadvantage! Then she goes back to more advantages! It would be easier to understand if all the advantages were put together, followed by all the disadvantages.

Or if I were reading a sample organized by importance, I might say this:

> **Teacher:** The writer seems to be telling the most important things about this topic at the beginning. So why is this unimportant little detail inserted here? It would be better if it came later on after all the important points are made.

Once I've identified what the problem is with the organization, I use my chart paper or SMART Board and a black marker to show how I would deconstruct or break down the report to create an outline or concept map based on the report's current structure. Then, I take a red marker and walk through—as I'm still thinking out loud—how I would reconstruct or rebuild the structure so it is more logical. If the changes are small, I mark up the deconstruction outline. If the changes are involved, I start fresh by creating a new outline.

Now it's time to use the outline I've just made to move sentences and paragraphs around in my draft. Again, I use my red marker to do this in front of students as I'm thinking out loud. Finally, I reread the report aloud to hear if it sounds fluent. I ask students if they have any suggestions for how I might revise the structure further.

Students Practice the Strategy

I review the steps of the Deconstruct–Reconstruct strategy with the students. I encourage them to construct a list of the steps or a checklist to keep in their writing notebooks. I guide them to include these steps:

1. Read the first draft out loud.
2. Identify the intended organization of the draft.
3. Ask: Does the draft reflect the intended organization? Is the organization logical, or could it be improved?
4. If the organization could be improved, deconstruct the draft by outlining its current structure.
5. Revise or reconstruct the outline so it makes sense.

6. Analyze the revised outline. Is the new organization logical?

7. If the organization of the outline is logical, reconstruct the draft to follow the new outline.

8. Read the new draft out loud. Is it better organized? Does it make better sense than the first draft?

Then I provide a short sample report that resembles the type of structure they are studying. Equipped with their list of steps of the Deconstruct–Reconstruct strategy, students practice the strategy on the sample report by following the process I've modeled for them. I walk around the class and offer support as they work.

Independent Writing

Students are now ready to independently try this strategy with their own report. If this is not their final draft, they will continue to independently apply this strategy as they complete their report. As I monitor their progress, I reteach the strategy or support them as needed. I keep a close eye on their progress to prevent their reports from getting unfocused or drastically disorganized.

Student Reflection

Report writing is done over time—sometimes days or even weeks. Therefore, to help me assess students' progress and understanding, I ask them to reflect on the process of revision. Specifically, I ask, "When is the last time you checked your structure? How is the Deconstruct–Reconstruct strategy working for you?"

MODIFYING THE MINI-LESSON

Adaptations for Writers Who Struggle

I frequently check in with my writers who struggle. I help them prevent their writing from becoming too disorganized by prompting them to check their organization and structure as they add information to their report. It is easier for these writers to think through smaller sets of information than larger sets. I support them as they work through the practice phase of the lesson several times with progressive drafts of their report. Each time, they update their outlines or maps to reflect the latest draft and then look for how to reorganize the pieces they've added. The task of transferring the report to a visual representation helps many struggling writers to stay focused on the topic.

Adaptations for English Language Learners

This strategy is very effective for English language learners because it takes a mass of narrative text and simplifies it to a visual representation that "cuts to the chase." I allow English language learners the choice to write the outline or concept map in their native language if it helps their comprehension. Using this method lets them think about content more than translating concepts and words.

Adaptations for Advanced Writers

I encourage advanced writers to compose their reports on computers. When students come to the minigroup lesson at the computer center, they open their report in Microsoft Word. Under the View tab, students click on Outline. Advanced writers can use the resulting outline to restructure their report following the process described in this chapter.

Microsoft Word also offers minicourses online to walk users through using their outlines to restructure their writing. To view these courses, click on the Help button. Type in "outline" and hit "Search." In the list that populates, click on Create a Document Outline. You'll see a button to start the course.

EXTENDING THE STRATEGY ACROSS THE CONTENT AREAS

The Deconstruct–Reconstruct strategy easily applies to writing reports in any content area. Students may also use the strategy when they work on oral presentations to ensure that their content flows and is easily understandable by listeners. They may use the resulting final outline as notes to guide them during the presentation.

RESOURCES FOR FURTHER READING

➤ Altieri, J. L. (2011). *Content counts! Developing disciplinary literacy skills, K–6.* Newark, DE: International Reading Association.

Visual literacy, which includes the use of visual aids such as outlines and concept maps, plays an important role in preparing students to live and work in a technologically rich world. Research shows that students spend more time engaged with technology than they do in school! Furthermore, students' ability to transmediate information from one symbol system to another—from report form to a visual form—enhances their ability to understand the material.

➤ Graham, S., MacArthur, C. A., & Fitzgerald, J. (Eds.). (2007). *Best practices in writing instruction.* New York: Guilford Press.

MacArthur's (2007) chapter on "Best Practices in Teaching Evaluation and Revision" in this edited volume of best practices in writing proposes that revision begins with evaluation. MacArthur writes, "The primary reason students have difficulty revising is that they do not know how to evaluate their writing" (p. 160).We must teach students how to evaluate their writing, using explicit criteria, and how to revise based on these criteria. The Deconstruct–Reconstruct strategy mini-lesson provides specific criteria for evaluating their writing and teaches them how to go about revising to meet these criteria.

Portal Writing 15
Helping Writers Rethink Their Writing

S. Rebecca Leigh

Portals are circled words that act like windows, making it possible for writers to see a variety of story ideas they might wish to pursue. The Portal Writing strategy provides opportunities for students to circle or box portal words of interest from an unfinished draft of a poem, short story, or personal narrative to serve as entry points to rethink and rework their piece. Students mask the remaining words with markers and study the portals as an alternative genre with the aim of finding the narrative's focus. The Portal Writing strategy offers students a creative approach to writing so they can reengage in their writing efforts.

WHY THIS STRATEGY IS IMPORTANT

Students often give up on their writing initiatives. Their drafts may start out well, but somewhere during the drafting stage students frequently abandon their narratives when they feel stumped, blocked, or simply unmotivated to finish what they have begun to write. I consider these half-finished drafts ideal for portal writing (Leigh, 2010).

When I work with young writers I notice how access to the aesthetic offers generative writing potential and, therefore, motivates students to continue writing. The Portal Writing strategy combines aesthetics with writing to help students revisit the stories in which they have lost interest. More than this, creating portals helps students look closely and reflectively at their word choices and notice how meaning can change when certain words are grouped together or tumble down a page in an informal order.

Creating portals helps students clarify their thinking by reflecting on the content of their writing from a different perspective. Seeing their writing from a portal perspective is important because portals open up possibilities for drafts and give students choices about how to proceed in their writing, such as whether to change a story slightly or dramatically alter it. The Portal Writing strategy provides students a way to see beyond their existing half-finished draft and to consider story directions anew.

THE MINI-LESSON

Materials Needed

- SMART Board, overhead projector, or large chart paper
- *The Humument* by Tom Phillips (2005) or a copy of a relevant poem or short paragraph
- *Newspaper Blackout* by Austin Kleon (2010) or a copy of an example newspaper article with words and phrases blackened out
- An unfinished poem or story to project on the SMART Board
- Dark, felt-tipped markers (chisel-tips are best because they cover considerable text with just a few strokes)
- A short poem or story to hand out (1 copy per student)
- 1 copy of Figure 15.3: Creating Portals: A Reproducible Checklist for Choosing Words That Can Drive Story for each student
- Students' writing folders
- Pencils
- 1 copy of Figure 15.4: After Portaling: Reproducible Questions to Help Me Revise My Writing for each student
- Glue or a stapler

Before I introduce the Portal Writing strategy to students, I use the SMART Board to show them two or three pages from an unfinished poem or story or from *The Humument* by Tom Phillips (2005) and a copy of a newspaper article with words and phrases blackened out, such as *Newspaper Blackout* by Austin Kleon's (2010) (see Figure 15.1 as an example). I invite students to read each page with me, and then we discuss how portals can illuminate story ideas.

To demonstrate what I call "portaling," I show students a copy of a story or poem I have started in my writer's notebook. Figure 15.2 is one example. I read what I have written and tell them I have not finished it because I feel stuck. Using this story example, I tell them I want to try a strategy called Portal Writing to help me with ideas about how to move forward with this piece. Next, I reread the story, asking students to tell me the words they like (e.g., the sound of words, the look of words, the meaning of words). As students say these words aloud, I circle them with my felt-tipped marker so students can see how to portal word choices. I also ask a student volunteer to come up to the SMART Board and circle some words on the story. Once we have decided we have enough portal words, I darken the remaining words with the felt-tipped marker and we read the portals together. This is where the chisel-tip marker works best because it can cover a lot of text with just a few strokes.

I ask students to note how particular words grouped together create interesting images in our mind. We group some of the words—*mushy velvet, kind apple,* and *mother courage*—and talk about what those groupings mean to us or make us think about. Next, I read all the circled words in order that we have portaled together: *mother, oozing, bruising, kind, good, reluctantly, mushy, velvet, apple, mold, courage.* Then the discussion takes off.

Figure 15.1   An Example of Portaling

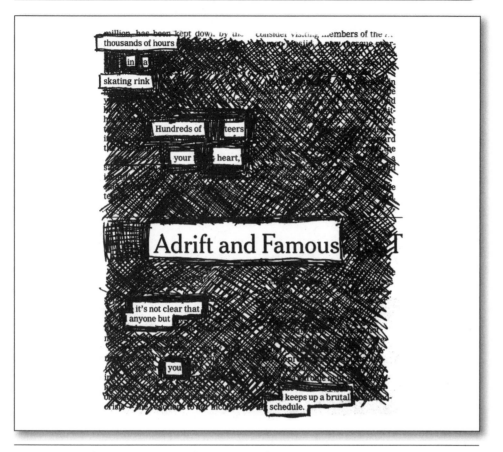

Image © Austin Kleon, 2007. Courtesy of 20x200/Jen Bekman Projects.

Figure 15.2   A First Draft of a Story About My Mother

My mother should have been a surgeon. When I was a kid, she would cut off the oozing, bruising part of an apple and kindly hand it to me. "Here, eat this," she would say smiling, "this part is still good." I would take it, though reluctantly, with eyes to the floor that read, "Do I have to?" I'd bite into the salvaged piece but remember the former mushy, wet part, a wounded skin of midnight velvet and yellow ochre. I'd watch my mother move on to a block of cheese, removing the moldy end with a careful, almost thoughtful look that I never understood. But sometimes, on days I felt brave, my eyes would read, "Why don't you eat it?" But of course I never, ever, had the courage to say *that* to my mother. Surgeons have knives!

Teacher: We can use these images to help us think about our story and where we want to take it. Creating portals in our writing can help us to see our writing in new ways.

We can use some of these circled portal words to help me think about how I want to continue writing my poem. I can use these exact words, but I do not have to. The purpose of circling words is to help me see my story with new eyes in a way that makes me want to finish it.

As we talk about these portals, most students suggest that I write about other oozing, bruising foods that my mother would salvage. But a few students notice a richer story brewing beneath the portals: *mother, kind, good,* and *courage.* They ask questions like these:

- What was her story?
- Why did she save food?
- Why was that important to her?

Our discussion about these portals helps me see how I could develop a story about my mother's childhood in postwar Europe, where food was scarce and cherished.

Next, I ask students to think about a story they have written that is still in draft form, much like the story about my mother. I ask them to identify the following:

1. Why they think they stopped working on it

2. How they think portal writing can help them revisit it

I close this part of the lesson by explaining to students how the strategy of Portal Writing is a creative way of rethinking their writing that can help them discover new story ideas and motivate them to write them.

Model the Strategy

I begin the lesson by distributing a copy of a short poem or personal narrative to each student.

Teacher:	I want you to read this silently to yourself and look carefully at the words in the piece. When I say *look carefully,* I mean look for words that hold a lot of meaning, like nouns and verbs. Then circle the words with a marker. You can also circle prepositions, such as *on* and *beneath,* or personal pronouns, such as *he* and *they,* but remember, you want to choose words to help you think about this story or poem in new ways.
	Remember, there is no right or wrong way to portal a story. The writer decides what words to choose, so select words that speak to you. Let's stop for a minute and look at a checklist that can help you make sure you diversify your choices.

On the SMART Board, I project a checklist that students can use to help them think carefully about their word choices, and we read it together (Figure 15.3).

As students create their own portals, I scaffold their efforts by walking around the room and answering questions they may have.

Once everyone has finished, I invite students to share suggestions with the whole group about how we could write a story from this piece. This allows

Figure 15.3   Creating Portals: A Reproducible Checklist for Choosing Words That Can Drive Story

> ☐ I selected verbs (e.g., words that express actions, events, or a state of being such as *run* or *cry*)
>
> ☐ I selected nouns (e.g., a person, place, or thing such as *house* or *cat*).
>
> ☐ I selected some adjectives (e.g., words that describe and identify such as *the **small** hat* or ***purple** mittens*).
>
> ☐ I selected some adverbs (e.g., words that modify verbs such as *I ran **quickly*** or *my brother waited **impatiently***).
>
> ☐ I selected some prepositions (e.g., words that link nouns, pronouns, and phrases such as *against* or *during*).
>
> ☐ I selected some conjunctions (e.g., words that also link words and phrases such as *and* and *when*).
>
> ☐ I selected some personal pronouns (e.g., words that refer to a specific person or thing such as *you, she,* or *we*).

students to hear the multiple story directions that are possible from the same text. I ask reflective questions, such as these:

- What do we notice when we portal a story?
- What kinds of words did each of us portal? Are they similar? Different?
- What do these words make us think about?
- What kind of images do they conjure up for us?
- How can we use these images to help us envision a new story?
- What kinds of questions did we ask ourselves about the text during the portal process?
- How do these questions help us think about genre?
- What directions do these portals give us?

These questions help students notice how creating portals can help clarify story, provide story ideas, and/or guide story direction.

Students Practice the Strategy

When I am certain students have developed an understanding for how portal writing works, I refer them to their writing folders: "Please take out one piece of writing that you would like to portal. This writing sample should be a story that you are kind of stuck on or want to develop further."

I photocopy these drafts so they will have access to their original. Next, students work individually to portal their stories from the photocopied text. Throughout the process, they may also ask a neighbor for feedback on some of their word choices or ask for ideas about how to rework their stories after they are finished creating portals. I carefully monitor students' progress with portaling and how those words help generate ideas for revision.

Independent Writing

At the beginning of this part of the mini-lesson, I give students a handout of questions that will help guide them as they work independently to revise their stories (Figure 15.4). I ask them to glue or staple these questions into their writing folders so they can refer to them when they need them. These questions help students think about their portals and how to use them as they revise their written work. In addition, these reflective questions gently challenge students to think about what they know about their stories and how they want to revise them.

Throughout this executing process, I remind students to use their portals to help them think about ways to improve their stories. I say, "Portals are like windows. They give us new ways of seeing our writing."

I encourage students to share their thinking with a partner before they revise their stories. Peer feedback offers a lens in writing that is particularly valuable in portal writing, given that a peer may interpret the meaning of a word or groups of words differently than the student writer. These kinds of differences, when shared, can catapult new thinking or offer new story direction that can motivate students to write. Here again, I continue to monitor students' understanding of the strategy and offer support to those who need additional help. I continue to observe, taking anecdotal notes about who is writing with ease and who requires additional support.

Student Reflection

Reflection is a process of becoming self-aware. Particular to this lesson on portal writing, reflection can lead to insights about the writing itself as well as insights about the student as an author. As a closure to the mini-lesson, I invite students to share with the whole group how they think portal writing supports them in the drafting process and how it helps them write independently. I ask students to think about and respond to the following questions:

- What am I coming to know about the connections between portal writing and revision?
- How does access to portal writing affect my writing or my thinking about language in general?

I value these responses because they help me refine the strategy in ways that best meet their needs as writers.

Figure 15.4   After Portaling: Reproducible Questions to Help Me Revise
My Writing

- Do the words construct a different story? The same story?
- Do the words magnify a person? A place? A mood? A voice?
- Do I notice a word I did not notice before?
- Does a word make me think differently about the story?
- Can a word be used to modify or change the title?
- Is there a word that changes the meaning of the story?
- Do any of the words I circled conjure up new words or images in my mind?

MODIFYING THE MINI-LESSON

Adaptations for Writers Who Struggle

I modify the strategy according to student need. For example, some students may not feel comfortable creating portals on their own. These students may find the freedom to choose words somewhat daunting, so I encourage them to seek support from peers on what to portal and why. I like to group these students with writers who feel comfortable creating portals. I believe this kind of scaffolding helps demystify any feelings of a right way to portal text.

Students who are reluctant to write at all may struggle with portal writing. For this reason, I like to introduce the strategy through texts from published authors whom students enjoy (e.g., J. K. Rowling, Stephanie Meyer). For reluctant writers in particular, it may be easier for students to discover ideas for writing from outside sources.

Students may also struggle with the step between creating portals and knowing how to use portals to drive new thinking in the revision process. Here again, I like to group students who demonstrate a range of ease with the strategy with ones who struggle so that they can support each other. In these groupings, I ask students to participate in discussions about word choice, story, and direction. These conversations serve generative purposes, as shared ideas become possibilities for writing.

Adaptations for English Language Learners

I modify the strategy for English language learners by encouraging them to draw their portals. I first ask students to portal words they know as sight words. Then we move on and talk about the portals and the ideas they present. Next, I ask students to illustrate these ideas. Drawing portals is a demonstration of visual thinking and can be used to further develop story ideas. In particular, drawing as a way of knowing encourages English language learners to transact with text through another communication system (i.e., transmediation). Our long-term goal is to shift these students from illustrating portal ideas to writing about them in their writer's notebooks.

Adaptations for Advanced Writers

I encourage advanced writers to look critically and reflectively at language in a variety of narrative forms—menus, maps, advertisements, recipes, and so on—that they can easily portal for ideas for writing. Advanced writers have the confidence to navigate texts with unique and different story or narrative structures. Access to a variety of texts also encourages self-sufficient writers to practice these unique forms in their own writing.

I also introduce students to texts written in other languages (e.g., Spanish newspaper articles, menus written in French, etc.). These texts can also be poems or stories written by children or pages photocopied from children's books. While this approach holds cultural significance for students in classes who speak more than one language, I encourage monolingual students to identify and portal words that look the same (e.g., *animal* in English and *animal* in Spanish) and words that look familiar (e.g., *crème* for *cream*). I also encourage students to search for cognates across languages (e.g., *night* and *nuit* in French). The purpose of this modification is to experience the pure enjoyment of language play through which we can access our imagination (Greene, 1995).

EXTENDING THE STRATEGY ACROSS THE CONTENT AREAS

Portal writing in the content area applies as students participate in writing expository pieces in history or science and in writing autobiography, memoir, and personal narrative in language arts (to name a few). Students who know how to portal as a way of seeing and improving their writing can use language throughout the content areas to generate ideas and facilitate new thinking.

RESOURCE FOR FURTHER READING

➢ Leigh, S. R. (2012). Re-seeing story through portal writing. *Journal of the Assembly on Expanded Perspectives in Learning, 17,* 83–94.

In the winter of 2010, I investigated the effectiveness of portal writing with 22 student participants in a Grade 4 classroom over a 6-week period. I collected and analyzed 94 samples of portal writing. Results indicate portal writing helped students re-see their writing in three ways: experience poetic form, develop new titles, and discover small-moment writing—that is, writing about one event and developing it fully into a focused, well-structured story rather than writing about an entire experience where the writer tries to cover multiple ideas at once (Calkins, 1994). Specifically, this study showed the positive impact of creating portals on students as writers. They (a) experienced revision as a creative process, (b) to detail in their writing by looking carefully at word choice and creating unique word combinations and phrases, (c) wrote with focus by using their juxtaposed words as aids in finding a story's focus, (d) reflected on the potential stories that emerged from their portals, and (e) reflected on form. Moreover, reluctant writers experienced joy in writing by creating their own texts from creating portals in texts other than their own.

Conferring With an Avatar 16

Chase Young and Lynda Swanner

Using this strategy, students work with text-to-speech software (Web 2.0 avatars*) to listen to how their writing sounds. Teachers can turn to this 21st-century method for proofreading when students do not read over their stories or are unaware of the revision or editing that is needed in their stories. Students can use this self-discovery strategy of revising and editing to privately critique their work before conferring with the teacher.

WHY THIS STRATEGY IS IMPORTANT

In our experience, students do not take enough time to read their own work carefully. This strategy gives students the opportunity to hear their writing as they have written it. This added step to the writing process promotes student accountability for their work. The following is an anecdote from one of Chase's classes to describe the process he used before he introduced students to avatars:

> The writing block has begun, and I am wielding my powerful red pen. Students approach apprehensively, ready for me to work my magic in editing. They have come to expect this ritual as part of the writing process. As always, I read their stories aloud and ask what changes they would like to make. The answer is usually the same: "None! It is perfect!"
>
> This response always prompts my red pen to prove them wrong. I go through their story, sentence by sentence, and make conventional changes out loud as students nod compliantly, but they are never truly aware of the necessary changes being made. They walk back to their

---

*Authors' Note: *Web 2.0* was declared the millionth English word in 2009. The term refers to an interactive Internet tool. In this chapter, we discuss the use of Web 2.0 avatars found on Voki.com. An avatar is a graphical representation of a computer user. On Voki.com, users can input text; their graphical representation turns into speech. Although avatars have many uses, in this strategy, students' avatars become their writing conference partners. A video of students using this strategy is available on YouTube: Conferring With an Avatar: Using Voki for Proofreading http://youtu.be/Y9gHpIH9RTA.

desks with their heads down, tail between their legs, and quietly adapt their writing to my specifications. And I feel good about my ability to edit. I have learned a lot while my students have learned nothing. This is particularly evident when they return to me with their next paragraph full of the same types of errors that I had fixed in their previous manuscripts.

This scenario was repeated daily in Chase's classroom—so often that even he almost believed this was how writing conferences were defined and conducted. Deep down, however, he knew that this strategy wasn't working.

In response to this daily struggle, we devised a strategy that motivates students to actively revise and edit their own writing prior to conferring with the teacher. This strategy helps them discover what they need to revise and edit, and it also empowers them as writers. They become aware of their own problems in writing, and they begin to self-regulate the writing process. In addition, student–teacher writing conferences are no longer filled with simplistic revision and editing issues. Instead, we can devote our focus during conference time to more complex issues and the craft of composing.

THE MINI-LESSON

Materials Needed

- An avatar site (e.g. Voki.com), prepared and assembled
- Desktop publishing software (e.g., Microsoft Word), optional
- A sample piece of writing that needs revision and editing
- Students' writing journals
- A pencil
- A pen

On the first day of implementing this strategy, we focus on the technology. We want students to explore Voki.com before they use it as a writing tool; this step eliminates its novelty. Before we bring students to the computer lab, we demonstrate the navigation of Voki.com. It does not take long, and the digital natives are eager to explore it for themselves. We give students free rein on the site, and they quickly master the technical aspects of the lesson. Soon they are prepared to dive into the writing piece.

Model the Strategy

On the second day, we model the Conferring With an Avatar strategy. We begin by choosing a piece of writing in need of revision and editing. Here is an example:

It was a summer nit the patio were perfect. Friends had gathered after a long hrd wek.

Using the copy and paste functions, we paste our sentences from Word into the Voki text box for the avatar to read. After listening to the avatar read the sentences, we engage students in discussion. The necessary edits stand out. The avatar has now become the red pen.

Students first notice the run-on sentence. When the avatar reads the paragraph, the lack of punctuation is clear. Students also notice the misspellings, because the avatar pronounces exactly what is written: *nit, hrd,* and *wek.* On a revising level, we analyze issues such as whether or not the story captures the reader's attention. We discuss possible revisions. We discuss the writing sample's strengths and weaknesses. Sentence by sentence, we look at conventions, misspellings, sentence structure, organization, and other opportunities for revising or editing. After we make the edits and revisions, we listen to the story again for clarity.

Students Practice the Strategy

In the next step, students create their avatar. It is important to limit this process because students—and teachers—could spend all day creating the perfect digital representation of themselves or the most gory, humorous, or crazy representation.

After students draft their first paragraph, they type it into Voki. Then, they make changes based on the avatar's rendering of their story. As an option, they can fix their story in Voki and bask in their glory and success. All of Chase's students make this choice on their own because they love to see their progress.

Because students have already conferred with themselves (as avatars), our role is to help students verbalize their specific changes and understand their edits. When we confer, we begin by asking, "What changes did you make after listening to your story?" Student responses vary and might include inserting additional punctuation, correcting the spelling, adding more information, and eliminating confusion. We are also happy when students relay how the avatar experience has confirmed their writing abilities and helped to build their self-confidence.

Independent Writing

After the initial whole-group usage, we embed this strategy into the proofreading step of the writing process. We require students to type their writing into Voki whenever it is evident that they have not critiqued their own writing. Later, this becomes a proofreading strategy students can access at anytime from their writing toolbox.

Student Reflection

The Conferring With an Avatar strategy is an example of reflection at its finest. In an objective way, students become self-aware of changes that need to be made to their writing. The reliance on the teacher's red pen is minimized.

When we meet with students, we encourage them to describe their changes and the thinking behind them. Here is an example of student–teacher discourse involving punctuation that occurred after the student conferred with an avatar:

Teacher:	What changes are you going to make?
Student:	I need more periods.
Teacher:	How do you know that?
Student:	It wasn't very good, because it went in one fast glob.

Here is an example of student–teacher discourse involving spelling:

Teacher:	What changes did you make?
Student:	I needed to fix some spelling errors. I needed to spell *grabbed* correctly.
Teacher:	How did you know it was spelled wrong?
Student:	It sounded wrong.
Teacher:	Do you remember how the avatar said it?
Student:	*Grabed.* [Student uses a long *a* sound.]
Teacher:	We know that you have to do WHAT to the consonant?
Student:	Double it!

Based on the avatar's rendering, students were able to reflect and make changes to their work without teacher direction.

MODIFYING THE MINI-LESSON

Adaptations for Writers Who Struggle

The Conferring With an Avatar strategy is based on individual abilities; therefore, adaptations are slight, if necessary. This is an excellent strategy for writers who struggle because individualized instruction meets writers where they are in their writing development. The avatar experience motivates struggling writers by affording them the chance to privately assess their own writing before peer or student-teacher conferring. The avatar is completely objective, free of judgment, and does not wield the almighty red pen.

Writers who struggle benefit from focused interaction with the avatar. We meet with these writers before they sit down with the avatar. We discuss what component of writing to focus on and help the student set goals. For example, if students recognize that they often inappropriately use run-on sentences, they need to listen carefully to how the avatar pauses at punctuation. Each time the avatar reads, students should focus on one goal only. After correcting that issue, they can choose another goal and listen to the piece again. This process helps struggling students revise and edit each piece in a manageable way.

Adaptations for English Language Learners

The oral aspect of the strategy supports English language learners (ELLs) through a scaffolded writing experience. We encourage ELL students to identify parts in their writing that do not sound right, circle them, and bring the information to the teacher conference. At that time, we help them analyze and understand why these parts sounded funny when the avatar read them.

Adaptations for Advanced Writers

Advanced writers in Chase's class type their entire story. Then, using the Conferring With an Avatar strategy, we encourage them to focus more on the craft of composing than on editing and proofreading. For example, Chase might ask students to listen for instances where a simile or additional description would enhance the story. Advanced writers are intrigued with the novelty of an avatar.

EXTENDING THE STRATEGY ACROSS CONTENT AREAS

Open-ended response items on standardized reading tests are now prevalent. Therefore, it is imperative that students know how to craft a well-articulated, succinct response to literature. This strategy helps students determine the general readability and efficiency of their responses to literature.

RESOURCES FOR FURTHER READING

➤ Morgan, M. (1999). *How to proofread and edit your writing: A guide for student writers*. Retrieved from ERIC database. (ED464346)

Proofreading strategies can be boring; therefore, students sometimes skip this necessary step in the writing process. Morgan suggests alternative proofreading strategies that motivate the writer and encourage a complete rethinking of the piece.

➤ Strauss, S., & Xiang, X. (2006). The writing conference as a locus of emergent agency. *Written Communication, 23*(4), 355–396. Retrieved from ERIC database. (EJ745067)

This article promotes agentive writers through self-evaluation and diagnosis of writing proficiency. The self-evaluative approach eliminates uncertainty, confusion, and negative views of student writing.

17 Writing Aloud

A Sound-Savvy Approach to Writing

Sandra K. Athans

The English Language Arts Common Core Standards (Common Core State Standards Initiative, 2011) encourages writing teachers to help students develop a *literary finesse*, an ability to use language correctly and commandingly. The Write-Aloud strategy is an auditory-based strategy to help students reflect thoughtfully on their writing so they can shape it effectively with finesse. To use the strategy, students whisper-read their writing aloud and examine and polish it based on the way it sounds. The strategy also prompts students to double-check their work through auditory and visual modalities. This double-checking often exposes previously undetected errors in mechanics or meaning. Students use the Write-Aloud strategy as they compose and edit their rough drafts; they also use it to polish their final copy.

The Write-Aloud strategy is similar to the Conferring With an Avatar strategy presented in Chapter 16, but it has different goals and benefits for students' writing. Students will benefit from learning both auditory approaches to improve their writing. The Write-Aloud strategy is also an alternative for students who write in classrooms with limited technology. As writers, we don't always have an avatar around to confer with!

WHY THIS STRATEGY IS IMPORTANT

For many years, I observed a large number of my students resist going back to edit and proofread their work by silently and carefully reading their drafts. I also noticed that students overlooked missing words, misplaced or omitted punctuation, and other errors I considered to be easily detectable. Peer collaborative editing often produced the same lackluster results.

I discovered that the Write-Aloud strategy helps students develop an ear for well-crafted writing. It provides them with a way to evaluate the effectiveness of their writing skills, such as their use of varied sentence structures and vibrant word choices. It also encourages them to reexamine their writing for meaning, clarity, and mechanics. Although teachers often model many aspects of writing by reading work aloud (Calkins, 1994; Spandel, 2008) or reading jointly with students (McCarrier, Pinnell, & Fountas, 2000; Wall, 2008), it is also a valuable technique for students to use independently or in small self-directed pairs.

Some students are more apt to detect ways to improve their writing if they hear their words aloud. Often, they catch errors they would miss with silent reading. Likewise, by whisper-reading their work aloud, students are more likely to develop an understanding of the rhythmical sound of thoughtful writing. They are also better able to determine ways to enhance the sound of their own writing voice.

As students progress in their ability to compose more first-draft writing on the computer, they often blend otherwise distinct stages of the writing process. Certainly, that is what many excellent experienced writers do as they go back and forth among the recursive stages of the writing process. But inexperienced student writers may not be able to handle the simultaneous challenge of getting thoughts down and expressing ideas well. The Write-Aloud strategy helps students improve the quality of their first-draft writing and thus prepares them for this challenge. The strategy helps them think through their ideas while they compose their work.

THE MINI-LESSON

Materials Needed

- One three-sentence passage that is well written and contains vivid words and richly developed sentences
- One three-sentence passage that contains simple sentences with little or no description
- An overhead projector
- A completed planning graphic organizer for a draft about a memorable childhood experience, prepared for projection on the overhead projector (see next entry)
- The start of the draft about a memorable childhood experience (I use a piece about feeding my family's chickens)
- Proofreading and editing checklists from students' writing notebooks
- Students' writing-in-progress folders
- Pencils
- Students' current drafts
- A sign marked Whisper Zone
- A conch shell

I begin the lesson by asking students to listen carefully as I read aloud two different three-sentence passages. (I often create these passages using student samples that I carefully adjust and make generic so the identity of the authors remains anonymous.) I intentionally do not ask students to listen for particular purposes. Following my reading, I ask them for their reaction to both passages. Students often claim that the well-constructed sentence passage sounds better and flows nicely. Some indicate that they got a clear picture of the ideas presented. Students often analyze phrases or words from the passage.

In our discussion of the second passage, students usually say it is "forgettable" or "boring." We discuss how their listening observations suggest that the quality of the passages is different and that it is easy to hear these differences.

> **Teacher:** So what you're also telling me is that we all have a wonderful writing tool that's practically right in front of our noses . . . but off to each side just a bit . . . our ears! Our ears can help us detect good writing and assist us in improving our writing.
>
> Now you will learn a new writing technique—the Write-Aloud strategy. It uses this new writing tool: our ears. This tool has many proofreading benefits. Our ears not only help us hear the sound of good sentences, but they can also do more. Our ears can also help us hear if we've forgotten to place a period at the end of a sentence. We can actually hear when we run one sentence into another if we forget to use a period. Also, we can easily hear if we leave out important words. We can hear when the meaning of our ideas is unclear or mixed up. Here's an example. I'm not terribly fond of spinach, yet I once wrote in a story, "I do like spinach." I mistakenly left out the word *not.* I certainly heard this error when I read my story aloud!

I then explain that they will see for themselves how the Write-Aloud strategy can help them improve the quality of their sentences and strengthen their proofreading skills. I also let them know that this strategy can be used throughout the writing process. It is even useful when they compose other types of writing that may not make use of the stages of a writing process, such as when they respond to on-demand writing prompts during content-area and other tests.

I conclude this introduction by sharing comments from one or two experienced writers who use variations of the technique to enhance their work. I quote one of our favorite authors, Pam Munoz Ryan (2010): "I can read my work silently and think it reads just fine, but when I hear it, I am often disappointed." I also enjoy selecting the words of a writing specialist, such as Lucy Calkins, who, I explain, crafts instructional writing books for teachers. Calkins (1994) says, "I see the shape of my words on the page. I listen to their sound" (p. 18).

Model the Strategy

In the modeling part of the mini-lesson, I project my writing activities on an overhead screen.

> **Teacher:** I'm going to model the strategy as it can be used during the drafting stage of writing my personal narrative. To do this, I'll also need the planning graphic organizer I completed yesterday.

I project an image of my graphic organizer.

> **Teacher:** A quick review of my organizer reminds me that I'm ready to begin the part about entering the chicken coop. As you'll see, I'll compose a few sentences aloud about entering the chicken coop, and I'll write them down as I compose them. Then I'll talk through changes I'm thinking about. Using the Write-Aloud strategy in this manner shows you how I listen to the sound of my words and consider the quality of what I'm writing. I use my ear to help shape my writing. You might say I write with my ear!

I compose my thoughts aloud and in writing.

> **Teacher:** I walked up the steps. I placed my hands on the doorknob. I listened for the sound of the rooster. Hmmm. I'm thinking these sentences sound very repetitive. Also, they sound kind of similar. I notice they all start the same way, and I notice they are kind of short and don't capture the pictures I see in my head. I could easily start one differently and add some details to another. I'll make these changes now and then continue my story while keeping these ideas in my mind.

I make three changes to the sentences. While adjusting my writing, I continue.

> **Teacher:** I crept up the cement steps very slowly and gently placed my hands on the doorknob. I held my breath as I pressed my ear to the door and listened for the rooster.

Since my fluency is choppy throughout the process of adjusting my writing, I reread the sentence over again, fluently.

> **Teacher:** That sounds much better. I will keep in mind the need to vary my sentence beginnings and to include rich details that capture the pictures I see in my mind.

Next, I encourage students to participate in my write-aloud. I ask them to help me complete my thoughts as I record our words.

> **Teacher:** We develop a rhythm in the writing. We won't need to go back and make changes to every sentence. We'll save that kind of fine-tuning for a later stage in the writing process. Instead, we'll listen as we write aloud and adjust our thoughts as we go along. This will make our first draft the best it can be.

I continue with my story, writing aloud and pausing as I search for words or adjust sentences by capturing ideas from my students. Each time I integrate student ideas, I stop briefly to discuss how the change enriched the sentence. Students typically agree that the sentences sound more concise, vivid, and interesting as we apply the Write-Aloud strategy.

After we compose a paragraph by applying the Write-Aloud strategy together, I introduce the proofreading element.

Teacher:	Now, why don't we proofread what we've written so far using the Write-Aloud strategy? This is a different use of the strategy. Of course, I will also proofread after I complete my entire first draft. But for now I'm going to practice proofreading with you so you can understand how the Write-Aloud strategy is also useful for this later stage in the writing process. Instead of composing by listening to our words, we will proofread by listening to our words.

I highlight specific areas of focus during the proofreading stage:

- Ideas
- Organization
- Sentence fluency
- Voice
- Word choice
- Conventions

I read aloud the passage with students and, inevitably, we find one or two errors or areas in need of improvement. As an example, while listening for effective word choice, I ask, "Does my word choice allow a reader to see, feel, or deeply experience something in my writing?" These reflective questions may be based on prompts used in the proofreading checklist in student's writing notebooks.

I close this segment by telling students we will revisit the use of the Write-Aloud strategy for this purpose later in the week, as we continue writing our narratives and working through the various stages of the writing process.

Students Practice the Strategy

During this part of the mini-lesson, students whisper-read a piece of their writing to practice the Write-Aloud strategy. I tell them to write aloud for two purposes:

1. To think through what their next sentence will be

2. To identify one way they might improve the quality of what they've written so far in their introduction

I allow about 3 minutes for this, and then we share some ideas.

I explain that although students will work at their seats today, I will set up a special area in the back of the classroom—the Whisper Zone—where they can use the technique without disturbing their neighbor. I tell them they may move to this special area to use the Write-Aloud strategy during any of the stages of the writing process.

As students work at their seats, I briefly scan the room and observe their behaviors. I find that initially some students have difficulty reading aloud and critically listening at the same time. This experience is new and may require some practice. Others struggle with reading and have difficulty juggling the tasks simultaneously. Using a computer, tape recorder, or even a writing partner or small peer group might help these students grow more comfortable or strengthen their fluency and word recognition skills so they are able to use the Write-Aloud strategy effectively. Used in conjunction with these aids, students can also flag questionable passages in their writing and return to edit them once they have read all the way through. Although the objective of using the Write-Aloud strategy is to encourage students to hear their words and to then make improvements, I sometimes find it necessary to establish these intermediary processes before this can happen.

Later in the week, I may introduce the use of whisper phones, cardboard dividers, and tape recorders for students who struggle to hear themselves. All these devices help students hear what they have written as they read their work aloud. A whisper phone works like a telephone but directs a student's spoken words to his or her own ear. They are inexpensive and sold through many educational supply companies. Some teachers even make their own whisper phones from plastic tubing. A cardboard divider enables a student to read aloud without concern that he or she may distract others in a quiet room. For now, I am conscientious about monitoring students as they practice independently so I can identify specific students who might benefit from the use of these other aids.

Independent Writing

To independently work on their writing using the Write-Aloud strategy, students may choose to work in the Whisper Zone throughout all stages of the writing process. I also demonstrate how students can use their editing and proofreading checklists from their writer's notebooks while using their ear to hear the areas that could be strengthened. These checklists reflect common writing practices and align with our districtwide writing rubric. To support their efforts, I hold miniconferences routinely and as needed.

Student Reflection

To encourage students to reflect on their progress using the Write-Aloud strategy, I call them back to our meeting area. I invite them to share their experiences. I typically ask volunteers to reflect on the process first. I ask, "What was it like for you to use the Write-Aloud strategy as you composed your narrative?" After several students share their ideas, I ask for volunteers to share passages or ideas to demonstrate ways in which they strengthened their writing or uncovered new insights about their writing skill or style. Next, I ask if any students were able to try the strategy as they proofread their work.

To conclude the mini-lesson, I hold up the conch shell and pause. As curiosity mounts, I ask, "Does anyone know why I selected a conch shell to remind you of the Write-Aloud strategy?" I take several answers, curious to learn if someone is familiar with the notion that the ocean can be heard when you hold a conch shell to your ear. If not, I make them aware of it. I close the lesson by saying that the conch shell will remind us of the almost magical role our ears play in hearing our writing. I say, "Just as we can hear the ocean in a conch shell, we can hear good writing. We can use our ears to help us shape, strengthen, and improve our writing." Then I invite the students to help me finish the statement. I begin and students typically chime in with me: "It's a tool that's right in front our nose . . . but off to each side just a bit!"

MODIFYING THE MINI-LESSON

Adaptations for Writers Who Struggle

Struggling writers benefit from additional support and scaffolds (Vygotsky, 1978) along with repeated practice (Pearson & Gallagher, 1983). If I find that students do not have the expertise to detect writing errors, I target one or two specific areas based on my ongoing review and analysis of an individual student's work. For example, if a student struggles with organizations of ideas, I encourage her to use the Write-Aloud strategy to hear if the sentences sound cohesive and united within a paragraph. Similarly, I might highlight a student's repeated use of the word *awesome* and instruct him to use the Write-Aloud strategy to (1) identify the problem and (2) remedy it

Limiting and targeting improvement areas help students detect and remedy errors that are unique in their writing.

Struggling writers also benefit from the peer support of their small writing group. Knowing they can choose to work in small groups or with a partner is comforting and motivating. Collaborative peer groups such as book clubs (Daniels, 2002) and literacy clubs have supported struggling readers for decades. Using a similar approach with struggling writers is also one way to adapt the strategy.

Adaptations for English Language Learners

I pair English language learners (ELLs) with a peer for guidance and support. I also invite these students to participate within a small group of guided writers using the Write-Aloud strategy. Sharing views about writing based on the way a passage sounds presents these learners with another avenue to strengthen all of their literacy skills.

Adaptations for Advanced Writers

I challenge advanced writers to use the Write-Aloud strategy to address more sophisticated areas of improvement in their writing, such as enhancing their voice, using figurative language, or incorporating complex sentence structures in their writing.

EXTENDING THE STRATEGY ACROSS THE CONTENT AREAS

Write-alouds can be used within science and social studies as students draft hypotheses, document observations and conclusions, or explain their understanding of a scientific event. Writers can apply the same strategy to ensure their meaning is clear. In social studies, students can rely on the technique to polish their written assignments. The Write-Aloud strategy can also be effective when used outside the writing process; it can help students develop an ear for stronger writing throughout the content areas.

RESOURCES FOR FURTHER READING

➤ Routman, R. (2005). *Writing essentials: Raising expectations and results while simplifying teaching.* New York: Heinemann.

Traditional write-alouds, most often associated with well-known literacy specialist Reggie Routman, receive merit among most literacy researchers. Teachers model their thoughts while constructing and editing a written piece to make their mental processes transparent. Although the intent of these practices is to model the critical-thinking process and stages involved in writing, the value of reading the written passages aloud to reach this objective is also key. As Routman advises, "Listen again, what do you hear that makes the writing outstanding?" (p. 21). Routman posits that listening to writing as a means of evaluating its quality is a viable strategy for developing writing skill.

➤ Saddler, B., & Asaro-Saddler, K. (2010). Writing better sentences: Sentence-combining instruction in the classroom. *Preventing School Failure, 54*(3), 159–163.

Developed in the 1960s as a writing intervention for struggling writers, sentence combining provides practice in rewriting basic sentences into forms that are more syntactically mature and varied (see Chapter 13 of this book). Through more than 80 studies, the researchers contend that sentence combining has positively influenced students' abilities to create more complex sentences of higher quality, improve revisions, and compose better story writing. Sentence combining relies on the practice of using hearing to detect correct usage, and it serves as an alternative to teaching formal grammar including parts of speech and sentence diagramming.

➤ Wall, H. (2008). Interactive writing beyond the primary grades. *The Reading Teacher, 62*(2), 149–152.

Interactive writing, developed in 1991 (McCarrier et al., 1999) to model and encourage independent practice in the writing process for the primary grades, is a technique in which a message is typically constructed aloud collaboratively by students and their teacher while students take turns as scribes. Recent studies suggest that positive effects of this technique are also evident at upper elementary grades. This study was undertaken in a third-grade classroom where the researcher served as the "more knowledgeable other" (Vygotsky, 1978), supervising the discussion and directing students' attention to potentially more sophisticated revisions in grammar, punctuation, and the writer's craft. The researcher noted that over time, the collaboratively constructed messages became more complex as students internalized the process and concepts. The investigation also demonstrated that interactive writing lessons, when used along with focused mini-lessons during writers' workshops, help to address teachers' concern for authentic instruction.

18 A Picture Is Worth a Thousand Words

Revising With Photographs

Noreen S. Moore

The Revising With Photographs strategy helps students understand what it means to "re-see" their writing after completing a first draft of a narrative piece. The strategy also prompts students to make substantial changes to their writing, if necessary, and it ultimately helps them experience the benefits of revision as part of the writing process. With this strategy, students learn to use personal photographs to generate new ideas, details, and improved word choice as part of the revision process.

WHY THIS STRATEGY IS IMPORTANT

Revision literally means to "see again" or to "re-see" (Richards & Miller, 2005). When I ask students to revise, they tend to approach revision as an editing, or cleaning up, assignment. For example, they equate revision with simple editing tasks, such as replacing vague words with more specific ones. It is critical for students to understand and value the true meaning of revision. Revising is at the heart of skilled writers' composing processes, and skilled writers engage in revision throughout the composing process (Fitzgerald, 1987; Hayes, 2004). Indeed, Donald Murray (1991) states that writing *is* revising.

Although revision can lead to better quality writing, students in Grades 4 through 8 do not do much substantial revision (Fitzgerald, 1987; McCutchen, Francis, & Kerr, 1997; Rijlaarsdam, Couzijn, & van den Bergh, 2004). Yet with appropriate instruction, these students can revise effectively (MacArthur, 2007).

When I teach revision, many students do not immediately realize that revision can help them improve the quality of their writing. As a result, many students treat revision as a tedious editing task. Students need instruction that helps them clearly understand what it means to revise as well as revision strategies that help them improve the overall quality of their writing.

A considerable number of writing strategies for revision focus on helping students learn to use evaluation criteria (e.g., Spandel, 2008). For example, instruction may focus on teaching students to self-evaluate their writing using a rubric. However, when I teach students to use rubrics and checklists, many struggle to use them effectively. Even if they understand the evaluation criteria on these tools, they have difficulty evaluating their writing objectively. Therefore, in addition to understanding evaluation criteria, my students need help distancing themselves from their writing to gain perspective before they can re-see their writing and apply evaluation criteria effectively. Like visual artists, my students need to step back from their writing and look at their work with a critical eye. When my students look at personal photographs related to their writing, they are able to experience the event they are writing about from a new angle; this helps them gain this distance from their original draft. Subsequently, they approach the revision task with fresh perspectives and new ideas.

THE MINI-LESSON

Materials Needed

- 1 copy of Figure 18.1: Reproducible Steps of the Revising With Photographs Strategy for each student
- 1 copy of Figure 18.2 Reproducible Sets of Cue Cards for the Revising With Photographs Strategy for each student
- Staplers or tape
- Students' writing notebooks
- Scissors
- Envelopes
- A model paper with revision marks (e.g., arrows indicating a moved sentence or two, sticky notes containing added text, a new introduction, etc.)
- A model paper with editorial marks (i.e., corrected spelling and punctuation marks)
- The teacher's first draft
- 3 to 5 photographs related to the teacher's first draft
- Chart paper and markers (or some other means of projecting the teacher's writing for all to see)
- Several photographs or pictures that relate to each student's first draft of a narrative (e.g., if a student writes about a summer vacation, he might bring in a picture that depicts the place he visited)
- Students' first drafts
- Pencils

Figure 18.1 Reproducible Steps of the Revising With Photographs Strategy

Steps for Revising With Photographs

1. Write a first draft.

2. Find photographs or images of the event or experience you have written about.

3. Brainstorm a list of words, phrases, and ideas that come to mind when you look at the photographs or images. Use cue cards to help you.

4. Star the words, phrases, and details that you would like to incorporate into your first draft.

5. Think about how these words, phrases, and details will change your draft.

6. Plan how you will use these words, phrases, or details in your first draft.

7. Revise your writing.

Figure 18.2   Reproducible Sets of Cue Cards for the Revising With Photographs
Strategy

Thinking About Images Cue Cards

1. When and where was this photo taken?	2. What senses does this photo evoke—sights, sounds, tastes, smells, and/or touch?
3. What words are the people saying to each other or to themselves?	4. What does this photo remind you of—person, place, or thing?

Revising With Photographs Strategy Steps Cue Cards

Step 1: Star the words, phrases, and details that you would like to incorporate in your first draft.	Step 2: How will these new ideas change your draft?
Step 3: Tell where you will add these in your draft.	Step 4: Rewrite this section of your first draft to incorporate your new ideas.

Prior to this mini-lesson, I give students a list of the steps in the strategy (Figure 18.1) and a set of cue cards to help them carry out the strategy procedures (Figure 18.2). Each cue card is numbered and scaffolds students through the steps in the strategy. Students staple the list into their writer's notebook, and I display this list during the entire mini-lesson. Students also cut the cue cards apart and store them in an envelope that can be taped or stapled into their writer's notebooks. The first set of cue cards prompts students to think about the photographs. The second set of cue cards is a series of steps to help students think about how to use these new ideas in their first drafts. I use these cue card phrases as I think aloud during the introduction and modeling portion of the lesson. I also refer students to these cards when they are practicing the strategy independently in pairs.

I begin the mini-lesson by discussing the difference between revising and editing. I show students two different papers, one that has revision marks and one that has editorial marks (see materials list). I explain that when writers make changes to spelling, grammar, and punctuation they are editing. When writers make larger changes to the ideas, content, and organization of their writing, they are revising. I ask the following questions:

- What paper is revised?
- What paper is edited?
- What do writers do when they revise?
- How does revision differ from editing?

Next, I write the word *revision* on chart paper and show students that the word contains two word parts: *re* and *vision*. We discuss what these word parts mean and create our own definition of *revision* (e.g., to see again). I explain that during revision, good writers

- find ways to take a step back from their writing,
- think about their topic and their purpose,
- get fresh new ideas, and
- return to see their original writing again.

We discuss how important it is for writers to take a break from their writing to get a fresh perspective on their topic. I explain that writers need to distance themselves from their writing, just like visual artists. I demonstrate how a painter might literally step back to look at her painting from a different perspective. I remind them that writers can step back from their writing in many ways. Specifically, they can

- do extra research on the writing topic,
- find inspiration by talking about the piece with peers,
- look at photographs or visual art related to the topic, and
- journal with a partner about these new experiences, and use new information gleaned to revise.

Next, I give students an example of two sentences I wrote in a first draft:

This summer I visited the lake. The weather was beautiful and I went kayaking.

Teacher: As I reread these sentences, I realize that I don't give my readers a sense of the beauty of the lake. I need to take a step back from, or distance myself from, this piece to discover what I really want to say about the lake and its beauty. To do this I will use the Revising With Photographs strategy.

I looked through photographs from my trip and found several that were inspirational to me. I taped them into my writer's notebook—have a look.

Next, I brainstormed a list of words, phrases, and images to describe the photographs. I wrote these ideas in my notebook next to my photographs. I used these new ideas to re-see my writing. Here's my revised story: "I spent my summer vacation in the most pristine nature preserve: Lake Serenity. The clear, still water framed with pure white lily pads invited me to kayak each morning."

We discuss as a group how the photographs gave me more information and inspiration to re-see my summer vacation and my writing.

To wrap up my introduction to the mini-lesson, I scaffold students in a similar exercise as they work in pairs to (1) come up with words, phrases, and images using my photographs and (2) offer alternate revisions of my original two sentences.

Students share their revised sentences and explain to the group how they used the strategy to alter the sentences. To conclude, we have a group discussion about the ways in which the strategy allows writers to distance themselves from their writing, gain fresh perspectives, and ultimately revise their writing effectively. If students express concern over not having photographs to match their writing, we discuss how pictures from books or the Internet can be used as well.

Model the Strategy

During the modeling phase of this lesson, I use a teacher-led think-aloud to break down the steps I previously discussed in the introduction. First, I show students two more sentences from my writing:

All of a sudden the sky grew dark and I could smell rain. The lake was rough and I was scared.

I read these sentences aloud and begin the think-aloud.

Teacher: In these two sentences I want to convey my fear. I was out on the water when a thunderstorm came up quickly. I had to act fast to get back to shore. However, when I reread these sentences, I don't think I convey my fear well. I just say the sky was dark and I was scared. I need to take a step back from my writing and gain distance, or a fresh perspective, by looking at my photographs from this vacation. I will use the Revising With Photographs strategy to help me.

I show students several photographs of my lake vacation.

Teacher: Not all these photographs are relevant to the part of my writing I want to revise, so I can set several pictures aside for now. There are two photographs that are relevant: the photo of a dark sky and the photo of me kayaking to shore. I am going to look at each photograph and brainstorm a list of words, images, and phrases about them.

I tape the photographs on chart paper and write my lists next to them. I think aloud as I come up with words and phrases for each photograph. For example, next to the dark sky photograph I write: "black as night, dismal, dark, Armageddon, end of the world, otherworldly, frightening, changed so quickly I felt like I was in a dream, or a nightmare." I ask students if they would like to add any words, images, or phrases to my own.

Finally, I think aloud about how I can revise my writing with the fresh ideas I came up with by looking at the photographs.

Teacher: Let me look at my first sentence again. When I looked at the photograph of the dark sky, I came up with many words and images that describe this scene as being otherworldly. I am going to revise this part of my writing to give my readers the sense that the color of the sky made me feel like the world was ending or that I was going into a different, frightening world. I'm going to write this on chart paper so you can follow along. Here's how I'll start. "The colors of the world around me changed suddenly. The once-blue and sunny sky was dark and dismal like something out of this world. As the sky grew increasingly black as night, I couldn't help thinking that this was the end of the world."

Next, I ask students what they would like to add to my revision or if they would revise this sentence differently. Once students understand the concept of revision and the strategy of Revising With Photographs, I feel comfortable teaching lessons in which we work on revising full paragraphs or larger sections of text.

Students Practice the Strategy

Next, students practice the strategy with my support. I give students two more sentences from my writing:

I kayaked through a small channel where fish jumped in front of me. The birds were singing all around me.

In addition, I show them two photographs that are related to this scene. Students work in pairs to (1) brainstorm a list of images, words, and phrases that describe the photographs and (2) use this information to revise my two sentences.

I use this time to observe and listen to students' conversations and field questions. Afterward, students share their revisions. I compliment students on their hard work, and we discuss any misconceptions or challenges I observed students having as they worked through the strategy.

Independent Writing

Students use their own photographs to revise parts of their first drafts. The list of strategy steps and the cue cards (Figures 18.1 and 18.2) help them through the process. In addition, I observe students and step in to help them if they are confused. Furthermore, students know that they can ask a peer for help if they have a question.

Student Reflection

I ask students to share their photographs and revisions with the group. Next, I give students time to reflect in their writer's notebooks. They write and then share what revision means to them. Afterward, I lead a discussion about how using Revising With Photographs can help them revise their writing. Finally, I ask students to talk about what is still challenging about this strategy, and we discuss how they can modify it if needed.

MODIFYING THE MINI-LESSON

Adaptations for Writers Who Struggle

Although writers may struggle for various reasons, many of the students I work with struggle because of a lack of motivation, difficulty self-regulating, or an ineffective stockpile of writing strategies. I address these issues in several ways. I provide students opportunities to work in pairs or on the computer to increase motivation (MacArthur, 2007). I also give them the following tools to scaffold and focus them on effectively completing the Revising With Photographs strategy.

First, I provide them with a goal-setting paper. On this paper, students record the goal of the strategy (i.e., to re-see my writing from a new perspective) as well as their own personal goals for using this strategy (e.g., complete it in one class period, complete without disruption, revise my writing so that it is better and I am proud of it, etc). Next, I direct them to use the set of steps in the strategy and the cue cards to help them apply the strategy. Specifically, I ask them to use these as a checklist; they must physically check off each step as they complete it. Finally, I require students to complete a written reflection stating whether they have achieved their goals and why. I do give all students the opportunity to use these tools, but I have found them to be particularly effective with my struggling writers.

Adaptations for English Language Learners

Due to their limited English language vocabulary, English language learners (ELLs) may need support brainstorming additional information, words, phrases, or images as they look at photographs. To address this, I have ELLs work with native English speaking partners to brainstorm. Specifically, ELLs can use the cue cards to interview their partners about their photographs and can then record the information in their notebooks so it is available for them to use as they revise their writing. It is also helpful to encourage ELLs to use thesauruses either on the computer (www.thesaurus.com) or in book format. These tools can help ELLs expand their vocabulary as they think about a topic from new perspectives.

Adaptations for Advanced Writers

My advanced writers tend to excel at using this strategy. Therefore, to keep their motivation high, I challenge them to use figurative language to express their ideas about the photographs. For example, I challenge them to come up with one of each of the following:

- Simile
- Metaphor
- Imagery
- Personification
- Alliteration
- Other types of figurative language we have been working on in class

I encourage them to use these in their writing pieces if it makes sense to do so.

Another way I challenge these writers is to encourage them to find a different way to distance themselves from their writing. For example, students can interview people in the school, community, or at home or do Internet research to find additional ways of looking at their topics.

EXTENDING THE STRATEGY ACROSS THE CONTENT AREAS

Students need to be able to revise their writing effectively in all content areas. The use of photographs to create distance between writers and their first drafts of writing can be used creatively across the curriculum to help students revise effectively. For example, in science, students can view pictures of lab procedures and materials as a way to help them think of additional information they need to include in their lab reports. In social studies, students can use photographs of time periods or people to help them think of additional information to include in research papers or biographies. It can also be effective for students to use additional distancing techniques after they complete a first draft. Specifically, students can conduct interviews, consult primary source materials, watch movies or YouTube clips, or study artwork as a way to help them gain perspective and think of new information to add or change their first drafts.

RESOURCES FOR FURTHER READING

> ➤ Holliway, R. D., & McCutchen, D. (2004). Audience perspective in young writers' composing and revising. In L. Allal, L. Chanquoy, & P. Largy (Eds.), *Revision: Cognitive and instructional processes* (pp. 157–170). Norwell, MA: Kluwer Academic.

Holliway and McCutchen found that elementary-age students revised their descriptive writing to improve its overall quality and level of detail after they participated in a special reading activity that helped them gain distance from or perspective on their first drafts. After writing first drafts, students read descriptions of tangram figures and tried to match the written descriptions to the correct figures from a set of four. When students guessed a match, they learned if the match was correct. Through this activity, students learned the characteristics that made descriptions effective, and they were then able to apply this information to improve their own descriptive writing.

> ➤ MacArthur, C. A. (2007). Best practices in teaching evaluation and revision. In S. Graham, C. A. MacArthur, & J. Fitzgerald (Eds.), *Best practices in writing instruction* (pp. 141–162). New York, NY: Guilford Press.

MacArthur argues that revision is an integral part of the writing curriculum for two reasons. First, there is evidence that experienced, skilled writers engage in revision during the composing process. Second, revision allows students and teachers an opportunity to spend more time on and reflect on a single piece of writing. In doing so, students can learn about the writing process. MacArthur outlines several evidence-based approaches for teaching revision effectively:

- Helping students to learn evaluation criteria and to self-evaluate
- Giving students critical reading opportunities
- Teaching students peer revising
- Coaching students to use strategies through strategy instruction
- Allowing students to use computers to write and revise
- Integrating strategy instruction combined with these other elements

Several of these techniques require students to distance themselves from their writing in order to revise it: using evaluation criteria and self-evaluation, engaging critical reading, and peer revising.

Section IV

Strategic Editing

The Finishing Touch

Writers edit their writing so it is smooth, reader-friendly, and as flawless as possible. Some writers prefer to edit recursively as they write. They want to fix problems with syntax (the order of the words in a sentence), parallel constructions (stating a list of ideas in grammatically similar form), wordiness, word choice, spelling, punctuation, and capitalization immediately before they move on with their writing. Others write their drafts nonstop and save editing for their last step. Although editing styles vary, logically, "polishing and editing come last" (Willis, 1993, p. 155).

Studies indicate that neither memorizing formal grammar rules nor learning how to diagram sentences are particularly useful to students when they edit their writing (Richards & Miller, 2005; Willis, 2000). "Most published authors don't know all of the formal rules of written language," note Richards and Miller (2005, p. 156). However, some people have an innate ability for editing. They even relish editing. Yet as developing writers, students struggle with editing their work.

How, then, might teachers help students learn to strategically, systematically, and independently edit their writing so they become adept and motivated about editing tasks? The chapters in this section offer strategies designed to help students identify changes necessary to make their writing clearer, recognize why these changes are necessary, and make appropriate adjustments.

As is the case with all the strategies offered in this book, each of the editing strategies in this section has been field-tested in Grades 4 through 8 classrooms. They also connect to the English/Language Arts Common Core Standards (see the Common Core Standards Chart on the inside cover of the book). We invite you to study your students' specific editing needs. Then, model and teach the editing strategies in this section that would benefit them. You and your students will appreciate how using editing strategies helps writers independently polish their writing and enables them to produce smooth, reader-friendly, and impeccable prose.

19 Revising and Editing Through Primary Sources

Nancy L. Williams and Kathleen Muir

The Revising and Editing Through Primary Sources strategy provides opportunities for students to revise and edit within an authentic context using a primary source as motivation. Students role-play being the framers of our country's Declaration of Independence as they collaborate to revise and edit a document and, eventually, their own writing. This strategy introduces students to the critical need for writers to revise and edit as they participate in a transdisciplinary unit on the American Revolution. This historical context provides students with a rationale for the need for revising and editing. Even Thomas Jefferson revised his work!

WHY THIS STRATEGY IS IMPORTANT

Students' abilities to revise and edit their writing are critical skills (see Common Core State Standards Initiative, 2011). Yet we have observed many students who are not motivated to revise and edit their writing. They view it as a task with little connection to the real world. They do not see authors revise and edit their work. Consequently, they may not believe authors engage in these stages of the writing process. They view their first draft as a completed work that needs no corrections, a process validated by high-stakes writing tests in which students are expected to ignore the concept of the writing process in general and create a first draft as a final product. Often, they think their stories and nonfiction texts are wonderful and do not need to be revised—with the possible exception of editing for spelling, grammar, and other conventions of written language. We believe that students need to recognize the importance of revising and editing their drafts and that writing, like all literacy skills, should be taught within a curricular context.

We created a framework that strengthens students' understanding and use of the processes of revising and editing. Our framework is connected to a fifth-grade social studies topic on the American Revolution, the writing process, and the 6+1 Traits. It is important to note that Kathie teaches within a transdisciplinary context. Similar to a thematic unit, transdisciplinary teaching and learning is contextualized within a particular topic—in this instance, the American Revolution. It differs because it is based on the concept that knowledge is gained through the synergy between the students and the teacher. It is value-added with elements of authenticity, constructivism, social justice, technology, and a transformation of information.

THE MINI-LESSON

Materials Needed

- A final copy of the Declaration of Independence, ready to project via a SMART Board or an overhead projector, or individual copies of the document to hand out (see www.archives.gov/exhibits/charters/charters_downloads.html)
- An edited draft of the Declaration of Independence (http://www.ushistory .org/declaration/document/rough.htm)
- A SMART Board
- Assorted intermediate-level literature on the topic of the American Revolution
- The grade-level social studies text
- A Patriot Points Checklist for student self-assessment (Figure 19.1 shows an example)
- Reference charts depicting guidelines for the writing process
- The 6+1 Traits—ideas, organization, voice, word choice, sentence fluency, and conventions—from the Northwest Regional Education Lab (see http:// educationnorthwest.org/resource/949)
- Students' writing folders
- Pencils

Kathie introduces the primary source, the Declaration of Independence, with a focus on the process the framers used to write this document.

Teacher: The framers of our country wrote the Declaration of Independence to boldly explain to their friends and their enemies why the colonies should separate from Great Britain immediately. They worked together as a committee. It was important to get the document written as clearly and precisely as possible to accurately represent the strong ideas and values they wanted to portray. There were fervent discussions and conferences among the members regarding precisely what words to use, how to structure sentences so readers would know exactly what they meant and not misunderstand anything, and how to make their points compelling and persuasive. These discussions resulted in several revisions to improve the document.

> Even though Thomas Jefferson was selected to author this critical document because of his excellent writing skills, he still needed to confer with other members of the committee to make the document as perfect as possible. His job was to represent the collected ideas of everyone on the committee. So it took time and many revisions before everyone could agree to what Jefferson had written. Let's take a minute to look at an edited draft of the Declaration of Independence.

This process helps students understand the need for revision, since the writing committee requested several drafts of the document from Thomas Jefferson before it was approved. She leads the class in chanting this mantra: "Thomas Jefferson needed to revise, and so do we!"

Model the Strategy

At this stage of the mini-lesson, Kathie points out the organization of the document (the preamble, rights, a list of grievances against the King of England, the conclusion, and the signatures) using the SMART Board and highlights these writing components as they relate to the writing process and the 6+1 writing traits—ideas, organization, voice, word choice, sentence fluency, and conventions. Next, she engages students in the discovery process, encouraging them to imagine being the framers of the document—Thomas Jefferson, John Adams, and Benjamin Franklin—as they review the final draft of the Declaration of Independence. They note how well Thomas Jefferson edited and revised for organization, choice of words, sentence fluency, and conventions. They discuss what makes the Declaration of Independence a strong, persuasive text. Students record comments from the committee regarding these writing skills. Kathie helps them notice the following:

- Various writing conventions, such as sentence structure and vocabulary
- Powerful, persuasive words that dominate the discussion, such as *declaration, independence, evident, unalienable, secure, instituted, sufferance, tyranny, absolved, solemnly, mutually,* and *consent*
- Different ways in which words were spelled during the American Revolution
- The varied lengths of sentences
- The overall active voice in the document (i.e., *We* hold these truths)

From students' observations and comments, we collaboratively create a Patriot Points Checklist as a class. Figure 19.1 shows a checklist created in Kathie's classroom. Yours may vary based on what your students notice about the document and the writing skills on which your class is currently working.

As the class creates the checklist, Kathie continually stresses the importance of revising and editing. She reminds students that the Declaration of Independence needed to be revised several times, even with Thomas Jefferson's famed ability to write.

Figure 19.1   Sample Patriot Points Checklist

Questions to Guide Revising and Editing	Did we?	Comments and Examples
Are the ideas organized?		
The beginning is interesting, and I want to read more.		
The writer stays on topic.		
Each paragraph contains a main idea and supporting details.		
There are smooth transitions from one paragraph to the next.		
The ending is logical and consistent with the document.		
Do the choice of words and sentence fluency reflect the style of the writer?		
The writing clearly conveys the intended meaning.		
The writer uses precise words.		
The writer uses strong, powerful, persuasive words.		
The writer uses descriptive words.		
The writer uses creative language (Example: metaphors, similes, personification, and onomatopoeia)		
The writer uses a mix of long and short sentences.		
Does the writer use the proper conventions of writing?		
Capitalization is used correctly.		
Punctuation is used correctly.		
The writing is easy to read.		
The writing is ready to be published.		

Students Practice the Strategy

In a simulation activity, Kathie places students in groups of three and tells them that they are a committee composed of John Adams, Benjamin Franklin, and Thomas Jefferson. With Kathie's help they role play these patriots. Kathie gives them a short essay chosen from their grade-level social studies text to revise and edit as a committee. Students use the Patriot Points Checklist to guide their revising and editing. Kathie monitors their collaboration and assists them as needed. As each group completes its revisions and edits, she asks them,

"How did the Patriot Points Checklist help you revise and edit?" This discussion helps students reflect on the purpose of these writing processes.

Independent Writing

Now, it's time for the students to use the Patriot Points Checklist in their own writing. Pretending they are Thomas Jefferson, they select a piece of writing from their student writing folders and apply the checklist.

Student Reflection

Kathie encourages students to share their use of the checklist with their committee and discuss how it helped them revise and edit. Again, this discussion gets students to think about the purpose of these writing processes. Members of each committee reflect and offer suggestions for each other's writing based on the Patriot Points Checklist. Kathie asks students to reflect as a class on how the Editing and Revising Through Primary Sources strategy has helped them as writers. Students then prepare their papers for final publication.

MODIFYING THE MINI-LESSON

Adaptations for Writers Who Struggle

Often, writers have difficulty with organization, creative language, and mechanics. Kathie reviews the comments and examples that students record in their Patriot Points Checklist to establish the content for individual conferences with writers who want to convey a message but experience difficulty. She uses the Writing Process Checklist (Figure 19.2) to analyze and guide their writing progress. Kathie affirms these students' ideas and thoughts and encourages them throughout the process from coming up with ideas to putting words on paper. She often serves as their scribe as they dictate their thoughts. She then walks them through the editing and revising processes, referring to class charts, language from the texts, and other references (e.g., dictionaries and thesauruses) as needed.

Adaptations for English Language Learners

A number of high-quality, high-interest, low-reading-level literature focuses on the American Revolution. These books provide students from diverse cultures and with linguistic differences an opportunity to learn about American history as they also acquire an understanding about English sentence structure and vocabulary. These materials offer English language learners (ELLs) appropriate forms of the English language in a variety of genres. Particularly, predictable texts and those with recurring refrains help ELLs understand various genres and language patterns they can use as prototypes for their own writing. As students use these books and other references for consultation, they become more comfortable with the historical facts on the topic, which in turn, assists in

Figure 19.2   Reproducible Writing Process Checklist

+ **Strong evidence**

× **Some evidence**

− **No evidence**

Questions	Teacher's Observations		
	Student A	Student B	Student C
Is the student able to map the story through prewriting strategies?			
Is the student able to orally tell the story in an organized way?			
Does the student refer to class charts and other references on the writing process?			
Does the student make the connection between the oral and written story?			
Does the student demonstrate increasing confidence in writing?			
Comments			

comprehension of primary source documents and enhances their ability to revise and edit their writing.

Adaptations for Advanced Writers

The structure of this strategy gives advanced writers opportunities to write complex pieces. The Declaration of Independence introduces students to sophisticated vocabulary that often sparks advanced writers' creativity and interest. Kathie encourages these students to consult reference materials and Internet sources to enhance their background knowledge on the Declaration of Independence and other historical documents. Then Kathie encourages them to include their extensive knowledge about a historical topic in their writing.

EXTENDING THE STRATEGY ACROSS THE CONTENT AREAS

As you might expect, Kathie uses this strategy throughout the academic year with other transdisciplinary units. For example, when students study the topic of ecology, she introduces them to the topic with newspaper and magazine articles about alternative energy and compares and contrasts the information with the content of the energy chapter in the science textbook. As a culminating unit activity, the students construct a model of a home of the future that uses green technology. Small groups of students then collaborate to write, revise, and edit an accompanying piece that describes their project. They also create and employ a Committee Green House Checklist (a variation of the Patriot Points Checklist) appropriate to the study of ecology to guide their revising and editing.

RESOURCES FOR FURTHER READING

➤ Williams, N. L., Connell, M., White, C. S., & Kemper, J. (2003). Real boats rock: A transdisciplinary approach for teacher preparation. *Action in Teacher Education, 24*(4), 95–101.

Transdisciplinary teaching and learning is an approach based on decades of research on thematic instruction. Multiple and appropriate content areas are taught in tandem, and authentic reading and writing materials are used in both approaches. Transdisciplinary teaching and learning, however, is a multifaceted model enhanced by collaboration, democratic classrooms, real-world experiences, technology, and the epiphany of learning. The authors of this article describe their partnership and construction of a novel approach to preservice teacher preparation. Literacy, science, social studies, and math methods courses were taught collaboratively within a field-based setting using common teaching themes. Preservice teachers worked in groups in planning and teaching ecologically valid and authentic lessons that incorporated these content areas. All stakeholders reported excitement about teaching and learning and stated that elementary students were motivated and more engaged in lessons. The authors advocate this approach in elementary classrooms as a solution to the criticism that many educators postulate regarding high-stakes testing and a narrowed curriculum.

> ➢ Goodman, K. S. (2003). Reading, writing, and written texts: A transactional sociopsycholinguistic view. In A. D. Flurkey & J. Xu (Eds.), *On the revolution of reading: The selected writings of Kenneth S. Goodman* (pp. 3–35). Portsmouth, NH: Heinemann.

In this chapter, Goodman reiterates the principle that the reader/writer is an active user of language. Through this orientation, teachers can examine the writing samples of their students and gain an understanding of writing development. Drawing on the transactional sociopsycholinguistic theory and model of reading, Goodman offers insights into miscue analysis, a process that provides insight into young writers' works. Goodman postulates that a writer creates new text that is influenced by individual values, experiences, and knowledge and, therefore, writes something that engages the writer in a transactional process in an effort to make sense to the audience. The processes of reading and writing are similar and should be considered to help students make sense of print.

20 Code Switching

An Editing Strategy

Rebecca Wheeler

The Code Switching Editing strategy builds on students' existing knowledge and their community dialect to add new knowledge in the form of Standard English. As they explore the concepts of *formal* and *informal* language, students learn that we all vary our speaking and writing styles to fit the setting and the occasion. In the Code Switching Editing strategy, students work with the linguistic strategies of contrastive analysis and code switching. Through contrastive analysis, students compare and contrast the grammar of the home to the grammar of the school to learn Standard English equivalents. In code switching, students learn to choose the grammar style to fit the setting and edit their papers appropriately.

WHY THIS STRATEGY IS IMPORTANT

Our schools expect all students to become adept in the Language of Wider Communication (LWC). To that end, the English language arts standards for every grade level require students to "demonstrate command of the conventions of Standard English grammar and usage when writing or speaking" (Common Core State Standards Initiative, 2011). The details of students' expected mastery evolves from Grade 1 through 12, but the expectation remains the same: Students need to master Standard English grammar.

Students who grow up speaking and writing in a vernacular dialect, such as African American Vernacular English (AAVE), may have difficulty acquiring Standard English with the traditional methods frequently used for teaching standard dialects in school. When African American students speak or write in the cadences and patterns of their home dialect, teachers typically assess their work in terms of Standard English and correct them accordingly. Yet experience and research demonstrate that the correction method does not succeed in teaching students Standard English grammar (Adger, Wolfram, & Christian, 2007; Rickford, 1999; Wheeler & Swords, 2006).

One basic insight from linguistics explains why: When vernacular-speaking students say or write *Mama jeep out of gas* or *My goldfish name is Scaley*, they are not making mistakes in their informal language Standard English; rather, they are following the grammar patterns of the home dialect (Wheeler, 2008).

By contrast, linguistically informed strategies, such as contrastive analysis and code switching, do succeed in teaching Standard English to dialectally diverse students (Rickford, 1999; Wheeler & Swords, 2006, 2010). The Code Switching Editing strategy helps students build on their existing knowledge and community English to add new knowledge in the form of Standard English. Students use this strategy in the editing stage of the writing process.

THE MINI-LESSON

Materials Needed

- SMART Board or flip chart
- Students' writing journals
- Samples of student writing that illustrate the vernacular past-time pattern
- Chart paper showing the code switching chart for showing past time (Figure 20.4 is an example)
- Chart paper showing a sample paragraph that illustrates examples of vernacular past-time uses

To match the needs of my students, I take time to analyze their speaking and writing patterns. To prepare for teaching the Code Switching Editing strategy, I build a code switching chart by finding and collecting examples of student writing showing vernacular past time (Figures 20.1 and 20.2).

Figure 20.1   Student Writing Illustrating African American Vernacular English Past-Time Patterns

Looking for the Hat
There was a boy he always wore a hat
ever when he was sleep. One day he woke up
and could not find his hat and his friends
want to see his new hat on his birthday.
He call his friends to help find the hat.

Source: Wheeler and Swords (2010, p. 100).

Figure 20.2   Student Writing Illustrating Past-Time Patterns

> name of the book was Camp rock.
> so I ask her can I trade her
> Book for my Bratz doll. She said
> it was not enough so I trade
> her for my mp3 player so we

Source: Wheeler and Swords (2010, p. 100).

For example, in student writing, I typically discover sentences such as the following:

- Yesterday I trade my MP3 player.
- We walk all around the school last night.
- Last Saturday, we watch that movie.
- I call my grandma two days ago.
- Martin Luther King talk to the people.

With these examples, I start to build our core graphic organizer, the code switching chart. This is a T-chart I will use to lead students in contrastive analysis between a local dialect and Standard English.

There are some tricks, however, to choosing what sentences go on the past-time chart. I look for sentences with "bare" verbs (verbs in the dictionary form) that take an *-ed* to show past tense in Standard English. But I want to be sure the informal sentences I choose illustrate past time and not other patterns often confused for past time. Thus, none of the examples in Figure 20.3 would go on my past-time chart. Why? Sentences 1 and 2 correspond to the Standard English perfect aspect (I have already turned . . . I had entered . . .). Sentence 3 corresponds to passive voice in Standard English (should be acknowledged), and Sentences 4 and 5 correspond to the Standard English use of past participle as adjective.

Figure 20.3   African American Vernacular English Patterns Often Confused for Showing Past Time

- I have already turn on the TV.
- I had enter the room.
- Aaliyah should be acknowledge for all of the wonderful thing she did.
- She was delight to come.
- She have a friend name Raven.

Source: Wheeler and Swords (2010, p. 101).

So I have a simple heuristic for figuring out what sentences go on the chart for showing past time and what sentences do not. I choose examples in which

- there is one and only one verb inside the main clause, and
- the verb is regular (i.e., if we translated it into Standard English, it would take an -*ed* ending).

That means I will not include any clauses that contain auxiliary verbs; I will also skip irregular verbs (see Wheeler & Swords, 2010, for more detail).

Figure 20.4 shows an example of a final code switching chart for showing past time. When I begin working with students, I use a chart such as this. Of course, I leave the grammar patterns blank until students discover them.

Figure 20.4   Showing Past-Time Patterns Chart

Past-Time Patterns	
Informal	**Formal**
Yesterday I trade my MP3 player.	Yesterday I trad<u>ed</u> my MP3 player.
We walk all around the school last night.	We walk<u>ed</u> all around the school last night.
Last Saturday we watch that movie.	Last Saturday we watch<u>ed</u> that movie.
I call my grandma two days ago.	I call<u>ed</u> my grandma two days ago.
Martin Luther King talk to the people.	Martin Luther King talk<u>ed</u> to the people.
The Pattern	**The Pattern**
Time words and phrases Common knowledge	Verb + -*ed*

Source: Excerpted from Wheeler and Swords (2010, p. 101).

Once I have the chart that fits my students' past-time needs, I analyze their editing needs. As noted previously, I have collected student writing, keeping an eye open for the range of grammar issues confronting our Standard English learners (SELs) (Wilkinson et al., 2011). Figure 20.5 shows an example of writing by a student named Tashawn; the essay contains a variety of issues. Specifically, in Tashawn's essay, I see examples of AAVE patterns for the following:

- Showing past time (Her mom call her . . . She open the door),
- Using be (She here, she here), and
- Showing possession (Yes said Annie mom; . . . and shouted Judy name).

Figure 20.5 African American Vernacular English Grammar Patterns Transferring Into Students' School Writing

It Is Time for
Me to come Now

"It is The Time That my friend Judy
come over said Annie" I can't wait
until she come said Annie" again as
her mom call her Down stairs ←Past time
oh Annie - come Down stairs it is time for
Dinner sad mom. but right befor Annie
said when is Judy coming. she heard
a knock on the Door Oh Boy
she here she here. Can I get ←Using Be
the Door. Yes said Annie mom ←Possessive
so Annie went to get the Door.
she open the Door And shouted ←Past time
Judy name out Three Times ←Possessive
Judy Judy Judy come on in
are you happy to be here with
me. Are you sad because you Left home
From North carlind did you miss Me
said Annie". yes said Judy do you want to
go to my Room . . .

Source: Wheeler and Swords (2010, p. xv).

Other students' essays show other AAVE features, including the following:

- Plurality (I have two sister.)
- Subject–verb agreement (I love her and she love me.)
- Was/were (We was going to the store.)
- Is/am/are (What is you fussin' about?)
- Habitual be (He be playing basketball every Thursday.)

These are common community dialect patterns I see year after year.

At this point, I have surveyed and assessed students' essays and reviewed my past experience, so I know what mini-lessons I need to teach. I will teach our SELs to distinguish their community English from Standard English for each of the top 10 patterns shown in Figure 20.6.

Figure 20.6   Top African American Vernacular English Patterns Transferring Into Student Writing

Noun patterns
• Possessive *The dog tail* vs. *The dog's tail*
• Plurality: "Showing more than one" *Three cat_* vs. *Three cats*

Verb patterns
• Showing past time (1) *I finish_* vs. *I finished*
• Subject–Verb Agreement *She walk_* vs. *She walks*
• Is/are *They is tall* vs. *They are tall*
• Was/were *You was sleeping* vs. *You were sleeping*
• A versus an *An rapper* vs. *A rapper* *A elephant* vs. *An elephant*
• Showing past time (2) *She seen the dog* vs. *She saw/had seen . . .*
• Be understood *He __ cool with me* vs. *He's cool with me*

These mini-lessons fit right into the writing process, because they foster students' abilities to choose their language to fit the setting.

I begin by reviewing what we have explored in previous lessons.

Teacher:	We have been talking about the terms *formal* and *informal*. Remember that *formal* is dressed up, or fancier, and *informal* is not dressed up, or casual. Someone used the word *casual* earlier this week. Who can tell me a time or occasion that you would wear something casual or speak informally? [Wheeler & Swords, 2010, p. 29]
Trevon:	When we play outside.
Kiara:	At soccer practice.
Jasmin:	I talk informally with friends.
Kendra:	Or family.

Teacher:	Who can tell me about some times and places when we might speak formally?
DeShawn:	With the principal.
Kendra:	With the mayor.
Alana:	With my minister.
Teacher:	Now let's think about actual examples of formal and informal speech. Who can give me an example of the difference?
DeShawn:	With my friends, I might say, "Yo' what's up?" but with the principal, I would say "Good Morning, Mr. Whitley."
Teacher:	That's right. Throughout each day, we choose language to fit the time and place. OK, so we've been exploring patterns in language—formal patterns and informal patterns. Today, we're going to talk about verbs. Let's talk about action! Who knows what an action verb is?
Trevon:	Something that we *do*, where we move around?
Teacher:	Yes, good! How about some examples?

Students readily respond with words such as *bake, laugh, talk, walk,* and so on. I write these on the SMART Board or a flip chart as students share their ideas.

Model the Strategy

To prepare for our grammar discovery, we begin by discussing the concept of past time.

Teacher:	What does *past time* mean? Can anyone give me an example of something that happened in the past—something that already happened?

Several students contribute, and then I reveal the code switching chart I have prepared for them based on their writing samples.

Teacher:	I'm going to model how we discover language patterns. I will read each example in the informal column. Listen carefully for how each sentence lets us know that the event happened in the past. Then, we'll talk about it together.

After reading all sentences in the informal column, I return to the first sentence.

Teacher:	"Yesterday, I trade my MP3 player." How does this show past time?
Kiara:	With the word *yesterday.*
Teacher:	Yes! The word *yesterday* tells us that the action happened in the past. Let's reread the next sentence. "We walk all around the school last night." How do we know this is set in the past?
Kendra:	*Last night* tells us it happened in the past.
Teacher:	Good work! Exactly. *Last night* also tells us the action has already taken place. Searching for clues like theses helps us discover when informal English shows past time.

Students Practice the Strategy

From this foundation, I guide students through a few moments of practice before they engage in independent practice with showing past time in both vernacular and Standard English.

Teacher:	We've explored the first two sentences on our chart discovering how informal English shows past time. Who would like to take over the teacher role for the next sentence?

Students volunteer. Misha comes up to the code switching chart.

Misha:	Class, how do we know "Last Saturday we watch that movie" happened in the past?
Class:	It says *Last Saturday.*
Misha:	Yes!

As she returns to her seat, Trevon comes up to take the teacher's role for "I call my grandpa two days ago." This leads to class discovery of past-time words and phrases.

Based on our work together, I continue.

Teacher:	Can anyone think of a rule to describe the past-time pattern in informal English?
DeShawn:	Look for words like *yesterday, last Saturday, two days ago.*
Teacher:	Yes, so maybe time words and phrases show past time! Let's write that rule at the bottom of our informal column!

	Ok! Good! Let's see if there's anything else we should look for. How about our last sentence: "Martin Luther King talk to the people." That one doesn't have any time words or phrases, but still, we know it's past. How come? How do you know it's past?
Misha:	Everyone knows that Martin Luther King was an important person in the past.
Teacher:	Oh! So we all just know! Yes! Let's call that our common knowledge. I'm going to write *common knowledge* under *The Pattern* for the informal column.
	So we see that informal English shows past time two ways—either by past-time words and phrases or by common knowledge. Great!
	Now that you've worked so well discovering the rule for showing past time in informal English, it's time to put your skills to work discovering the pattern for formal English past time. Let's look to see how the formal sentences are different from the informal ones. Talk about it with your partner. Compare what's similar between the two sentences, and then look for what's different. Once you find a difference, try to express it as a pattern. Then check each sentence to make sure your pattern really works.

In this way, students discover that both informal English and formal English have rules for showing past time. Code switching charts for this and our other code switching lessons stay up on the classroom walls for students' use during the writing process. Students consult the wall charts as they're writing their essays. They learn to choose formal English in research and formal papers, and informal English as they're creating character and voice in narrative writing. In this way, students expand their linguistic repertoires and come to own their own language choices.

Independent Writing

The Code Switching Editing strategy usually spans four sessions. Students first discover and define the grammar pattern (e.g., showing past time as demonstrated in this chapter). In Session 2, students work to classify formal and informal patterns. Students apply knowledge from Session 1 as they create sample sentences to fit the context (Figure 20.7):

Figure 20.7   Fitting your language to context

Pretend you are

1. talking to your best friend

2. writing a paper you plan to publish

3. giving a speech to the whole school

4. talking to your mom

5. talking to the principal

Source: Wheeler and Swords (2010, p. 110).

Students first choose a context and then build their own formal or informal sentences to fit that setting. As students explain their choices and the pattern they used, they deepen their understanding of how to fit language to time, place, audience, and purpose.

In Lessons 3 and 4, students edit multiple sentences. First, we all work together to edit a paragraph on chart paper. Then in our culminating lesson, students apply their understanding to their own writing. They choose one of their own essays, seek any instances of informal English past-time pattern, and then code switch to Standard English.

Student Reflection

In a wrap-up, students reflect on what was easy and what was hard as they worked to add Standard English to their linguistic toolboxes. Sometimes, I build a new code switching chart with only part of the rules filled in and then ask students to fill in the rest of the rules and explain how the rules fit the examples in the chart. Or I might ask students what was easy or what was hard for them to understand as we explored past-time patterns. Typically, some students say they were comfortable because they've been using the charts for many weeks now. Others say it was a little hard figuring out how to work the grammar patterns.

MODIFYING THE MINI-LESSON

Adaptations for Writers Who Struggle

The Code Switching Editing strategy primarily serves students who speak a vernacular or regional dialect. It helps these students to become aware of their existing knowledge (the grammar patterns of the home) and to add the grammar patterns of Standard English as used in school. With this knowledge, students practice editing their essays to choose the language appropriate to the purpose and audience.

Adaptations for English Language Learners

The linguistic insights and strategies in the Code Switching Editing strategy extend immediately to the writing of English language learners (ELLs). Of course, when students from other language backgrounds write in English, we see the influence of their native language. For instance, Spanish speakers may use many more instances of the postnominal genitive (e.g., *the house of Carmen*), whereas native English speakers would prefer *Carmen's house* precisely because Spanish uses the *of* construction. Similarly, Russian speakers may omit the verb *be* (e.g., *He big man*) because Russian does not use *be* in such sentences. The linguistic insights and strategies of contrastive analysis and code switching immediately apply as we can help nonnative English speakers to identify the pattern they are following and then add the Standard English pattern to their repertoire.

Adaptations for Advanced Writers

The Code Switching Editing strategy serves advanced writers as well. When I extend this lesson to diverse grammar structures, students gain the tools for the following core language standard: "Compare and contrast the varieties of English (e.g., *dialects, registers*) used in stories, dramas, or poems" (Common Core State Standards Initiative, 2011). As advanced writers work with the Code Switching Editing strategy, they gain the skills to truly understand the structure of different dialects in the literature they read. Since language helps create character and voice, students are well served in the literature classroom.

EXTENDING THE STRATEGY ACROSS THE CONTENT AREAS

As I teach in the content areas, I note the vernacular patterns students use in their writing, and I respond in the margins with linguistically informed techniques. For instance, if a student uses informal patterns for showing past time or for showing possession or plurality in social studies or science, I make a note in the margin: "Code switch to formal English!" Supported by code switching lessons, teachers in all subject areas can help students choose the language to fit the setting: the time, place, audience, and communicative purpose.

RESOURCES FOR FURTHER READING

➤ Turner, K. H. (2009). Flipping the switch: Code-switching from text speak to Standard English. *English Journal, 98*(5), 60–65.

Turner draws on Wheeler and Swords's (2006, 2010) work in code switching to offer methods for bringing their secondary students metacognitive awareness about their language use. As students become more conscious of when and where they use text language, they learn to code switch to choose the language style to fit the setting (see http://www.ncte.org/library/NCTEFiles/PD/Consulting/WheelerEJMay2009.pdf).

➤ Wheeler, R., & Swords, R. (2010). *Code-switching lessons: Grammar strategies for linguistically diverse writers*. First Hand Curriculum Series. Portsmouth, NH: Heinemann.

Wheeler and Swords offer hands-on, minute-by-minute lesson plans for teaching the top 10 vernacular grammar patterns transferring into student writing. Each lesson includes a unit opener that provides concrete tips on how to recognize and teach issues such as subject–verb agreement, showing past time, possessive, plurals, and so on. These tips will help teachers feel ready to respond to the grammar needs of their children, and the lessons will show them how to integrate dialect into the reading and writing classroom.

The Imagine, Describe, Resolve, and Confirm (IDRC) Strategy to Develop Students' Story Writing Abilities

21

Lindsay Sheronick Yearta, Katie Stover, Lynne Newton, and Karen Wood

The Imagine, Describe, Resolve, and Confirm (IDRC) strategy provides a "bridge" for students to make connections between reading and writing as they learn to write cohesive stories While they plan their first draft of a story, students use the IDRC chart to record the images of the setting, characters, and problems they visualize (imagine), note how they would describe the images in detail (describe), and brainstorm resolutions for problems that face the characters (resolve). Finally, authors use the ideas from the chart to revise and finish their first drafts and then confirm or refute their resolutions (confirm).

WHY THIS STRATEGY IS IMPORTANT

Through the IDRC strategy, students become familiar with the parts of the story, or story grammar. These elements include identifying the setting, character, and problems in a story (imagine and describe), and the resolution or ending of the story (resolve and confirm).

It is important for students to have opportunities to use concrete organizers to use as a framework, or writing tool, for reference as they begin to write. We explain to students that when we write, just like when we read, we continually monitor our comprehension—and our readers' potential for understanding—of the story. We do this by asking ourselves, "Do I understand what's going on? Does this make sense? Will my reader understand what I mean?" When we detect confusion, we stop writing and go back to reread what we wrote. In addition, "chunking" the text—thinking of it in terms of story elements—helps to develop organization in writing. The IDRC strategy helps students plan their stories in terms of how story elements (characters, settings, problems, solutions) relate to each other

THE MINI-LESSON

Materials Needed

- Several copies of *Owl Moon,* by Jane Yolen
- Copies of the IDRC Strategy Chart (Figure 21.1), one for each student
- Rough draft of a story by the teacher
- Students' writing notebooks
- Students' unfinished first drafts
- A document camera with a copy of the IDRC Strategy Chart (Figure 21.1) or chart paper with IDRC Strategy Chart

Model the Strategy

We always make sure students understand the concepts of characters, setting, problems, and solutions prior to reading and writing with the IDRC strategy. Once this is established, we begin.

Teacher: Today we are going to learn a new writing strategy that will help us plan and edit our writing. It's called the IDRC strategy. The letters *IDRC* stand for *imagine, describe, resolve,* and *confirm.* This strategy will help us learn how to write better descriptions of what we want our readers to imagine or visualize when they read our stories..

To model the strategy, we use *Owl Moon* by Jane Yolen (1987), a realistic fiction text that is rich in imagery and descriptive vocabulary. This story is about a little girl and her father who venture out on a cold moonlit winter night looking for a great horned owl. We introduce the book and give students a brief overview without going into too much detail. We want our students to engage in the discovery process of unfolding the story themes through the use of the IDRC strategy. We look at the cover and the illustrations contained within the

Figure 21.1 Reproducible IDRC Strategy Chart

Name _____ Date

Strategy	Instructions	Acronym	My Notes
Imagine	Close your eyes and imagine the scene, characters, and problems that you plan to place in your story. What do you see, feel, hear, smell?	I	
Describe	Describe your visual image by writing the details of what you see in your mind.	D	
Resolve	Use these details to resolve what might happen next.	R	
Confirm	After finishing the story, confirm (or refute) your resolution.	C	

book without reading the text. Next, we ask students to think about the following questions:

- What it would be like to be the little girl?
- What it would be like to be the father?
- How would it feel to be out on a cold snowy night?
- Why are they looking for the owl?

At this point, we emphasize how the author uses descriptive words and phrases that help readers form a mental picture of the setting, characters, and the events, thereby engaging the students in the story. For example, Yolen (1987) writes,

There was no wind. The trees stood still as giant statues. Our feet crunched over the crisp snow and little gray footprints followed us. (n.p.)

Pointing out the author's use of such rich vocabulary helps students transfer this skill to their own writing.

Next, we distribute copies of the IDRC Strategy Chart (Figure 21.1). Students use this chart to record their thoughts for each of the four steps. The first three stages—imagine, describe, and resolve—develop the story elements of the setting, characters, problems, themes, and the sequence of events before reading the text. The last part, the confirm phase, is where students confirm or refute how characters' solve their problems. Here's how we walk students through each part of the strategy:

Teacher:	The first step of the strategy is imagine. Close your eyes and listen to the story using your senses. Imagine you are in the story, right there in the middle of the action with the characters. Identify what feelings, tastes, smells, and sights surround you in the story.

In this way, we scaffold students' learning by guiding them to make connections between their personal experiences and the text.

Teacher:	Close your eyes and tell me how you imagine the little girl feels.
Susie:	She feels nervous and excited because she is going on an adventure.
John:	Her feet are cold, and she is a little scared.
Teacher:	Good imagining. Now let's imagine you are the father.
Tamika:	I feel strong and brave.
Scott:	I'm smart, and I know what I am doing.
Teacher:	I love the way you describe the characters. Now, let's think about the setting. That is where the story occurs.

Tia:	It is cold, and the ground is snow covered, and the moon is shining.
Anna:	The air smells clean and my face is cold. I like the softness of my mittens.
Emily:	I can hear twigs snapping under my feet, but it's mostly quiet.
Rachael:	The woods are dark and scary.
Teacher:	Where do you think they are going?
Scott:	They are going to look for an owl.
Teacher:	How do you know they are looking for an owl?
Marquis:	Because the word *owl* is in the title and owls live in the woods.

We introduce students to imaging in this way because it plays a crucial role for students as they begin to organize and plan their own writing. We find that as they write, students have much to say; however, they are still learning how to organize their thoughts in a coherent structure. Consequently, their written compositions tend to be disjointed and jump from one thought to another. To address this, we've found that imagining scenes from an existing story such as *Owl Moon* provides the students with rich descriptors of the characters, setting, and the plot of the story from which to pull ideas to extend their thinking and write about.

We write student responses on the board for all to share. Students then record their own responses in the *I*, for imagine, row of their IDRC Strategy Chart. Figure 21.2 shows a sample of an IDRC Strategy Chart completed for this exercise.

The *describe* step of the strategy provides the model for students to expand on their thoughts yet stay on topic when they write. In their own writing, students are often reluctant to describe, add detail, or expand their thoughts without encouragement and guidance (Wood & Endres, 2004). Consequently, it is crucial that we prompt them to describe their sensory images through modeling and strategic demonstration to expand their thoughts. As we read *Owl Moon*, we prompt students with phrases and questions such as the following:

- Tell me more about why you felt the little girl was scared or excited.
- Why do you think the father felt brave and strong?
- Why were they looking for the owl?
- Why do you think the story was set in the woods on a cold moonlit night?
- What do we know about owls?

Students record their response on their IDRC Strategy Chart in the *D*, for describe, row.

The third step is *resolve*, which involves getting students to use their prior knowledge to anticipate what might occur next. The resolve phase focuses on the story element of identifying the problem or event faced by the characters and brainstorming possible solutions. Some of the probing questions we ask include the following:

- How do you think the little girl felt as they went deeper and deeper into the woods?
- What do you think are some things the father will do to find the owl?
- Do you think they will find the owl?
- What do you think they will do when they find the owl?

Again, students record their predicted resolutions in *R*, for resolve, row on the IDRC Strategy Chart. These predicted resolutions are critical to help them gain meaning from connected text

At this stage, we divide students into small groups to read the story. Then we ask them to confirm their predicted resolutions. Students think aloud and explain to the whole class why their resolutions were either plausible or not. Students defend their resolutions by providing evidence from the book as support. Then they make entries in the *C*, for confirm, row of the chart.

Figure 21.2 Sample IDRC Strategy Chart

I	• I can hear twigs snapping, but it's mostly quiet. • The air smells clean and crisp. I can smell a pine tree. • It's very cold; my hands feel frozen like when I make snowballs. I can also feel the softness of the mittens. • The little girl probably feels excited, like she is going on an adventure. She might be scared or nervous. • The dad probably feels calm because he has probably done this before. • I think the owl will look like a large bird with big eyes. I think he will have lots of feathers and a sharp beak.
D	• The little girl will probably be excited because it seems like it is late at night, and I get excited when I am allowed to stay up past my bedtime. • I think she probably feels like she is going on an adventure because they are all alone out in the woods. I play with my friends in the woods, and we pretend like we're going on adventures.
R	• I think the little girl will be nervous, cold, and excited when they begin their adventure. • As they go deeper and deeper in the woods, she will probably become more nervous. • I predict that they will find the owl. The title of the book makes me think they will. • I predict that they do find the owl because I think her dad will hear the owl making a noise and they will see it, and then I think that they will take pictures of the owl.
C	• The girl was cold when they began their adventure, and I know this because the author descriptively tells us that the little girl is cold. It seems like she got more nervous as they went deeper into the woods, but she stayed brave because you have to be brave when you go owling. • They did find an owl. Dad found the owl by making owl noises, and the owl answered him back. They did not take pictures though; they just watched in awed silence. • I think that they went owling because it was a way for the girl and her dad to spend time together.

After students use the IDRC Strategy Chart to analyze the story, we make the reading–writing connection by modeling how we apply the chart to our writing.

Teacher:	Here's how I use the IDRC strategy to revise and finish a rough draft of a story I have started. You'll see that I'm going to use the same process, the same steps, and the same chart that we used with *Owl Moon*. That's because reading and writing involve similar processes. I have started a story about my favorite place, which is my backyard. I love to tend my flower and vegetable gardens there. It's a pretty good story, but I know it can be more interesting and tell a better story if I describe my backyard in more detail. So that's why I'm going to use the IDRC strategy. It will help me write more descriptively so readers get a better picture of what I'm saying.

I read the rough draft aloud and then continue.

Teacher:	Let's use the IDRC strategy to make this a better story. The first step is *I* for imagine. I close my eyes and create a mental image of my backyard as I watch the movie of my story come to life in my mind. I also make notes about what I saw in my mental images in the imagine row.

I use a document camera (chart paper showing the IDRC Strategy chart can also be used) to display the IDRC Strategy Chart as I write down my responses to these questions in the appropriate row for students to see.

Teacher:	The second step is *D* for describe. I describe, or tell more, about mental images I saw in my head when I was visualizing and imagining the story. I ask myself some sensory questions that will help me think about different aspects of my backyard: "What smells or sounds are around me?" "What do I see when I am there?" "How do I feel when I am there?" I pick a part of my story to stretch out and describe with elaboration. I imagine more details as I rewind the movie in my mind.

I write my responses to my questions in the D row for describe.

Teacher:	The third step is *R* for resolve. I think about what could happen next now that I've described my story. I identify the problems characters are facing and make predictions about how these problems will be resolved. I write them in the resolve row. Now, it is time to use my notes in the IDR rows to revise and finish my story.

I explain how I review my notes and use ideas from the IDR rows to add richer descriptions of characters, settings, and actions. Then I consider my predicted resolutions and decide how to finish the story.

After completing my first draft, I summarize my experience.

> **Teacher:** Finally, I reread my story and confirm or refute the resolutions I brainstormed earlier. The IDRC strategy has helped me not only grow as a writer, but develop as a reader. It helped me ask thoughtful questions about my writing, practice useful skills, and make connections to my personal experiences

This strategy helps the reader establish a purpose for reading; it provides the connection to stay on course, focusing on relevant facts and discarding irrelevant facts. The same constructs can be applied to writing. The IDRC strategy helps the writer establish a purpose for writing. It provides the connection to stay on topic, writing about relevant facts and omitting irrelevant facts.

Students Practice the Strategy

As we move toward letting students apply this strategy to their own writing independently, we review the IDRC process with them again and then hand out fresh charts. We help them select an unfinished first draft from their writing notebook to practice the strategy. To support their first attempts with the strategy, we discuss their sensory images pertaining to the characters, setting, and plot of the story. We ask prompting questions such as these:

- How did the character feel? Why?
- How do you know the character felt a certain way?
- What did the setting convey about the plot?

We pair students with a partner so they can help each other through the steps in this practice phase of the mini-lesson. Students find it helpful to talk about their mental imaging as they collaborate to describe, form questions about details, identify characters' problems, and brainstorm resolutions to predict what will happen next in the story.

Independent Writing

Now, it's time for students to independently use the IDRC Strategy Chart to revise and complete their own stories. Again, we hand out fresh copies of the chart. As students work through the steps, we are available to answer questions, monitor their understanding of the strategy, listen, and provide feedback. At the end of the process, we invite students to share their revised work with the class

Student Reflection

During a whole-class discussion, we ask specific students questions to prompt reflection about the strategy and the underlying constructs:

- How are the organizational thought processes we use when we read the same as those we use when we write?
- How did the IDRC strategy help you write more descriptively?
- How does making predictions about things we are reading—even our own stories—help us?
- How do the four parts of the IDRC strategy work together to help us improve our writing? For example, how do your thought processes become more organized and relevant as you move from the imagine phase to the describe and resolve phases?

MODIFYING THE MINI-LESSON

Adaptations for Writers Who Struggle

We have had great success using the IDRC strategy with struggling writers. Typically, we pair the struggling writer with a partner. This partner can be a fellow peer, parent volunteer, a classmate, a tutor, or any other willing participant. The partner provides the scaffolding that the struggling writer needs to be successful. It is common for struggling writers to have difficulty with transcribing thoughts from the mind to the paper. Partners can help alleviate this issue. Specifically, the struggling writer vocalizes the descriptions, and the partner records them on paper. An additional way that the partner can help is to provide prompts. We encourage partners to ask questions such as these:

- Can you tell me what else you see in your mind?
- How else might you resolve what happens next?
- How do you think Jane Yolen would describe that?

The use of the graphic organizer, which is embedded in the strategy, as well as the extra support that the partner provides enables struggling writers to be successful with the use of the IDRC strategy.

Adaptations for English Language Learners

This strategy is easily adapted for English language learners. We encourage ELLs to represent the imagine and resolve phases through illustrations. After the illustrations are completed, the ELL students use them as a catalyst for writing what was represented through the drawings. We write important words from the storybook on index cards in view of the students so they have visual access to the words when they begin the writing process.

Another way we adapt the IDRC strategy for ELLs is to have students orally communicate thoughts to the teacher, peer partner, or tutor who then transcribes for the student. Working in communal writing groups is also helpful for

ELLs because they receive assistance from fellow students, who become models of the composing process. Sometimes they write the entire form; sometimes they write only sections. As the student progresses, we reduce the amount of scaffolding in place.

Adaptations for Advanced Writers

The IDRC can be adapted to better serve advanced writers as well. We sometimes modify the strategy for our advanced writers by allowing the *R* in IDRC to stand for *research.* After our advanced writers have imagined and described, we encourage them to research some of their details to have a richer, more authentic piece of writing. In doing so, our students have the opportunity to enhance their writing and develop their research skills at the same time.

After students describe the images mentally, they use a range of print and digital informational resources to research aspects of the images. We ensure that our students have access to resources such as trade books, Internet resources, and encyclopedias.

Here's an example: Ryan, a fifth grader, wrote about a trip to a local beach that he took over spring break. He used this story as a catalyst to imagine and describe an exciting beach trip to a foreign country. He chose to write about a beach in Italy. He used his research time to discover the Amalfi Coast. He researched factual information about the Amalfi Coast and wove the details into his story. As a result, Ryan deepened his knowledge, authenticated his writing, and was incredibly proud of his final product.

EXTENDING THE STRATEGY ACROSS THE CONTENT AREAS

The IDRC strategy is versatile and can be tweaked and used in any subject area. For instance, it might be applied in the social studies classroom with the introduction of a new topic. Students in a class studying World War II might imagine what it would have been like to be Jewish during this time period. Students then use the whole strategy to write a story or an essay on this topic.

Students can also complete an IDRC Strategy Chart in their science journals. They can imagine what might happen at the beginning of a science experiment, describe using information from the text or prior knowledge, identify and resolve problems, and finally, confirm whether or not their resolutions (hypotheses) were plausible.

RESOURCES FOR FURTHER READING

➤ Vygotsky, L. (1962). *Thought and language.* Cambridge, MA: MIT Press.

Vygotsky believed that social context is critical to the development of mental processes and the acquisition of knowledge. He believed that children learn mental processes through shared experiences with adults and knowledgeable others. The Zone of Proximal Development includes all the functions and activities that a child or learner can perform only with the assistance of someone else. Teachers scaffold students by demonstrating the skill and assisting with the work. After giving students several exposures to a particular task, the teacher gradually releases the responsibility to the student. Eventually, the teacher withdraws the scaffolding so the student can perform the task independently.

➢ Gambrell, L. B., & Jawitz, P. B. (1993). Mental imagery, text illustrations, and children's story comprehension and recall. *Reading Research Quarterly, 28*(3), 265–276.

Successful use of comprehension strategies depends on the reader's ability to employ specific strategies to derive meaning from the text. These strategies include making predictions, summarizing, making inferences, drawing conclusions, generating questions, and monitoring for understanding. Gambrell and Jawitz posit that mental imagery has also been identified as a strategy for enhancing reading comprehension performance. Creating mental images before reading enhances students' prior knowledge, which enables them to make connections to the text. Furthermore, the authors suggest that combining the strategies of mental imagery and attention to text illustrations enhances the cognitive processing of text.

22 Probable Passages

Using Story Structure to Write and Revise a Predictive Passage

Katie Stover, Jean Payne Vintinner, Crystal P. Glover, and Karen Wood

The ability to capture ideas in writing, especially in response to reading, is essential for students to effectively communicate their understanding. The Probable Passages strategy (Wood & Taylor, 2006) actively engages students with reading and writing through the creation and revision of a written predictive passage based on their understanding of key elements of story structure. It provides a framework for students to compose a written prediction of the text they will read. After reading, students revise their writing to construct an accurate summary of the text.

WHY THIS STRATEGY IS IMPORTANT

Students in Grades 4 through 8 must be able to recognize story structure, or the elements that tie fiction together. All well-written stories have characters, settings, problems, and solutions. Characters have goals and attempt to reach their goals. Stories present outcomes—success or failure of characters' attempts to reach goals—and a well-defined ending (Mandler & Johnson, 1977; Stein & Glenn, 1979).

Although these students usually have little difficulty recognizing story elements in fiction, they may need guidance to include all the elements in their own writing. When we provide students with opportunities to identify story structure as they read or listen to fiction, we give them a cognitive framework that helps them write their own stories that contain all the necessary story elements.

THE MINI-LESSON

Materials Needed

- Several copies of the blank Probable Passages Concept Frame (Figure 22.1) for each student
- Several copies of the blank Probable Passages Passage Form (Figure 22.2) for each student
- Chart paper or a projector to model the strategy
- One copy of Figure 22.3: Reproducible Chart for Key Terms Categorized by Story Elements in the Concept Frame, prepared for display or projection
- One copy of the Concept Frame for making predictions
- One copy of the Concept Frame for amending work after reading
- Copies of the text being studied
- A list of terms from the text that are significant to students' comprehension of the story or novel (e.g., words that relate directly to elements of the story and previously unknown words that students will need to know to fully understand the text) (Figure 22.4)

Model the Strategy

To support students' application of the Probable Passages strategy, we provide a large version of a blank concept frame (Figure 22.1) on chart paper or illuminated by on an overhead or computer projector so that as we model the strategy, everyone can see our work. We also hand out blank copies for students to fill in for themselves as we work.

Our first step is to determine the students' understanding of story elements. We select a story (or stories) we have previously read and discussed and then ask them to identify each of the elements listed on the handout as it applies to that story. We ask questions such as the following:

- Where and when did the story take place?
- What happened as a result of the characters' actions?

If any students seem to struggle with these concepts, we view this discussion as a great opportunity to work collaboratively as a class to define and provide examples of each of these building blocks of stories (Wood & Taylor, 2006).

As we talk with students about how characteristics of stories can influence our ability to understand them, we pose a series of questions that push students to explicitly define aspects of story elements. For example:

- How do you learn about a character?
- How would you gather information about a setting?

Figure 22.1   Reproducible Probable Passages Concept Frame

Name _____ Date _____

Probable Passages Concept Frame
Setting Character Problem Solution Ending

Figure 22.2   Reproducible Probable Passages Passage Form

Passage Form
The story takes place _____.
_____ is a character in the story who _____.
A problem occurs when _____.
After that, _____.
Next, _____.
The problem is solved when _____.
The story ends with _____.

Figure 22.3 Reproducible Chart for Key Terms Categorized by Story Elements in the Concept Frame

Setting	Character	Problem	Solution	Ending

We also explain how understanding story elements—what words such as *character, setting,* and *problem* mean and how they interact with each other—can support comprehension of a story.

Once we are sure that students understand the store elements, we model the Probable Passages strategy in front of the class, using the list of words we've prepared in advance. For the text *Bud, Not Buddy* by Christopher Paul Curtis (1999), which will be the example we explore throughout this chapter, we selected words that identify characters, settings, and themes integral to the plot; we also included words we thought students might not be familiar with (Figure 22.4).

Figure 22.4   Key Terms From *Bud, Not Buddy* (Curtis, 1999)

Depression	Jazz	Herman Calloway
Orphanage	Suitcase	Prejudice
Locomotive	Bud (not Buddy)	Flyer
Shantytown	On the lam	Michigan

To begin, we explain that they will use their knowledge of words to predict what will happen in the novel *Bud, not Buddy* by writing a short passage of what is the most *probable result* based on the information we will provide them.

To ensure that students understand the task, we think aloud a sample response.

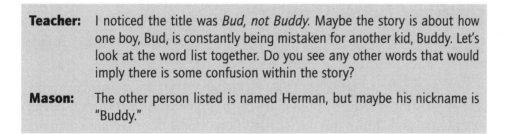

Teacher: I noticed the title was *Bud, not Buddy*. Maybe the story is about how one boy, Bud, is constantly being mistaken for another kid, Buddy. Let's look at the word list together. Do you see any other words that would imply there is some confusion within the story?

Mason: The other person listed is named Herman, but maybe his nickname is "Buddy."

Then we work together to use the words from the list to fill out the story element chart (Figure 22.3). For instance, as we discuss the remaining story elements, we point out that the words that may be slotted in the Problem category may be words that have a negative connotation, whereas words for the Solution category may be more positive in nature.

We then continue, discussing as a group what each of the words on the list might mean and how they might be related. When a word fits within more than one category, we encourage students to discuss their reasoning, extend their understanding of the words, and make decisions about what fit is best. Figure 22.5 shows an example of a completed chart.

Figure 22.5 Key Terms Categorized by Story Elements in the Concept Frame

Setting	Character	Problem	Solution	Ending
Michigan orphanage shantytown	Bud Herman Calloway	on the lam depression prejudice suitcase (not Buddy)	locomotion	jazz flyer

Our next step involves modeling and thinking aloud how we fill in the Passage Form (Figure 22.2).

We begin by looking at the story frame that begins, "The story takes place . . ." We think aloud while referencing our story element chart (Figure 22.5).

Teacher:	I notice that *Michigan, orphanage,* and *shantytown* are the places we determined as our setting. If I want to write a beginning sentence for my predictive passage so my readers know where the story is happening, I may write, "The story takes place in an orphanage in Michigan." Now let's look at the character category. Who do you think Bud is?
Mollie:	Maybe he is the student.
Teacher:	Great! What about Herman?
Jordi:	Hmm, maybe he is Bud's friend.
Teacher:	Do all these characters look like they would be at an orphanage?
Jordi:	Maybe. I'm not really sure what an orphanage is.
Teacher:	So do you think there is another setting?
Tim:	Well, we mentioned there is also a shantytown.

We continue to scaffold students' predictions about the characters, setting, and plot and eventually use this knowledge to create an entire Probably Passage storyline (Figure 22.6). It is often beneficial to model this step more than once to scaffold the process.

Figure 22.6 Sample Probable Passage

The story takes place at an orphanage in Michigan. Bud is a character in the story who is depressed because he is mistaken for Buddy. A problem occurs when Bud goes on the lam. After that he loses his suitcase. Next, Bud and Herman go to live in a shantytown. The problem is solved when they take a ride on a locomotive and return to their hometown. The story ends when the boys take a flyer and get to hear jazz music with their families.

After we complete the probable passage, we ask students to read the selected text to make comparisons between our predictions and what actually happens in the story. Students may read individually or in pairs, based on their abilities, their familiarity with the strategy, and the length of the text. When they are finished, the class gathers again so we can model how to reflect on the similarities and differences between the predictions and the text. Together, we amend both the Concept Frame and the Probable Passage Form to reflect the actual events in the story. Figure 22.7 shows an example of amended forms.

Figure 22.7   Amended Concept Frame and Probable Passage

Setting	Character	Problem	Solution	Ending
Michigan Depression era	Bud Herman Calloway	orphanage prejudice shantytown on the lam	suitcase flyer locomotion	jazz

The story takes place during the Depression era in Michigan. Bud, not Buddy, is a character in the story who is living in an orphanage because his mother has died and he can't find his father. A problem occurs when Bud decides to go on the lam and search for his father. After that he visits a shantytown and hops on a locomotive while trying to find his dad. Next, Bud tries to find Herman Calloway, who he believes is his dad, because his mom had a flyer for his jazz band. The problem is solved when Bud finally finds Herman, based on information he found on the flyer he now keeps the flyer in his suitcase. The story ends when Bud realizes Herman, still a jazz musician, is his grandfather.

Students Practice the Strategy

To help scaffold students' application of this strategy, we revisit the procedure the next day with a different text. During practice, we guide students to preview the text to find words that are new, interesting, or seem relevant to the story based on what they may already know from the title or illustrations. They use these self-selected words to complete blank copies of the Concept Frame and then fill in new copies of the Passage Form, predicting a possible storyline. Once again, students read the selection individually or in pairs, and then they work together to make appropriate changes to their probable passage summary.

Independent Writing

At this stage, students are responsible for completing all phases of this strategy with the least amount of support necessary. We may select the text or leave the decision to students. Their tasks are to

- apply their understanding of the strategy to scan the text for suitable terms,
- use their knowledge of story structure to create a prediction that seems plausible,

- build their vocabulary as they contextualize the terms to place them into the Concept Frame correctly, and
- synthesize their predictions with what actually happens in the text, identifying the similarities and differences between the two.

In some cases, individuals or small groups make require additional support. We encourage students to make connections to other words and other stories and employ fix-up strategies when they struggle with comprehension. During the entire process, we guide students as they develop their comprehension skills while interacting with text and improve their writing skills as they record both their predictions and the actual plot.

Student Reflection

To help students understand the value of this strategy, we ask them to compare their Probable Passages with their classmates' work. This step offers many benefits:

- As students evaluate together what terms they chose and why they chose them, they are exposed to their classmates' thinking processes, which helps expand their own vocabulary and comprehension.
- By sharing their Probable Passages, students gain exposure to multiple narrative models for writing.
- Predicting possible plotlines provides students with a purpose for reading that improves metacognitive skills and increases comprehension.
- Reading and writing practice in a low-risk collaborative environment allows students to build motivation and self-efficacy in the classroom.

MODIFYING THE STRATEGY

Adaptations for Writers Who Struggle

Struggling writers benefit from modeling and guided writing activities (Brotherton & Williams, 2002). To support students who have difficulty writing, we adapt the Probable Passages strategy to include extensive teacher modeling and guided writing support. Interactive writing is a form of guided writing that involves teacher modeling and encourages student participation (McCarrier, Pinnell, & Fountas, 1999). Using this method, we jointly construct a probable passage with students using a "shared pen" approach. Through the mutual creation of a probable passage, struggling writers contribute to the production of a quality writing piece in a supportive, nonthreatening context. As these students experience success in the writing process, they are more likely to view themselves as successful writers.

Adaptations for English Language Learners

To help English language learners (ELLs) achieve success with probable passages, we tailor instruction to address their specific needs. As we introduce key vocabulary from the story, we help ELLs make connections to familiar and unfamiliar concepts. This is easily achieved through background-building strategies such as previewing pictures and activating schema. For example, prior to reading the story, we engage ELLs in a picture walk to help them become familiar with the context of the story. During the picture walk, we highlight concepts that are unfamiliar to the students. Once these connections are established, we proceed through the Probable Passages strategy using a Language Experience Approach (Stauffer, 1970). In this approach, students receive grammatically correct models of written passages that are inclusive of the students' first language yet increase their understanding of key concepts and vocabulary from the story.

Adaptations for Advanced Writers

Advanced writers require less scaffolding throughout the probable passage experience. In fact, they are often capable of constructing a probable passage individually or in pairs. In this case, they may skip the step where the whole class constructs a passage together. We also modify the requirements of the probable passage for advanced writers to include their prediction of minor events that lead up to the major problem in the story. Often, we ask them to justify in writing the thinking behind their predictions.

EXTENDING THE STRATEGIES ACROSS THE CONTENT AREAS

The Probable Passages strategy supports students in content area classes as well. In social studies, students can create hypotheses of what they believe to be true about various historical figures and events based on their present level of knowledge. This activity not only allows students to make predictions about what they are preparing to read, it also provides teachers with an opportunity to pre-assess student knowledge and identify misconceptions. After the reading, students compare their predictions with actual events and discuss their reasoning.

The Probable Passages strategy can help students in math classes as they attempt to tackle word problems. By assessing all the possible information provided in a word problem, students predict possible computations. This step allows them to evaluate the possible problem from many angles. When they tackle the actual problem, they can choose the most efficient solution. The Probable Passages strategy supports any content area in which students must make sense of new material and ideas.

RESOURCES FOR FURTHER READING

➢ Rumelhart, D. E. (1980). Schemata: The building blocks of cognition. In R. J. Spiro (Ed.), *Theoretical issues in reading comprehension* (pp. 35–58). Hillsdale, NJ: Lawrence Erlbaum.

The concept of schema theory relates to the categorization and storage of new knowledge in the brain. This knowledge is broken down into meaningful structures in memory as an organized way to facilitate recall of knowledge. This system of organized prior knowledge into related networks of information is referred to as *schemata.* To acquire new information during reading, for example, it is necessary to tap into prior knowledge to make connections with the new learning.

➤ Pearson, P. D., & Gallagher, M. (1983). The instruction of reading comprehension, *Contemporary Educational Psychology, 8,* 317–344.

The Gradual Release Model introduced by Gallagher and Pearson is an effective way to guide students through an instructional framework that leads to deeper understanding and successful learning. After direct instruction and guidance, students learn by doing. The teacher scaffolds the learning until the students can implement the skill or strategy independently; this process helps students understand the skills and strategies being taught. This is what occurs during the Probable Passages strategy as the teacher models and demonstrates through the use of think-aloud and then, eventually, eliminates the scaffolds so students can work on their own.

References

Achieve, Inc. (2005). *Rising to the challenge. Are high school graduates prepared for college and work?* Washington, DC: Author.

ACT. (2005). *Crisis at the core: Preparing all students for college and work.* Iowa City, IA: Author.

Adger, C. T., Wolfram, W., & Christian, D. (2007). *Dialects in schools and communities.* Mawah, NJ: Lawrence Erlbaum.

Aliki. (1985). *Mummies made in Egypt.* New York, NY: HarperCollins.

Alliance for Excellent Education Issue Brief. (2006). *Reading and writing in the academic content areas.* Retrieved from http://www.all4ed.org/files/ReadingWritingAcad Content.pdf

Altieri, J. L. (2011). *Content counts! Developing disciplinary literacy skills, K–6.* Newark, DE: International Reading Association.

American Psychological Association. (2010). *Publication manual of the American Psychological Association* (6th ed.). Washington, DC: American Psychological Association.

Ansary, T. (1997). *Mysterious places.* Portland, ME: J. Weston Walch.

Applebee, A., & Langer, J. A. (1987). *How writing shapes thinking: A study of teaching and learning.* Urbana, IL: National Council of Teachers of English.

Baker, L., & Wigfield, A. (1999). Dimensions of children's motivation for reading and their relations to reading activity and reading achievement. *Reading Research Quarterly, 34,* 452–477.

Baldwin, C. (2008). *Teaching the story: Fiction writing in grades 4–8.* Gainesville, FL: Maupin.

Barnes, D. (1992). *From communication to curriculum* (2nd ed.). Portsmouth, NH: Heinemann.

Berninger, V. W., Nagy, W., & Beers, S. (2010). Child writers' construction and reconstruction of single sentences and construction of multi-sentence texts: Contributions of syntax and transcription to translation. *Reading and Writing, 24,* 151–182. doi:10.1007/s11145–010–9262-y

Boers, F., Eyckmans, J., Kappel, J., Stengers, H., & Demecheleer, M. (2006). Formulaic sequences and perceived oral proficiency: Putting a lexical approach to the test. *Language Teaching Research, 10*(3), 245–261.

Borko, H. (2004). Professional development and teacher learning: Mapping the terrain. *Educational Researcher, 33*(8), 3–15.

Brotherton, S., & Williams, C. (2002). Interactive writing instruction in a first grade Title I literacy program. *Journal of Reading Education, 27*(3), 8–19.

Calkins, L. (1994). *The art of teaching writing.* Portsmouth, NH: Heinemann.

Carlson, L. (1995). *Cool salsa: Bilingual poems on growing up Hispanic in the United States.* New York, NY: Fawcett.

Cassidy, J., & Cassidy, D. (2009). What's hot for 2009. *Reading Today, 26*(4), 1, 8, 9.

Cassidy, J., & Cassidy, D. (2010). What's hot for 2010. *Reading Today, 27*(3), 1, 8, 9.

Cassidy, J., & Lovelace, D. J. (2011, October/November). More about the 2012 what's hot what's not literacy survey. *Reading Today,* 16–21.

Chalk, J., Hagen-Burke, S., & Burke, M. (2005). The effects of self-regulated strategy development on the writing process for high school students with learning disabilities. *Learning Disability Quarterly, 28*(1), 75–87.

Chapman, M. (1997). *Weaving webs of meaning: Writing in the elementary school.* Toronto, Ontario, Canada: ITP Nelson.

Coker, D. (2007). Writing instruction for young children: Methods targeting the multiple demands that writers face. In S. Graham, C. S. MacArthur, & J. Fitzgerald (Eds.), *Best practices in writing instruction* (pp. 101–118). New York, NY: Guilford Press.

Coles, R. (1995). *The story of Ruby Bridges.* New York, NY: Scholastic.

Collins, J. L. (1998). *Strategies for struggling writers.* New York, NY: Guilford Press.

Common Core State Standards Initiative. (2011). *Common core state standards for English language arts & literacy in history/social studies, science, and technical subjects.* Retrieved from http://www.corestandards.org

Cornwell's writing guide. (2008–2009). Retrieved from http://www.scasd.org/cms/lib5/PA01000006/Centricity/Domain/1369/WritingGuide.pdf

Curtis, C. P. (1999). *Bud, not Buddy.* New York, NY: Delacorte Books.

Daniels, H. (2002). *Literature circles: Voice and choice in book clubs and reading groups.* Portland, ME: Stenhouse.

De La Paz, S., & Graham, S. (2002). Explicitly teaching strategies, skills and knowledge: Writing instruction in middle school classrooms. *Journal of Educational Psychology, 94,* 687–698.

Dorfman, L. R., & Cappelli, R. (2007). *Mentor texts: Teaching writing through children's literature, K–6.* Portland, ME: Stenhouse.

Dworin, J. E. (2006). The Family Stories Project: Using funds of knowledge for writing. *Reading Teacher, 59*(6), 510–520. doi:10.1598/RT.59.6.1

Englert, C. S., Mariage, T. V., & Dunsmore, K. (2006). Tenets of sociocultural theory in writing instruction. In C. A. MacArthur, S. Graham, & J. Fitzgerald (Eds.), *Handbook of writing research* (pp. 208–221). New York, NY: Guilford Press.

Fine, J. C. (2004). Reciprocal mapping: Scaffolding students' literacy to higher levels. In A. Rogers & E. M. Rogers (Eds.), *Scaffolding literacy instruction: Strategies for K–4 Classrooms* (pp. 88–104). Portsmouth, NH: Heinemann.

Fitzgerald, J. (1987). Research on revision in writing. *Review of Educational Research, 57,* 481–506.

Fitzgerald, J., & Amendum, S. (2007). What is sound writing instruction for multilingual learners? In S. Graham, C. A. MacArthur, & J. Fitzgerald (Eds.), *Best practices in writing instruction* (pp. 289–307). New York, NY: Guilford Press,

Fletcher, R. (1993). *What a writer needs.* Portsmouth, NH: Heinemann.

Fletcher, R., & Portalupi, J. (2007). *Craft lessons: Teaching writing K–8.* New York, NY: Stenhouse.

Fontenot, J., & Carney, K. (2008). *Blueprint for exceptional writing.* Boston, MA: Pearson Education.

Fuchs, D., & Fuchs, L.S. (2001). Responsiveness-to-intervention: A blueprint for practitioners, policymakers, and parents. *Teaching Exceptional Children, 38*(1), 57–61.

Gambrell, L. B. (1982, December). *Induced mental imagery and the written expression of young children.* Paper presented at International Reading Conference, Clearwater Beach, FL. Retrieved from ERIC database. (ED 228632)

Gambrell, L. B., & Jawitz, P. B. (1993). Mental imagery, text illustrations, and children's story comprehension and recall. *Reading Research Quarterly, 28*(3), 265–276.

Ganske K., Monroe, J. K., & Strickland, D. S. (2003). Questions teachers ask about struggling readers and writers. *The Reading Teacher, 57*(2), 118–128.

Goodman, K. S. (2003). Reading, writing, and written texts: A transactional sociopsycholinguistic view. In A. D. Flurkey & J. Xu (Eds.), *On the revolution of reading: The selected writings of Kenneth S. Goodman* (pp. 3–35). Portsmouth, NH: Heinemann.

Graham, S., & Harris, K. (2005). Improving the writing performance of young struggling writers. *Journal of Special Education, 39*(1), 19–33.

Graham, S., & Harris, K. R. (2007). Best practices in teaching planning. In S. Graham, C. A. MacArthur, & J. Fitzgerald (Eds.), *Best practices in writing instruction* (pp. 119–140). New York, NY: Guilford Press.

Graham, S., & Herbert, M. A. (2010). *Writing to read: Evidence for how writing can improve reading.* A Carnegie Corporation Time to Act Report. Washington, DC: Alliance for Excellent Education. Retrieved from http://72.47.207.55/files/WritingToRead.pdf

Graham, S., MacArthur, C. A., & Fitzgerald, J. (Eds.). (2007). *Best practices in writing instruction.* New York, NY: Guildford Press.

Graham, S., & Perin, D. (2007a). A meta-analysis of writing instruction for adolescent students. *Journal of Educational Psychology, 99,* 445–476. doi:10.1037/0022–0663.99.3.445

Graham, S., & Perin, D. (2007b). *Writing next: Effective strategies to improve writing of adolescents in middle and high schools.* A Report to Carnegie Corporation of New York. Washington, DC: Alliance for Excellent Education.

Graves, D. H. (1994). *A fresh look at writing.* Portsmouth, NH: Heinemann.

Greene, M. (1995). *Releasing the imagination.* San Francisco, CA: Jossey-Bass.

Gregorian, V. (2010). Forward. In S. Graham & M. A. Hebert, *Writing to read: Evidence for how writing can improve reading.* A Carnegie Corporation Time to Act Report. Washington, DC: Alliance for Excellent Education.

Gutman, D. (2007). *The homework machine.* New York, NY: Simon & Schuster Children's.

Hammann, L. A., & Stevens, R. J. (2003). Instructional approaches to improving students' writing of compare-contrast essays: An experimental study. *Journal of Literacy Research, 35*(2), 731–756. doi:10.1207/s15548430jlr3502_3

Hampton, S., & Resnick, L. B. (2009). Effective writing. In *Reading and writing with understanding* (pp. 55–72). Newark, DE: National Center on Education and the Economy and University of Pittsburgh.

Harris, K. R., & Graham, S. (1992). Self-regulated strategy development: A part of the writing process. In M. Pressley, K. R. Harris, & J. Guthrie (Eds.), *Promoting academic competence and literacy in school* (pp. 277–309). New York, NY: Academic Press.

Harris, K., Graham, S., Brindle, M., & Sandmel, K. (2009). Metacognition and children's writing. In D. J. Hacker, J. Dunloskey, & A. Graesson (Eds.), *Handbook of metacognition in education* (pp. 131–153). Abingdon, Oxon, UK: Routledge.

Hayes, J. R. (2004). What triggers revision? In L. Allal, L. Chanquoy, & P. Largy (Eds.), *Revision: Cognitive and instructional processes* (Vol. 13, pp. 9–20). Norwell, MA: Kluwer.

Heller, R. (1999). *The reason for a flower.* New York, NY: Grosset & Dunlop.

Hillocks, G., Jr. (1986). *Research on written composition.* New Directions for Teaching. Urbana, IL: National Council of Teachers of English.

Hoffner, H., Baker, E., & Quinn, K. B. (2008). Lights, cameras, pencils! Using descriptive video to enhance writing. *The Reading teacher, 61*(7), 576–579.

Holliway, R. D., & McCutchen, D. (2004). Audience perspective in young writers' composing and revising. In L. Allal, L. Chanquoy, & P. Largy (Eds.), *Revision: Cognitive and instructional processes* (pp. 157–170). Norwell, MA: Kluwer Academic.

Hong Xu, S. (2005). *Trading cards to comic strip: Popular culture texts and literacy learning in grades K–8*. Newark, DE: International Reading Association.

Hunt, K. W. (1965). *Grammatical structures written at three grade levels* (Research Rep. No. 3). Champaign, IL: National Council of Teachers of English.

Jacques, B. (1994). *The bellmaker: A novel of Redwall*. New York, NY: Ace Books.

Kam'enui, E. J., Carnine D. W., Dixon, D. C., Simmons, D. C., & Coyne, M. D. (2002). *Strategies for teaching students that accommodate diverse learners*. Columbus, OH: Merrill.

Keck, C. (2006). The use of paraphrase in summary writing: A comparison of L1 and L2 writers. *Journal of Second Language Writing, 15*(4), 261–278.

Kleon, A. (2007). The figure skater [Framed art]. A blackout poem. Retrieved from http://www.20x200.com/artworks/1733-austin-kleon-the-figure-skater

Kleon, A. (2010). *Newspaper blackout*. New York, NY: Harper.

Kolln, M. (1999). Cohesion and coherence. In C. R. Cooper & L. Odell (Eds.), *Evaluating writing: The role of teachers' knowledge about text, learning, and culture* (pp. 93–113). Urbana, IL: National Council of Teachers of English.

Leigh, S. R. (2010). Cut up, cover up, and come away with ideas for writing! ReadWriteThink [Lesson plan]. Retrieved from http://www.readwritethink.org/classroom-resources/lesson-plans/cover-come-away-with-30617.html

Leigh, S. R. (2012). Re-seeing story through portal writing. *Journal of the Assembly on Expanded Perspectives in Learning, 17*, 83–94.

Lemke, M., Sen, A., Pahlke, E., Partelow, L., Miller, D., Williams, T., . . . Jocelyn, L. (2004). *International outcomes of learning in mathematics literacy and problem solving: PISA 2003 Results from the U.S. perspective* (NCES 2005–003). Washington, DC: U.S. Department of Education, Institute of Educational Sciences, National Center for Educational Statistics.

Lenski, S. D., & Johns, J. L. (2004). *Improving writing: Strategies, assessments, and resources*. Dubuque, IA: Kendall/Hunt.

MacArthur, C. A. (2007). Best practices in teaching evaluation and revision. In S. Graham, C. A. MacArthur, & J. Fitzgerald (Eds.), *Best practices in writing instruction* (pp. 141–162). New York, NY: Guilford Press.

Mandler, J., & Johnson, N. (1977). Remembrance of things parsed: Story structure and recall. *Cognitive Psychology, 9*, 111–151.

Marzano, R. J., Pickering, D. J., & Pollock, J. E. (2004). *Classroom instruction that works: Research-based strategies for increasing student achievement*. Alexandria, VA: Association for Supervision and Curriculum Development.

McCarrier, A., Pinnell, G. S., & Fountas, I. (1999). *Interactive writing: How language and literacy come together, K–2*. Portsmouth, NH: Heinemann.

McCarrier, A., Pinnell, G. S., & Fountas, I. C. (2000). *Interactive writing*. Portsmouth, NH: Heinemann.

McCutchen, D., Francis, M., & Kerr, S. (1997). Revising for meaning: Effects of knowledge and strategy. *Journal of Educational Psychology, 89*, 667–676.

Mellon, J. C. (1967). *Transformational sentence-combining: A method for enhancing the development of syntactic fluency in English composition*. Champaign, IL: National Council of Teachers of English.

Meyer, B. J. F. (1982). Reading research and the composition teacher: The importance of plans. *College Composition and Communication, 33*, 37–49.

Meyer, B. J. F., Brandt, D. M., & Bluth, G. J. (1980). Use of the top-level structure in text: Key for reading comprehension of ninth-grade students. *Reading Research Quarterly, 16*, 72–103.

Meyer, B. J. F., & Freedle, R. O. (1984). Effects of discourse types on recall. *American Educational Research Journal, 21*, 121–143.

Meyer, B. J. F., Middlemiss, W., Theodorou, E., Brezinski, K. L., McDougall, J., & Bartlett, B. J. (2002). Effects of structure strategy instruction delivered to fifth-grade children via the Internet with and without the aid of older adult tutors. *Journal of Educational Psychology, 94,* 486–519.

Meyer, B. J. F., Wijekumar, K., Middlemiss, W., Higley, K., Lei, P., Meier, C., & Spielvogel, J. (2010). Web-based tutoring of the structure strategy with or without elaborated feedback or choice for fifth- and seventh-grade readers. *Reading Research Quarterly, 45,* 62–92. Retrieved from http://dx.doi.org/10.1598/RRQ.45.1.4

Morgan, M. (1999). *How to proofread and edit your writing: A guide for student writers.* Retrieved from ERIC database. (ED464346)

Murray, D. (1991). *The craft of revision.* Austin, TX: Holt, Rinehart, & Winston.

National Center to Improve the Tools of Educators. (2001). Assessed December 2010. Online. idea.uoregon/edu/-ncite

National Commission on Writing. (2003). *The neglected "R": The need for a writing revolution.* New York, NY: College Entrance Examination Board. Retrieved from http://www.vantagelearning.com/docs/myaccess/neglectedr.pdf

Neville, D. (1985). The effects of sentence-combining and kernel-identification training on the syntactic component of reading comprehension. *Research in the Teaching of English, 19,* 37–61.

Newell, G. E., Koukis, S., & Boster, S. (2007). Best practices in developing writing across the curriculum program in the secondary school. In S. Graham, C. A. MacArthur, & J. Fitzgerald (Eds.), *Best practices in writing instruction* (pp. 74–100). New York, NY: Guilford Press.

Nickell, J. (2000, April). The secrets of Oak Island. *Skeptical Inquirer: Investigative Files, 24*(2). Retrieved from http://www.csicop.org/si/show/secrets_of_oak_island/

Norton, D. (2007). *Literacy for life.* Boston, MA: Pearson.

Oczkus, L., Baura, G., Murray, K., & Berry, K. (2006). Using the love of "poitchry" to improve primary sudents' writing. *The Reading Teacher, 59*(5), 475–479.

O'Hare, F. (1973). *Sentence combining.* Champaign, IL: National Council of Teachers of English.

Olinghouse, N. G., Zheng, J., & Reed, D. M. (2010). Preparing students for large-scale writing assessments. In G. A. Troia, R. K. Shankland, & A. E. Heintz (Eds.), *Putting writing research into practice: Applications for teacher professional development* (pp. 17–44). New York, NY: Guilford Press.

Olson, L. (2006). A decade of effort. *Quality Counts, 25,* 8–10, 12, 14, 16, 18–21.

Organisation for Economic Co-operation and Development. (2000). *Literacy in the information age: Final report of the adult literacy survey.* Paris, France: Author.

Page-Voth, T. (2010). Effective professional development for teachers of struggling writers. In G. Troia, R. Shankland, & A. Heinz (Eds.), *Putting writing research into practice: Applications for teacher professional development* (pp. 229–256). New York, NY: Guilford Press.

Patel, P., & Laud, L. (2009). Helping students to add detail and flair to their stories. *Preventing School Failure, 54*(1), 2–9.

Pearson, P. D., & Gallagher, M. (1983). The instruction of reading comprehension. *Contemporary Educational Psychology, 8,* 317–344.

Persky, H. R., Daane, M. C., & Jin, Y. (2003). *The nation's report card: Writing 2002* (NCES 2003–529). Washington, DC: U.S. Department of Education Office of Educational Research and Improvement, National Center for Educational Statistics. Retrieved from http://nces.ed.gov/nationsreportcard/pdf/main2002/203529.pdf

Phillips, T. (2005). *The humument: A treated Victorian novel.* London: Thames & Hudson.

Reutzel, D. R., & Cooter, R. B. (2009). *The essentials of teaching children to read: The teacher makes the difference.* Boston, MA: Allyn & Bacon.

Richards, J. C., & Lassonde, C. A. (2011). *Writing strategies for all primary students: Scaffolding independent writing with differentiated mini-lessons.* San Francisco, CA: Jossey-Bass.

Richards, J., & Miller, S. (2005). *Doing academic writing in education: Connecting the personal with the professional.* New York, NY: Routledge, Taylor & Francis.

Richardson, J. S., Morgan, R. F., & Fleener, C. E. (2012). *Reading to learn in the content areas.* Belmont, CA: Wadsworth Cengage.

Rickford, R. (1999). *African-American vernacular English: Features, evolution, educational implications.* Malden, MA: Wiley-Blackwell.

Rijlaarsdam, G., Couzijn, M., & van den Bergh, H. (2004). The study of revision as a writing process and as a learning-to-write process: Two prospective research agendas. In L. Allal, L. Chanquoy, & P. Largy (Eds.), *Revision: Cognitive and instructional processes* (Vol. 13, pp. 189–208). Norwell, MA: Kluwer.

Rombauer, I. S., Becker, M. R., & Becker, E. (2006). *The joy of cooking.* New York, NY: Scribner.

Routman, R. (2005). *Writing essentials: Raising expectations and results while simplifying teaching.* Portsmouth, NH: Heinemann.

Rumelhart, D. E. (1980). Schemata: The building blocks of cognition. In R. J. Spiro (Ed.), *Theoretical issues in reading comprehension* (pp. 35–58). Hillsdale, NJ: Lawrence Erlbaum.

Ryan, P. M. (2010). Pam Muñoz Ryan on the writing process [Web blog message]. Retrieved from http://forum.teachingbooks.net/?p=3764

Saddler, B., & Asaro-Saddler, K. (2010). Writing better sentences: Sentence-combining instruction in the classroom. *Preventing School Failure, 54*(3), 159–163.

Schleppegrell, M. J. (2004). Characterizing the language of schooling. In *The language of schooling: A functional linguistics perspective* (pp. 1–20). Mahwah, NJ: Erlbaum.

Skinner, E. N., & Hagood, M. C. (2008). Developing literate identities with English language learners through digital storytelling. *The Reading Matrix, 8*(2), 12–38.

Spandel, V. (2008). *Creating young writers: Using the six traits to enrich writing process in primary classroom.* New York, NY: Pearson.

Stauffer, R. G. (1970). *The language-experience approach to the teaching of reading.* New York, NY: Harper & Row.

Stein, N., & Glenn, C. (1979). An analysis of story comprehension in elementary school children. In R. D. Freedle (Ed.), *Advances in discourse processes: Vol. 2. New directions in discourse processing* (pp. 53–119). Norwood, NJ: Ablex.

Strauss, S., & Xiang, X. (2006). The writing conference as a locus of emergent agency. *Written Communication, 23*(4), 355–396. Retrieved from ERIC database. (EJ745067)

Strickland, D. S., Ganske, K., & Monroe, J. K. (2002). *Supporting struggling readers and writers: Strategies for classroom intervention 3–6.* Portland, ME: Stenhouse.

Strong, R., Silver, H., & Robinson, A. (1995). What do students want (and what really motivates them)? *Educational Leadership, 53*(1), 8–12. Retrieved from http://www.ascd.org/publications/educational-leadership/sept95/vol53/num01/Strengthening-Student-Engagement@-What-Do-Students-Want.aspx

Strong, W. (1986). *Creative approaches to sentence combining.* Theory & Research Into Practice Series. Urbana, IL: National Council of Teachers of English.

Taplin, S. (2010). *Mummies & pyramids.* New York, NY: Usborne Books.

Teaching paraphrasing improves reading comprehension. (n.d.). Retrieved from http://online.edfac.unimelb.edu.au/LiteracyResearch/pub/Projects/MDaly.pdf

Tompkins, G. E. (2010). *Literacy in the middle grades: Teaching reading and writing to fourth through eighth graders* (2nd ed.). Upper Saddle River, NJ: Allyn & Bacon.

Troia, G. A. (2007). Introduction: Research on writing-knowledge development, effective interventions, and assessment. *Reading and Writing Quarterly, 23,* 203–207.

Troia, G. A., & Graham, S. (2002). The effectiveness of a highly explicit, teacher directed strategy instruction routine: Changing the writing performance of students with learning disabilities. *Journal of Learning Disabilities, 35,* 290–305.

Troia, G. A., Shankland, R., & Heintz, A. (2010). *Putting writing research into practice: Applications for teacher professional development.* New York, NY: Guilford Press.

Troia, G. A., Shankland, R. K., & Wolbers, K. A. (2012). Motivation research in writing: Theoretical and empirical considerations. *Reading & Writing Quarterly: Overcoming Learning Difficulties, 28,* 5–28.

Turner, K. H. (2009). Flipping the switch: Code-switching from text speak to Standard English. *English Journal, 98*(5), 60–65.

Vitale, M., King, F., Shontz, D., & Huntley, G. (1971). Effect of sentence-combining exercises upon several restricted written composition tasks. *Journal of Educational Psychology, 62*(6), 521–525.

Vygotsky, L. (1962). *Thought and language.* Cambridge, MA: MIT Press.

Vygotsky, L. S. (1978). *Mind in society: The development of higher psychological processes* (M. Cole, V. John-Steiner, S. Scribner, & E. Souberman, Eds. & Trans.). Cambridge, MA: Harvard University Press.

Wall, H. (2008). Interactive writing beyond the primary grades. *The Reading Teacher, 62*(2), 149–152.

Wheeler, R. (2008). Becoming adept at code-switching. *Educational Leadership, 65*(7), 54–58.

Wheeler, R. S., & Swords, R. (2006). *Code-switching: Teaching Standard English in urban classrooms.* Urbana, IL: National Council of Teachers of English.

Wheeler, R., & Swords, R. (2010). *Code-switching lessons: Grammar strategies for linguistically diverse writers.* First Hand Curriculum Series. Portsmouth, NH: Heinemann.

Wilkinson, C., Miciak, J., Alexander, C., Reyes, P., Brown, J., & Giani, M. (2011). *Recommended educational practices for Standard English learners.* Austin: University of Texas at Austin, Texas Education Research Center.

Williams, N. L., Connell, M., White, C. S., & Kemper, J. (2003). Real boats rock: A transdisciplinary approach for teacher preparation. *Action in Teacher Education, 24*(4), 95–101.

Willis, M. (1993). *Deep revision: A guide for teachers, students, and other writers.* New York, NY: Teachers and Writers Collaborative.

Wood, K. D., & Endres, C. (2004). Motivate student interest with the imagine, elaborate, predict, and confirm (IEPC) strategy. *The Reading Teacher, 58*(4), 346–357.

Wood, K. D., & Taylor, D. B. (2006). *Literacy strategies across the subject areas.* Boston, MA: Allyn & Bacon.

Wray, A. (2000). Formulaic sequences in second language teaching: Principle and practice. *Applied Linguistics, 21*(4), 463–489.

Wray, A. (2008). *Formulaic language: Pushing the boundaries.* Oxford, UK: Oxford University Press.

Writer's workshop: Making writing a lifelong habit for elementary students, grades 4–6. (2012). Retrieved from http://www.teachersfirst.com/lessons/writers/writer-4.php

Yolen, J. (1987). *Owl moon.* New York, NY: Scholastic.

Index

Achieve, Inc., 4
ACT, 4
Action verbs, 48
Adger, C. T., 196
Advanced writers
  Big Idea Checklist strategy, 88
  Blueprint Graphic Organizers, 40
  Buddies Build It Stronger strategy, 144
  Code Switching Editing strategy, 206
  Color-Coding Sources strategy, 15
  Conferring With an Avatar strategy, 167
  Creating Rounded Characters Through
      Cartoon Connections strategy,
      123–124
  Deconstruct-Reconstruct strategy, 154
  genre charts, 52 (figure), 52–53
  I-Can! Chart strategy, 26
  Imagine, Describe, Resolve, and Confirm
      (IDRC) strategy, 216
  paraphrasing strategies, 113
  Portal Writing strategy, 161–162
  Probable Passages strategy, 227
  quilting strategy, 100
  reciprocal text structure mapping, 65
  Revising and Editing Through Primary
      Sources strategy, 194
  Revising with Photographs strategy, 184
  Structure strategy, 134
  Team Writing strategy, 107
  Thanks for the Memories! strategy, 75–76
  Write-Aloud strategy, 174
African American Vernacular English
      (AAVE), 196, 197 (figure), 198 (figure),
      199–201, 200 (figure), 201 (figure)
Alexander, C.
  see Wilkinson, C.
Aliki, 13
Alliance for Excellent Education Issue Brief, 2
Altieri, J. L., 154
Amendum, S., 100
American Psychological Association, 15
Ansary, T., 127
Applebee, A., 89
Appropriate tools, 43–44
Asaro-Saddler, K., 144–145, 175

Auditory-based strategies, 168–175
Avatars, 163–167

Baker, E., 116
Baker, L., 102
Baldwin, C., 6
Barnes, D., 94
Bartlett, B. J., 136
Baura, G., 67
Becker, E., 47
Becker, M. R., 47
Beers, S., 145
Bellmaker, The (Jacques), 68
Berninger, V. W, 145
Berry, K., 67
Bibliographic style, 15
Big Idea Checklist strategy, 78–89, 80–82
      (figure), 84 (figure), 85 (figure),
      87 (figure)
Blueprint Graphic Organizers, 28–41, 31–33
      (figure), 36 (figure), 37 (figure), 39
      (figure)
Bluth, G. J., 126
  see also Meyer, B. J. F.
Boers, F., 123
Borko, H., 5
Boster, S., 94
Brainstorming, 88, 182, 184, 212
Brandt, D. M., 126
  see also Meyer, B. J. F.
Brezinski, K. L., 136
Brindle, M., 19, 27
  see also Harris, K. R.
Brotherton, S., 226
Brown, J.
  see Wilkinson, C.
Buddies Build It Stronger strategy,
      137–145, 139 (figure)
Bud, Not Buddy (Curtis), 223, 223 (figure),
      224 (figure), 225 (figure)
Bunting, E., 75
Burke, M., 113

Calkins, L., 162, 169, 170
Cappelli, R., 42, 43

Carlson, L., 75
Carnegie Corporation of New York, 4
Carney, K., 29, 40–41
Carnine D. W., 40
Cartoon connections
   see Creating Rounded Characters Through
     Cartoon Connections
Cassidy, D., 3
Cassidy, J., 3
Cause-and-effect expository writing, 56, 57
   (figure), 62, 64 (figure)
Chalk, J., 113
Chapman, M., 42, 53
Character development, 116–125, 118–119
   (figure), 208–216
Chart paper
   Blueprint Graphic Organizers, 30
   Code Switching Editing strategy, 197
   Deconstruct-Reconstruct
     strategy, 150, 152
   I-Can! Chart strategy, 19
   Imagine, Describe, Resolve, and Confirm
     (IDRC) strategy, 213
   Probable Passages strategy, 219
   Revising with Photographs strategy, 182
Chisel-tip markers, 156
Christian, D., 196
Citation styles, 15
Code Switching Editing strategy, 196–206,
   197–198 (figure), 199 (figure), 200
   (figure), 201 (figure), 204 (figure)
Cognates, 161–162
Coker, D., 42
Coles, R., 56, 62
Collaborative teams, 103–107, 112
College Board, 1
Collins, J. L., 6
Color-Coding Sources strategy, 11–15
Colored computer fonts, 12–14
Colored folders, 30
Colored index cards, 12–14
Common Core of Standards, 1, 11, 67, 137,
   148, 168
Common Core State Standards Initiative,
   137, 168, 188, 206
Compare-and-contrast signal words, 132
Conch shell, 169, 173
Conferring With an Avatar strategy,
   163–167
Connell, M., 194–195
Cooter, R. B., 65
Cornwell's writing guide, 108
Couzijn, M., 176
Coyne, M. D., 40
Craft charts
   see I-Can! Chart strategy
Creating Rounded Characters Through
   Cartoon Connections, 116–125,
   118–119 (figure)
Cross-content strategies

Big Idea Checklist strategy, 88
Blueprint Graphic Organizers, 40
Buddies Build It Stronger strategy, 144
Code Switching Editing strategy, 206
Color-Coding Sources strategy, 15
Conferring With an Avatar strategy, 167
Creating Rounded Characters Through
   Cartoon Connections strategy, 124
Deconstruct-Reconstruct strategy, 154
genre charts, 53
I-Can! Chart strategy, 27
Imagine, Describe, Resolve, and Confirm
   (IDRC) strategy, 216
paraphrasing strategies, 115
Portal Writing strategy, 162
Probable Passages strategy, 227
quilting strategy, 100
reciprocal text structure mapping, 65
Revising and Editing Through Primary
   Sources strategy, 194
Revising with Photographs strategy, 184
Structure strategy, 134–135
Team Writing strategy, 107
Thanks for the Memories! strategy, 76
Write-Aloud strategy, 174
Cue cards, 180
Curtis, C. P., 223, 223 (figure)

Daane, M. C., 3
Daniels, H., 174
Declaration of Independence,
   189–190, 194
Deconstruct-Reconstruct strategy, 149–154,
   150 (figure), 151 (figure)
De La Paz, S., 4
Demecheleer, M., 123
Descriptive reciprocal map, 58 (figure)
Differentiated instruction, 2
Direct quotations, 108–112, 110 (figure)
Distancing strategies, 177, 180–181, 184
Ditto marks, 22
Dixon, D. C., 40
Document camera, 208, 213
Dorfman, L. R., 42, 43
Drafting strategies
   Buddies Build It Stronger strategy,
     137–145, 139 (figure), 143 (figure)
   Creating Rounded Characters Through
     Cartoon Connections, 116–125,
     118–119 (figure)
   first drafts, 91–92
   importance, 91–92
   paraphrasing strategies, 108–115, 110
     (figure), 114 (figure)
   quilting strategy, 93–101, 95 (figure)
   Structure strategy, 126–136, 128 (figure),
     129–131 (figure)
   Team Writing strategy, 102–107
Dunsmore, K., 54
Dworin, J. E., 75

Editing strategies
    Code Switching Editing strategy, 196–206, 197–198 (figure), 199 (figure), 200 (figure), 201 (figure), 204 (figure)
    Conferring With an Avatar strategy, 163–167
    Deconstruct-Reconstruct strategy, 149–154, 150 (figure), 151 (figure)
    Imagine, Describe, Resolve, and Confirm (IDRC) strategy, 207–217, 209 (figure), 212 (figure)
    importance, 147–148, 187
    Portal Writing strategy, 155–162, 157 (figure), 159 (figure), 160 (figure)
    Probable Passages strategy, 218–228, 220–222 (figure), 223 (figure), 224 (figure), 225 (figure)
    Revising and Editing Through Primary Sources strategy, 188–195, 191 (figure), 193 (figure)
    Revising with Photographs strategy, 176–185, 178–179 (figure)
    Write-Aloud strategy, 168–175
Endres, C., 211
Englert, C. S., 54
English Language Arts Common Core Standards, 1, 11, 137, 148, 168
English language learners (ELLs)
    Big Idea Checklist strategy, 88
    Blueprint Graphic Organizers, 38, 40
    Buddies Build It Stronger strategy, 144
    Code Switching Editing strategy, 205
    Color-Coding Sources strategy, 15
    Conferring With an Avatar strategy, 167
    Creating Rounded Characters Through Cartoon Connections strategy, 123
    Deconstruct-Reconstruct strategy, 153–154
    genre charts, 52, 52 (figure)
    I-Can! Chart strategy, 26
    Imagine, Describe, Resolve, and Confirm (IDRC) strategy, 215–216
    paraphrasing strategies, 113
    Portal Writing strategy, 161
    Probable Passages strategy, 226–227
    quilting strategy, 100
    reciprocal text structure mapping, 65
    Revising and Editing Through Primary Sources strategy, 192, 194
    Revising with Photographs strategy, 184
    Structure strategy, 134
    Team Writing strategy, 107
    Thanks for the Memories! strategy, 75
    Write-Aloud strategy, 174
Evaluation criteria, 177
Expository writing
    Big Idea Checklist strategy, 78–89, 80–82 (figure), 84 (figure), 85 (figure), 87 (figure)

    Color-Coding Sources strategy, 15
    paraphrasing strategies, 108–115, 110 (figure), 114 (figure)
    quilting strategy, 93–101, 95 (figure)
    reciprocal text structure mapping, 55–62, 57–61 (figure), 63–64 (figure)
    signal words, 62, 63 (figure)
    structural characteristics, 55–56
Eyckmans, J., 123

Fine, J. C., 66
First drafts
    Deconstruct-Reconstruct strategy, 149–154
    strategies, 91–92
    Write-Aloud strategy, 168–175
    see also Revision strategies
Fitzgerald, J., 100, 154, 176
Fleener, C. E., 17
Fletcher, R., 67, 89
Fontenot, J., 29, 40–41
Foreshadowing, 24
Fountas, I., 169, 175, 226
Fox, Terry, 150 (figure)
Francis, M., 176
Freedle, R. O., 56
Fuchs, D., 5
Fuchs, L.S., 5

Gallagher, M., 174, 228
Gambrell, L. B., 76, 217
Ganske, K., 2, 3, 4, 6, 19, 27
    see also Strickland, D. S.
Genre charts, 42–54, 45–46 (figure), 49 (figure), 51 (figure), 52 (figure)
Giani, M.
    see Wilkinson, C.
Glenn, C., 218
Goodman, K. S., 195
Gradual Release Model, 228
Graham, S., 1, 2, 3, 4, 5, 6, 19, 27, 101, 113, 137, 154
    see also Harris, K. R.
Graphic organizers
    Blueprint Graphic Organizers, 28–41, 31–33 (figure), 36 (figure), 37 (figure), 39 (figure)
    Code Switching Editing strategy, 198
    Color-Coding Sources strategy, 15, 16 (figure)
    genre charts, 50, 52, 53
    importance, 28–29
    reciprocal text structure mapping, 55
    Write-Aloud strategy, 171
Graves, D. H., 124
Greene, M., 162
Gregorian, V., 2
Group work, 102–107, 112, 140–142, 174
Gutman, D., 123

Hagen-Burke, S., 113
Hagood, M. C., 116
Half-finished drafts, 155
Hammann, L. A., 126, 135–136
Hampton, S., 5
Harris, K. R., 1, 5, 19, 26, 27, 101, 113
Hayes, J. R., 176
Heintz, A., 1, 2
Heller, R., 56, 62
Herbert, M. A., 137
Highlighters, 12–14, 127
Higley, K.
    see Meyer, B. J. F.
Hillocks, G., Jr., 137
Hoffner, H., 116
Holliway, R. D., 185
Homework Machine, The (Gutman), 123
Hong Xu, S., 124–125
Humument, The (Phillips), 156
Hunt, K. W., 137
Huntley, G., 137

I-Can! Chart strategy, 18–27, 20 (figure),
    22 (figure), 24 (figure), 25 (figure)
Imagine, Describe, Resolve, and Confirm
    (IDRC) strategy, 207–217, 209 (figure),
    212 (figure)
Independent writing
    Big Idea Checklist strategy, 87
    Blueprint Graphic Organizers, 31–33
        (figure), 35, 36 (figure), 37 (figure),
        39 (figure)
    Buddies Build It Stronger strategy, 142
    Code Switching Editing strategy, 204
        (figure), 204–205
    Color-Coding Sources strategy, 14
    Conferring With an Avatar strategy, 165
    Creating Rounded Characters
        Through Cartoon Connections
        strategy, 122
    Deconstruct-Reconstruct strategy, 153
    genre charts, 49 (figure), 50
    I-Can! Chart strategy, 23–24
    Imagine, Describe, Resolve, and Confirm
        (IDRC) strategy, 214
    paraphrasing strategies, 111–112
    Portal Writing strategy, 160
    Probable Passages strategy, 225–226
    quilting strategy, 99
    reciprocal text structure
        mapping, 64–65
    Revising and Editing Through Primary
        Sources strategy, 192
    Revising with Photographs strategy, 183
    Structure strategy, 133
    Team Writing strategy, 106
    Thanks for the Memories! strategy, 73
    Write-Aloud strategy, 173
Index cards, 12–14
Interactive writing, 175

Invention strategies
    Big Idea Checklist strategy, 78–89,
        80–82 (figure), 84 (figure),
        85 (figure), 87 (figure)
    Blueprint Graphic Organizers, 28–41,
        31–33 (figure), 36 (figure),
        37 (figure), 39 (figure)
    Color-Coding Sources strategy,
        11–17, 16 (figure)
    genre charts, 42–54, 45–46 (figure),
        49 (figure), 51 (figure), 52 (figure)
    I-Can! Chart strategy, 18–27, 20 (figure),
        22 (figure), 24 (figure), 25 (figure)
    reciprocal text structure mapping, 55–66,
        57–61 (figure), 63–64 (figure)
    Thanks for the Memories! strategy,
        67–77, 69 (figure), 70–71 (figure),
        74 (figure)

Jacques, B., 68
Jawitz, P. B., 217
Jefferson, Thomas, 190
Jin, Y., 3
Jocelyn, L.
    see Lemke, M.
Johns, J. L., 4
Johnson, N., 218
Joy of Cooking (Rombauer, Becker, and
    Becker), 47

Kam'enui, E. J., 40
Kappel, J., 123
Keck, C., 115
Kemper, J., 194–195
Kerr, S., 176
King, F., 137
Kleon, A., 156, 157 (figure)
Kolln, M., 101
Koukis, S., 94

Langer, J. A., 89
Language Experience Approach, 227
Language of Wider
    Communication (LWC), 196
Language play, 161–162
Lassonde, C. A., 15, 16 (figure), 20 (figure),
    31–33 (figure), 39 (figure), 45–46
    (figure), 51 (figure), 57–61 (figure),
    63 (figure), 69 (figure), 74 (figure),
    80–82 (figure), 95 (figure), 110 (figure),
    114 (figure), 118–119 (figure), 128
    (figure), 129–131 (figure), 139
    (figure), 178–179 (figure), 193
    (figure), 209 (figure), 220–222 (figure)
Laud, L., 77
Leigh, S. R., 155, 162
Lei, P.
    see Meyer, B. J. F.
Lemke, M., 2
Lenski, S. D., 4

Literary devices, 70–71
Lovelace, D. J., 3

MacArthur, C. A., 154, 176, 183, 185
Mandler, J., 218
Mariage, T. V., 54
Marzano, R. J., 41
Materials
    Big Idea Checklist strategy, 79, 80–82
        (figure)
    Blueprint Graphic Organizers, 29–30,
        31–33 (figure)
    Buddies Build It Stronger strategy, 138,
        139 (figure)
    Code Switching Editing strategy, 197,
        197–198 (figure)
    Color-Coding Sources strategy, 12
    Conferring With an Avatar strategy, 164
    Creating Rounded Characters Through
        Cartoon Connections strategy,
        116–117, 118–119 (figure)
    Deconstruct-Reconstruct strategy, 150,
        150 (figure), 151 (figure)
    genre charts, 43–44, 45–46 (figure)
    I-Can! Chart strategy, 19, 20 (figure)
    Imagine, Describe, Resolve, and Confirm
        (IDRC) strategy, 208, 209 (figure)
    paraphrasing strategies, 109, 110 (figure)
    Portal Writing strategy, 156, 157 (figure),
        159 (figure), 160 (figure)
    Probable Passages strategy, 219, 220–222
        (figure), 223 (figure), 224 (figure),
        225 (figure)
    quilting strategy, 94, 95 (figure)
    reciprocal text structure mapping, 56,
        57–61 (figure)
    Revising and Editing Through Primary
        Sources strategy, 189, 191 (figure)
    Revising with Photographs strategy, 177,
        178–179 (figure)
    Structure strategy, 127, 128 (figure),
        129–131 (figure)
    Team Writing strategy, 103
    Thanks for the Memories! strategy, 68, 69
        (figure)
    Write-Aloud strategy, 169
McCarrier, A., 169, 175, 226
McCutchen, D., 176, 185
McDougall, J., 136
Meier, C.
    see Meyer, B. J. F.
Mellon, J. C., 137
Mentor texts
    genre charts, 42–43, 53
    I-Can! Chart strategy, 19
    reciprocal text structure mapping, 55–65,
        57–61 (figure), 63–64 (figure)
    Structure strategy, 126
    Thanks for the Memories! strategy, 75
Metacognition, 19, 26

Metaphors, 71
Meyer, B. J. F., 56, 126, 132, 136
Miciak, J.
    see Wilkinson, C.
Middlemiss, W., 136
Miller, D.
    see Lemke, M.
Miller, S., 147, 176, 187
Mini-lessons
    Big Idea Checklist strategy, 79–88,
        80–82 (figure), 84 (figure),
        85 (figure), 87 (figure)
    Blueprint Graphic Organizers, 29–40,
        31–33 (figure), 36 (figure), 37
        (figure), 39 (figure)
    Buddies Build It Stronger strategy,
        138–144, 139 (figure), 143 (figure)
    Code Switching Editing strategy, 197–198
        (figure), 197–206, 199 (figure), 200
        (figure), 201 (figure), 204 (figure)
    Color-Coding Sources strategy, 11–15
    Conferring With an Avatar strategy,
        164–167
    Creating Rounded Characters Through
        Cartoon Connections strategy,
        116–124, 118–119 (figure)
    Deconstruct-Reconstruct strategy, 150
        (figure), 150–154, 151 (figure)
    genre charts, 43–53, 45–46 (figure), 49
        (figure), 51 (figure), 52 (figure)
    I-Can! Chart strategy, 19–26, 20 (figure),
        22 (figure), 24 (figure), 25 (figure)
    Imagine, Describe, Resolve, and Confirm
        (IDRC) strategy, 208–216, 209
        (figure), 212 (figure)
    paraphrasing strategies, 109–113, 110
        (figure), 114 (figure)
    Portal Writing strategy, 156–162, 157
        (figure), 159 (figure), 160 (figure)
    Probable Passages strategy, 219–227,
        220–222 (figure), 223 (figure), 224
        (figure), 225 (figure)
    quilting strategy, 94–100, 95 (figure)
    reciprocal text structure mapping, 56–65,
        57–61 (figure), 63–64 (figure)
    Revising and Editing Through Primary
        Sources strategy, 189–194, 191
        (figure), 193 (figure)
    Revising with Photographs strategy,
        177–184, 178–179 (figure)
    Structure strategy, 127–134, 128 (figure),
        129–131 (figure)
    Team Writing strategy, 103–107
    Thanks for the Memories! strategy, 68–76,
        69 (figure), 70–71 (figure), 74
        (figure)
    Write-Aloud strategy, 169–174
Modeling strategies
    Big Idea Checklist strategy, 83–86, 84
        (figure), 85 (figure), 87 (figure)

Blueprint Graphic Organizers, 33–35
Buddies Build It Stronger strategy,
    140–141
Code Switching Editing
    strategy, 202–203
Color-Coding Sources strategy, 12–14
Conferring With an Avatar strategy,
    164–165
Creating Rounded Characters Through
    Cartoon Connections strategy,
    120–122
Deconstruct-Reconstruct strategy,
    151–152
genre charts, 47–49, 49 (figure)
I-Can! Chart strategy, 19–22, 20 (figure),
    22 (figure), 24 (figure), 25 (figure)
Imagine, Describe, Resolve, and Confirm
    (IDRC) strategy, 208–214
paraphrasing strategies, 111
Portal Writing strategy, 158–159
Probable Passages strategy, 219–225,
    220–222 (figure), 223 (figure), 224
    (figure), 225 (figure)
quilting strategy, 97–99
reciprocal text structure mapping, 62
Revising and Editing Through Primary
    Sources strategy, 190, 191 (figure)
Revising with Photographs strategy,
    181–182
Structure strategy, 132–133
Team Writing strategy, 104
Thanks for the Memories! strategy, 68–74,
    69 (figure), 70–71 (figure), 74
    (figure)
Write-Aloud strategy, 170–172
Monroe, J. K., 2, 3, 4, 19, 27
    see also Ganske, K.; Strickland, D. S.
Morgan, M., 167
Morgan, R. F., 17
Motivated writers, 102–103
Mummies & Pyramids (Taplin), 13
Mummies Made in Egypt (Aliki), 13
Murray, D., 176
Murray, K., 67

Nagy, W., 145
Narrative stories, 28–29, 67, 72–73, 74
    (figure)
National Center for Educational Statistics,
    233
National Center to Improve the Tools of
    Educators, 38, 40
National Commission on Writing, 1
National Writing Project initiative, 137
Neville, D., 137
Newell, G. E., 94
Newspaper Blackout (Kleon), 156
Nickell, J., 127
No Child Left Behind Act (2001), 1
Norton, D., 75

Oczkus, L., 67
O'Hare, F., 137
Olinghouse, N. G., 4
Olson, L., 2
Organisation for Economic Co-operation
    and Development (OECD), 4
Organization strategies, 11–13, 78–89,
    93–94
Owl Moon (Yolen), 208, 210–212

Page-Voth, T., 112
Pahlke, E.
    see Lemke, M.
Paraphrasing strategies, 108–115, 110
    (figure), 114 (figure)
Partelow, L.
    see Lemke, M.
Partner Writing, 106
Past-Time Patterns Chart, 198 (figure),
    198–199, 199 (figure)
Patchworking, 108
Patel, P., 77
Patriot Points Checklist, 190–192,
    191 (figure)
Pearson, P. D., 174, 228
Peer interaction, 52, 73, 160, 174
Peha, S., 68
Perin, D., 2, 3, 4, 6, 137
Persky, H. R., 3
Personal narratives, 28–29, 67, 72–73,
    74 (figure)
Persuasive writing, 126–136, 129–131
    (figure)
Phillips, T., 156
Photograph-based revision strategies,
    176–185, 178–179 (figure)
Pickering, D. J., 41
Pinnell, G. S., 169, 175, 226
Plagiarism, 108
Planning strategies, 28–29
Pollock, J. E., 41
Portalupi, J., 67
Portal Writing strategy, 155–162, 157
    (figure), 159 (figure), 160 (figure)
Poster paper, 94, 98
Predictive writing
    see Probable Passages strategy
Prewriting rubrics, 73, 74 (figure)
Primary sources, 188–195
Probable Passages strategy, 218–228,
    220–222 (figure), 223 (figure),
    224 (figure), 225 (figure)
Problem-and-Solution reciprocal map,
    61 (figure)
Problem-and-Solution signal words, 132
Procedural writing, 44, 48, 49 (figure)
Proofreading strategies
    Conferring With an Avatar strategy,
        163–167
    Write-Aloud strategy, 168–175

Quilting strategy, 93–101, 95 (figure)
Quinn, K. B., 116
Quotations, direct, 108–112, 110 (figure)

Reading resources
    Big Idea Checklist strategy, 89
    Blueprint Graphic Organizers, 40–41
    Buddies Build It Stronger strategy,
        144–145
    Code Switching Editing strategy, 206
    Color-Coding Sources strategy, 15, 17
    Conferring With an Avatar strategy, 167
    Creating Rounded Characters Through
        Cartoon Connections strategy,
        124–125
    Deconstruct-Reconstruct strategy, 154
    genre charts, 53–54
    I-Can! Chart strategy, 27
    Imagine, Describe, Resolve, and Confirm
        (IDRC) strategy, 216–217
    paraphrasing strategies, 115
    Portal Writing strategy, 162
    Probable Passages strategy, 227–228
    quilting strategy, 101
    reciprocal text structure mapping, 66
    Revising and Editing Through Primary
        Sources strategy, 194–195
    Revising with Photographs strategy, 185
    Structure strategy, 135–136
    Team Writing strategy, 107
    Thanks for the Memories! strategy, 76–77
    Write-Aloud strategy, 175
Reason for a Flower, The (Heller), 56, 62
Recipe writing, 46 (figure), 47–48,
    49 (figure)
Reciprocal text structure mapping, 55–66
Reed, D. M., 4
Reference documentation, 108
Report structures, 150–151, 151 (figure)
Reproducible forms
    Big Idea Checklist strategy, 80–82 (figure)
    Blueprint Graphic Organizers, 31–32
        (figure), 39 (figure)
    Buddies Build It Stronger strategy,
        139 (figure)
    Cause-and-Effect Reciprocal Map,
        57 (figure)
    Compare-and-Contrast Reciprocal Map,
        60 (figure)
    Creating Rounded Characters Through
        Cartoon Connections strategy,
        118–119 (figure)
    Deconstruct-Reconstruct strategy,
        151 (figure)
    Descriptive Reciprocal Map, 58 (figure)
    direct quotation checklist, 110 (figure)
    expository writing, 95 (figure)
    genre charts, 45 (figure), 46 (figure),
        51 (figure)
    I-Can! Chart strategy, 20 (figure)

    Imagine, Describe, Resolve, and Confirm
        (IDRC) strategy, 209 (figure)
    Narrative Scoring Rubric, 32 (figure)
    paraphrasing strategies, 110 (figure),
        114 (figure)
    Portal Writing strategy, 159 (figure), 160
        (figure)
    Portfolio Entry Slip, 51 (figure)
    Prewriting Rubric, 74 (figure)
    Probable Passages strategy, 220–222
        (figure)
    Problem-and-Solution Reciprocal Map, 61
        (figure)
    quilting strategy, 95 (figure)
    Recipe Writing Checklist, 46 (figure)
    reciprocal text structure mapping, 57–61
        (figure)
    Report Structure Patterns, 151 (figure)
    Revising with Photographs strategy,
        178–179 (figure)
    rounded characters, 118 (figure)
    self-regulated learning, 119 (figure)
    Sensory-Details Chart, 69 (figure), 74
        (figure)
    Sequence Reciprocal Map, 59 (figure)
    signal words, 63 (figure)
    Structure strategy, 129 (figure)
    Writing Observation Checklist for
        Sentences and Paragraphs,
        139 (figure)
    Writing Process Checklist, 193 (figure)
    Writing Reflection Questionnaire,
        39 (figure)
Resnick, L. B., 5
Reutzel, D. R., 65
Revising and Editing Through Primary
    Sources strategy, 188–195, 191
    (figure), 193 (figure)
Revising with Photographs strategy, 176–185
Revision strategies
    Buddies Build It Stronger strategy,
        144–145
    Conferring With an Avatar strategy,
        163–167
    Deconstruct-Reconstruct strategy,
        149–154, 150 (figure), 151 (figure)
    importance, 147–148
    Portal Writing strategy, 155–162, 157
        (figure), 159 (figure), 160 (figure)
    Probable Passages strategy, 218–228
    Revising and Editing Through Primary
        Sources strategy, 188–195, 191
        (figure), 193 (figure)
    Revising with Photographs strategy,
        176–185, 178–179 (figure)
    Write-Aloud strategy, 168–175
    see also Strategic editing
Reyes, P.
    see Wilkinson, C.
Richards, J., 147, 176, 187

Richards, J. C., 15, 16 (figure), 20 (figure), 31–33 (figure), 39 (figure), 45–46 (figure), 51 (figure), 57–61 (figure), 63 (figure), 69 (figure), 74 (figure), 80–82 (figure), 95 (figure), 110 (figure), 114 (figure), 118–119 (figure), 128 (figure), 129–131 (figure), 139 (figure), 178–179 (figure), 193 (figure), 209 (figure), 220–222 (figure)

Richardson, J. S., 17

Rickford, R., 196, 197

Rijlaarsdam, G., 176

Robinson, A., 107

Rombauer, I. S., 47

Routman, R., 26, 27, 175

Rubrics
  Blueprint Graphic Organizers, 32 (figure)
  Creating Rounded Characters Through Cartoon Connections strategy, 119 (figure)
  self-regulated learning, 119 (figure)
  Thanks for the Memories! strategy, 74 (figure)

Rumelhart, D. E., 227–228

Ryan, P. M., 170

Saddler, B., 144–145, 175

Sandmel, K., 19, 27
  see also Harris, K. R.

Scaffolding strategies
  Buddies Build It Stronger strategy, 142–144
  Creating Rounded Characters Through Cartoon Connections strategy, 122
  Imagine, Describe, Resolve, and Confirm (IDRC) strategy, 210
  Portal Writing strategy, 158
  Probable Passages strategy, 224–225
  quilting strategy, 99
  Revising with Photographs strategy, 180–181
  Thanks for the Memories! strategy, 73
  Write-Aloud strategy, 174

Schema theory, 228

Schleppegrell, M. J., 66

Sen, A.
  see Lemke, M.

Sensory-details chart, 67–77, 69 (figure), 70–71 (figure), 74 (figure)

Sentence-combining strategies, 137–145, 175

Sequence reciprocal map, 59 (figure)

Shankland, R. K., 1, 2, 102

Shontz, D., 137

Signal words, 62, 63 (figure), 65, 127, 131–132

Silver, H., 107

Similes, 71

Simmons, D. C., 40

Skinner, E. N., 116

Small-moment writing, 162

Smart Boards
  Big Idea Checklist strategy, 79
  Blueprint Graphic Organizers, 30
  Code Switching Editing strategy, 197
  Deconstruct-Reconstruct strategy, 150
  paraphrasing strategies, 109
  Portal Writing strategy, 156
  reciprocal text structure mapping, 56
  Revising and Editing Through Primary Sources strategy, 189
  Team Writing strategy, 103
  Thanks for the Memories! strategy, 68

Spandel, V., 67, 169, 177

Spielvogel, J.
  see Meyer, B. J. F.

SpongeBob, 116–117, 120, 121–122

SpongeBob SquarePants, 116

Squidward, 116, 120, 121–122

Standard English learners (SELs), 199

Standard English usage, 196–206, 197–198 (figure), 199 (figure), 200 (figure), 201 (figure)

Stauffer, R. G., 227

Stein, N., 218

Stengers, H., 123

Stevens, R. J., 126, 135–136

Sticky notes, 94, 97–98, 99

Story dialogue, 21–22, 22 (figure)

Story elements, 218–228, 220–222 (figure), 223 (figure), 224 (figure), 225 (figure)

Story of Ruby Bridges, The (Coles), 56

Strategic editing
  Code Switching Editing strategy, 196–206, 197–198 (figure), 199 (figure), 200 (figure), 201 (figure), 204 (figure)
  Imagine, Describe, Resolve, and Confirm (IDRC) strategy, 207–217, 209 (figure), 212 (figure)
  importance, 187
  Probable Passages strategy, 218–228, 220–222 (figure), 223 (figure), 224 (figure), 225 (figure)
  Revising and Editing Through Primary Sources strategy, 188–195, 191 (figure), 193 (figure)
  see also Editing strategies

Strauss, S., 167

Strickland, D. S., 2, 3, 4, 19, 25, 27
  see also Ganske, K.

Strong, R., 107

Strong, W., 137

Structure strategy, 126–136, 128 (figure), 129–131 (figure), 218–228

Struggling writers
  Big Idea Checklist strategy, 88
  Blueprint Graphic Organizers, 38
  Buddies Build It Stronger strategy, 142–144, 143 (figure)
  Code Switching Editing strategy, 205

Color-Coding Sources strategy, 15
Conferring With an Avatar strategy, 166–167
Creating Rounded Characters Through Cartoon Connections strategy, 123
Deconstruct-Reconstruct strategy, 153
genre charts, 52
I-Can! Chart strategy, 25–26
Imagine, Describe, Resolve, and Confirm (IDRC) strategy, 215
paraphrasing strategies, 112–113, 114 (figure)
Portal Writing strategy, 161
Probable Passages strategy, 226
quilting strategy, 100
reciprocal text structure mapping, 65
Revising and Editing Through Primary Sources strategy, 192, 193 (figure)
Revising with Photographs strategy, 183
Structure strategy, 133–134
Team Writing strategy, 106
Thanks for the Memories! strategy, 75
Write-Aloud strategy, 174
Student practice
Big Idea Checklist strategy, 86–87
Blueprint Graphic Organizers, 35, 36 (figure), 37 (figure)
Buddies Build It Stronger strategy, 141–142
Code Switching Editing strategy, 203–204
Color-Coding Sources strategy, 14
Conferring With an Avatar strategy, 165
Creating Rounded Characters Through Cartoon Connections strategy, 122
Deconstruct-Reconstruct strategy, 152–153
genre charts, 49–50
I-Can! Chart strategy, 23
Imagine, Describe, Resolve, and Confirm (IDRC) strategy, 214
paraphrasing strategies, 111
Portal Writing strategy, 159
Probable Passages strategy, 225
quilting strategy, 99
reciprocal text structure mapping, 62
Revising and Editing Through Primary Sources strategy, 191–192
Revising with Photographs strategy, 182–183
Structure strategy, 133
Team Writing strategy, 104–106
Thanks for the Memories! strategy, 72–73
Write-Aloud strategy, 172–173
Student reflection
Big Idea Checklist strategy, 87–88
Blueprint Graphic Organizers, 36, 38, 39 (figure)
Buddies Build It Stronger strategy, 142
Code Switching Editing strategy, 205
Color-Coding Sources strategy, 14

Conferring With an Avatar strategy, 165–166
Creating Rounded Characters Through Cartoon Connections strategy, 122
Deconstruct-Reconstruct strategy, 153
genre charts, 50, 51 (figure)
I-Can! Chart strategy, 24–25
Imagine, Describe, Resolve, and Confirm (IDRC) strategy, 215
paraphrasing strategies, 112
Portal Writing strategy, 160
Probable Passages strategy, 226
quilting strategy, 99
reciprocal text structure mapping, 65
Revising and Editing Through Primary Sources strategy, 192
Revising with Photographs strategy, 183
Structure strategy, 133
Team Writing strategy, 106
Thanks for the Memories! strategy, 73
Write-Aloud strategy, 173
Student writing achievement, 1
Swords, R., 196, 197, 197–198 (figure), 199, 199 (figure), 200 (figure), 201, 204 (figure), 206
Synthesizing process, 96–97

Taplin, S., 13
Taylor, D. B., 218, 219
Teaching paraphrasing improves reading comprehension, 115
Team Writing strategy, 102–107
Text-to-speech software, 163–167
Thanks for the Memories! strategy, 67–77, 69 (figure), 70–71 (figure), 74 (figure)
Theodorou, E., 136
Thesauruses, 109
Think-alouds
Buddies Build It Stronger strategy, 140–141
genre charts, 48–49
quilting strategy, 97, 99
report structure patterns, 152
Revising with Photographs strategy, 181–182
Thanks for the Memories! strategy, 75
Write-Aloud strategy, 171
Tompkins, G. E., 3
Transdisciplinary teaching, 189, 194–195
Transition words, 150
Treasure pit exercise, 127–133, 128 (figure)
Troia, G. A., 1, 2, 4, 102, 107
Turner, K. H., 206

Unmotivated writers, 102–103

van den Bergh, H., 176
Vernacular dialect, 196–197, 197 (figure), 198 (figure), 199–201, 200 (figure), 201 (figure)

Viacom, 116
Vitale, M., 137
Voki.com, 164–165
Vygotsky, L. S., 103, 174, 175, 216–217

Wall, H., 169, 175
Web 2.0 avatars, 163–167
Wheeler, R. S., 196, 197, 197–198 (figure),
    199, 199 (figure), 200 (figure), 201,
    204 (figure), 206
Whisper-reading, 168–175
White, C. S., 194–195
Wigfield, A., 102
Wijekumar, K.
    see Meyer, B. J. F.
Wilkinson, C., 199
Williams, C., 226
Williams, N. L., 194–195
Williams, T.
    see Lemke, M.
Willis, M., 187
Wolbers, K. A., 102
Wolfram, W., 196
Wood, K. D., 211, 218, 219
Word bank, 142, 143 (figure)
Wray, A., 123
Write-Aloud strategy, 168–175
Writer's workshop: Making writing a lifelong
    habit for elementary students, grades
    4–6, 113
Writing genres, 42–44
Writing Observation Checklist for Sentences
    and Paragraphs, 139 (figure)
Writing Process Checklist, 192, 193 (figure)
Writing-strategy instruction
    background information, 1–6

Big Idea Checklist strategy, 78–89,
    80–82 (figure), 84 (figure), 85
    (figure), 87 (figure)
Blueprint Graphic Organizers, 28–41,
    31–33 (figure), 36 (figure), 37
    (figure), 39 (figure)
Buddies Build It Stronger strategy,
    137–145, 139 (figure), 143 (figure)
Color-Coding Sources strategy, 11–17, 16
    (figure)
Creating Rounded Characters Through
    Cartoon Connections strategy,
    116–125, 118–119 (figure)
genre charts, 42–54, 45–46 (figure), 49
    (figure), 51 (figure), 52 (figure)
I-Can! Chart strategy, 18–27, 20 (figure),
    22 (figure), 24 (figure), 25 (figure)
paraphrasing strategies, 108–115, 110
    (figure), 114 (figure)
quilting strategy, 93–101, 95 (figure)
reciprocal text structure mapping, 55–66,
    57–61 (figure), 63–64 (figure)
Structure strategy, 126–136, 128 (figure),
    129–131 (figure)
Team Writing strategy, 102–107
Thanks for the Memories! strategy, 67–77,
    69 (figure), 70–71 (figure),
    74 (figure)
see also Revision strategies

Xiang, X., 167

Yolen, J., 75, 208, 210

Zheng, J., 4
Zone of proximal development (ZPD), 217

About the Authors

 **Janet C. Richards**, a former K–6 teacher, is a professor in the Department of Childhood Education and Literacy Studies at the University of South Florida. She is senior editor of the *Journal of Reading Education* and served as a volunteer literacy scholar in emerging nations through the International Reading Association and USAID. She was selected as a visiting scholar at the University of Victoria, British Columbia, Canada. This is Richards's 10th book and her third with Cynthia Lassonde.

 **Cynthia A. Lassonde** is a professor in the Elementary Education and Reading Department at the State University of New York College at Oneonta, where she teaches undergraduate and graduate courses in literacy and special education. Formerly, she taught elementary language arts for more than 20 years. As a writer, she is the author of numerous articles published in professional journals and has authored and edited 11 books on children's writing and literacy leadership. She is also editor of *Excelsior: Leadership in Teaching and Learning*, a scholarly teacher education journal, and was awarded the SUNY Chancellor's Award for Excellence in Teaching in 2010. She is most fortunate to be the mom of three beautiful daughters and the wife of the love of her life!

About the Contributors

Sandra K. Athans is a National Board Certified practicing classroom teacher with over 10 years' experience teaching reading and writing at the elementary level. She is the author of several teacher-practitioner books on literacy: *Quality Comprehension* (International Reading Association), *Fun-tastic Activities for Differentiating Comprehension Instruction* (International Reading Association), and *Motivating Every Student in Literacy* (Eye on Education). She has presented her research at the International Reading Association and the National Council of Teachers of English Conferences. She is also a children's writer and has published her short stories in national magazines. Her first children's book will be published next year. She earned an MA in elementary education from Manhattanville College. She is currently completing her MS in Education II—Literacy Education at Le Moyne College.

Joanne Durham has been a teacher, reading specialist, literacy staff developer, Reading Recovery site coordinator, and reading/language arts supervisor in Prince George's County Public Schools, Maryland, where she currently coordinates reading comprehension and writing workshop projects with a focus on Title I schools. She has taught or supported writing in classrooms K–8. She has also taught writing courses at Trinity University in Washington, D.C. for K–12 teachers. Her poetry has been published in *Language Arts* and the *Journal of Reading Recovery*, and her articles about teaching have been printed in *The Reading Teacher* and other publications.

Joyce C. Fine, associate professor of reading/language arts at Florida International University, is the program leader for Reading Education and teaches undergraduate and graduate courses. Joyce has worked in school settings with teachers and students to develop reading and writing for diverse populations of students. She has published chapters in NCTE's *Alternatives to Grading Student Writing,* edited by Stephen Tchudi; *Scaffolding Literacy Instruction: Strategies for K–4 Classrooms,* edited by Adrian Rodgers and Emily M. Rodgers; *Writing Strategies for All Primary Students: Scaffolding Independent Writing With 25 Differentiated Mini-Lessons,* by Janet C. Richards and Cynthia A. Lassonde; and numerous articles in various professional journals.

Jennifer A. Fontenot is a 35-year veteran teacher-consultant in public education. She has also been a full-time faculty member at Marywood University in Scranton, Pennsylvania, and an adjunct faculty member at Eastern Michigan University. In addition, she holds a position as a corporate English language trainer where she instructs writing and presentation skills to automotive executives who promote global car development.

Sandra Gandy is an assistant professor in the MA in Reading program at Governors State University. She has taught undergraduate and graduate classes in reading and writing across grade levels.

Crystal P. Glover is a lecturer and adviser in the department of Reading and Elementary Education at the University of North Carolina at Charlotte. Crystal is a National Board Certified Teacher and Certified Reading Specialist. She has 10 years' experience as a primary grades teacher and is currently pursuing a PhD in curriculum and instruction with a focus in urban literacy. Her research interests include culturally responsive literacy instruction for students of color, urban teacher preparation, and the oral and written language development of children in poverty.

Jane Hansen, professor at the University of Virginia, started to study children as writers/readers in 1981, morphed her research into writers/readers as self-evaluators, and now researches students as writers across the curriculum. In her articles and books, she writes in detail about what writers do in the natural settings of classrooms designed to promote their engagement. Currently, she directs the Central Virginia Writing Project, which provides courses, writing experiences, and professional development for elementary, middle, and high school teachers and students—all of whom are writers.

Gabriel C. Horn is an elementary teacher at Joplin Elementary in Boise, Idaho. As a current fourth-grade teacher, he encourages his students to appreciate the craft of writing and understand the nuances of various writing genres. He holds a master's of arts in curriculum and instruction from Boise State University. His thesis focused on the use of tools such as rubrics to scaffold writing for his students, particularly during planning and revision processes.

Jennifer Ireland, a National Board Certified teacher, is department chair of a multidisciplinary team of middle school teachers. Previously a sixth- and seventh-grade teacher, she currently teaches eighth-grade reading and English in the Sumner School District in Sumner, Washington. She has presented her work on the integration of reading in the content areas of science and social studies at the Washington Library and Media Conference. She completed her MEd, specializing in integrated curriculum and reading, at the University of Washington. Her research interests focus on integrating the structure strategy into middle school curricula.

Mariah Kraus is a graduate student in the MA in Reading program at Governors State University; an elementary teacher who has taught reading and writing to at-risk third-, fourth-, and fifth-grade students in south suburban Chicago; and a former education administrator for Chicago Public Schools.

S. Rebecca Leigh is an assistant professor of reading and language arts at Oakland University in Rochester, Michigan. Her current research, in the elementary and secondary grades, focuses on how access to art serves as a pathway to literacy learning and its impact on students as writers. Her work has appeared in *Language Arts,* the *Journal for Learning Through the Arts, English Journal, ReadWriteThink,* and the *Journal of Adolescent and Adult Literacy.*

Susan D. Martin is a professor in the Literacy Department at Boise State University. She taught writing as an elementary teacher for 18 years—10 of which were spent in Grades 4 and 5. She now teaches both undergraduate and graduate courses on writing and writing instruction. In these courses, teachers and teacher candidates create writing portfolios across a broad range of genres. Genre charts are used as models for classroom teaching. Her research interests include effective elementary writing instruction and teacher education in writing instruction.

Bonnie J. F. Meyer, professor of educational psychology at The Pennsylvania State University, studies text structure, the Structure strategy, reading, writing, and decision making. She has classroom teaching experience at the sixth-grade level and as an elementary and middle school resource teacher and school psychologist. Additionally, she has over 50 publications about the Structure strategy and its effects on understanding and applications for reading or writing. Her current research, funded by the Institute for Education Sciences of the U.S. Department of Education, is focused on Structure strategy instruction for students in Grades 4 through 8. She has served on editorial boards for *Discourse Processes,* the *Journal of Educational Psychology,* the *Reading Research Quarterly, Cognition and Instruction,* the *Educational Psychologist,* and the *Journal of Literacy Research* and is a Fellow in the American Psychological Association, the American Educational Research Association, and the American Psychological Society.

Noreen S. Moore is an assistant professor of special education, language, and literacy at The College of New Jersey. Her current research interests are K–12 writing strategies and instruction, writing and technology, and the vocabulary development of young children. She has presented her research at national and international literacy conferences. Her most recent publications include research on vocabulary instruction for preschool children.

Kathleen Muir is currently a literacy coach at Dr. John D. Long Middle School in Pasco County, Florida. Her research interests include the teaching of writing as a real-world experience and content literacy. She has presented her work at the Florida Reading Association, Florida Council for the Social Studies, and the Florida Association for Curriculum Development. She is completing her master's in reading at the University of South Florida.

Lynne Newton is a literacy specialist for the Charlotte Mecklenburg School System in Charlotte, North Carolina.

Melissa Ray is a doctoral candidate in educational psychology at The Pennsylvania State University. Melissa received her MA in teaching English as a second language from the University of Illinois at Urbana–Champaign. Prior to attending Penn State, Melissa was a developmental English instructor at Pasco-Hernando Community College in Hernando County, Florida, teaching reading, writing, and English as a second language. Her primary research interests are reading comprehension, literacy development, and literacy instruction.

Krishna Seunarinesingh is a lecturer in teaching of language arts at The University of the West Indies, St. Augustine, Trinidad and Tobago. His research explores adolescent motivation to read, use of authentic texts in primary schools, and school discourses. His most recent work examines the vocabulary of English B texts used at high schools in the Caribbean.

Allison Stone is a fifth-grade teacher in Miami, Florida. She recently graduated with a master's of science degree in reading from Florida International University.

Katie Stover began her career as an elementary teacher, then worked as a literacy coach, and is currently pursuing her PhD in curriculum and instruction in urban literacy at the University of North Carolina at Charlotte. She also teaches undergraduate courses in reading and writing pedagogy and has published articles about literacy teaching and literacy coaching in *The Reading Teacher* as well as other publications.

Todd Sundeen is an assistant professor at the University of Northern Colorado in the School of Special Education. He previously taught writing to students in Grades 6 through 8 for 7 years. The primary themes for his research are focused on written expression strategy instruction for students with diverse learning needs. He is specifically interested in the impact of explicit strategy instruction for students with mild and moderate disabilities who have difficulty planning and prewriting.

Lynda Swanner has been a teacher, library media specialist, and literacy staff developer. She is currently the English language arts and reading coordinator in McKinney Independent School District in McKinney, Texas. She coordinates the curriculum, instruction, and assessments for all elementary teachers in the district. She is also a literacy consultant for many Texas school districts. Over the years, she has presented many workshops that integrate technology and literacy for the International Society for Technology in Education.

Jean Payne Vintinner is a clinical assistant professor of reading in the Department of Reading and Elementary Education at the University of North Carolina at Charlotte. Before teaching at the university, she taught English and remedial reading in the public schools for a decade, leading to research interests, professional development, and publications in motivating adolescents to read and the relationship between reading ability and behavior.

Rebecca Wheeler is a professor of English language and literacy at Christopher Newport University in Newport News, Virginia. She specializes in teaching Standard English in dialectally diverse classrooms. Wheeler, a literacy consultant and spokesperson for the National Council of Teachers of English (NCTE), has consulted for public schools K -14 from New York to New Orleans and from Chicago and Baltimore to Arkansas. Recent publications include *Code-Switching: Teaching Standard English in Urban Classrooms* (NCTE, 2006), "Becoming Adept at Code-Switching" in *Educational Leadership* (April 2008), and "Factoring AAVE Into Reading Assessment and Intervention" in *The Reading Teacher* (March 2012).

Nancy L. Williams is an associate professor in the Department of Childhood Education and Literacy Studies at the University of South Florida. Her research interests include transdisciplinary teaching and learning, vocabulary, and preservice teacher preparation in literacy. She has been published in *The Reading Teacher* and *Action in Teacher Education.* She has presented at the annual conferences of the American Educational Research Association, the National Reading Conference, and the International Reading Association.

Karen Wood is a professor and the graduate program coordinator at the University of North Carolina at Charlotte. She received her doctorate in reading education from the University of Georgia and is a former middle school teacher and K–12 literacy specialist. She is the author of over 200 publications that have appeared in journals such as *Literacy Research and Instruction, The Reading Teacher,* the *Journal of Adolescent and Adult Literacy,* and *Reading and Writing Quarterly.* She is the author and originator of the "Research to Practice" column in the *Middle School Journal.* Her most current books are *Literacy Instruction for Adolescents: Research-Based Practices* (Guilford Press) and *Guiding Readers Through Text: Strategy Guides in "New Times"* (International Reading Association). She is currently working on another book on peer talk. Her research interests include translating research and theory into classroom practice, integrated instruction, vocabulary, and comprehension.

Lindsay Sheronick Yearta is a fifth-grade teacher in Rock Hill, South Carolina. She is also a doctoral candidate at the University of North Carolina at Charlotte working toward a PhD in curriculum and instruction in urban literacy. Her current research interests include culturally relevant pedagogy in higher education, teacher education, and vocabulary acquisition and retention of kindergarten through Grade 12 students.

Chase Young is an elementary reading specialist for McKinney Independent School District and a doctoral student at the University of North Texas. As a reading specialist and previously a second-grade teacher, he has experience teaching writing and sharing his knowledge through professional development.

CORWIN

A SAGE Company

The Corwin logo—a raven striding across an open book—represents the union of courage and learning. Corwin is committed to improving education for all learners by publishing books and other professional development resources for those serving the field of PreK–12 education. By providing practical, hands-on materials, Corwin continues to carry out the promise of its motto: **"Helping Educators Do Their Work Better."**